THE DARK WITHIN US

A MESSAGE FROM CHICKEN HOUSE

Would you trust a demon you met at a party? What if it was the only way to find your lost soul? Jess Popplewell takes us on a tough journey to Hell and back, but also shows us a world of love on the way. Darkly funny, original stuff from a great new voice.

BARRY CUNNINGHAM
Publisher
Chicken House

THE DARK WITHIN US

JESS POPPLEWELL

Chicken House

2 Palmer Street, Frome, Somerset BA11 1DS
www.chickenhousebooks.com

First published in Great Britain in 2024
Chicken House
2 Palmer Street
Frome, Somerset BA11 1DS
United Kingdom
www.chickenhousebooks.com

Chicken House/Scholastic Ireland, 89E Lagan Road, Dublin Industrial Estate,
Glasnevin, Dublin D11 HP5F, Republic of Ireland

Cover design by Micaela Alcaino
Typeset by Dorchester Typesetting Group Ltd
Printed in Great Britain by Clays, Elcograf S.p.A

FSC
www.fsc.org
MIX
Paper | Supporting responsible forestry
FSC® C018072

1 3 5 7 9 10 8 6 4 2

British Library Cataloguing in Publication data available.

PB ISBN 978-1-915947-18-5
eISBN 978-1-915947-20-8

For Jade, obviously.

1

THE TWINS

Chloe-Lee and Joey were in a warehouse on an abandoned industrial estate when social services found them, about as far north and west in England as it's possible to go without a) crossing the border into Scotland or b) falling in the sea. How they got there no one could say, not least because the children themselves seemed to have no intention of telling.

The social-work team set up an emergency fostering arrangement with their newest recruit, one Martha Garstang, the Site Manager at the nearby Elrick Park holiday centre. This arrangement, agreed over steaming mugs of tea in hushed tones, was for the best. The trauma of it – living in a draughty old warehouse! That had to be the reason they were so – well, none of the team wanted to use the word, but it hung over their desks anyway – *creepy*.

The fresh air and serene greenness of Elrick Park should do them good.

Decision made, all that was left to do was paperwork. Not usually anyone's favourite task, but also somehow worse today because no one wanted to be in the team's cheerless, windowless interview room with these children.

Ultimately, a social worker named Jim drew that shortest of straws, leading the small children into the claustrophobic space. He kept the door open and let them sit closest to it, as per protocol, trying to ignore the sensation of being trapped in there with them.

'How old are you, Joey?' Jim asked.

The little boy took a seat on one of the grey plastic chairs, glanced over at his sister and grinned a closed-lipped grin before replying.

'How old do we look?'

Jim, for what it's worth, was newly qualified and perhaps oughtn't to have been handling a case this delicate. Perhaps, therefore, he could be forgiven for demanding that Joey stop being so bloody facetious and just answer him.

The thing is, as Jim *looked* at Joey, he wasn't sure the little boy seated in front of him was a little boy at all. The clothes didn't help; Joey had on a pair of corduroy trousers the colour of damp sand. He had a long-sleeved white shirt made of heavy linen, and braces held the trousers up at the front. Hanging over the back of his chair was a tweed jacket, the kind with leather elbow patches.

Where the hell the kid had found one of those to fit

him, Jim had not the foggiest. The fact he sat there in his shirtsleeves also revealed something else: on the inside of one of Joey's wrists was what appeared to be a tattoo. Which was impossible: who would tattoo a child? And yet there it was, a fine-line rendering of a feather.

Overall, the effect was of someone significantly older than the youthful boy sitting in front of him on a plastic chair, swinging his legs.

His sister was no better. She also had a wrist tattoo, perhaps even stranger than her brother's, depicting as it did an anatomically correct human heart.

The tattoos had to be those temporary ones you sometimes saw inside lollipop wrappers. It was the only explanation, because they could absolutely be no older than . . .

'About . . . ten?' Jim hazarded.

'Really?' Joey seemed surprised. 'I suppose ten will do. Don't you think so, Chloe-Lee?'

'I'm happy to be ten for the time being,' the girl replied with a sharp nod.

'We'll probably be ten for a while,' Joey warned her.

'So be it.'

So, Jim – rather out of his depth but relieved to have an answer – marked them both as being ten on his forms.

'Do you know your parents' names?'

'Not really, no,' Chloe-Lee answered. 'I should think they're dead by now. What kills most ineffectual human parents?'

'Oh, er . . . I don't know.' Jim swallowed, sure he *should* have this information, but in the presence of the twins, all his training seemed to have flown out of his head. He was, however, confident that even if he could remember, it would not be appropriate to tell Chloe-Lee.

'In that case, I suppose you ought to write that. We don't know our parents' names or whereabouts. At any rate, they won't be back for us.'

She smiled at him then, and Jim recoiled. Not because of what she said, although it *was* strange, but because for the first time he noticed Chloe-Lee's teeth – straight, white and uniformly, terrifyingly, pointed.

The blood leached from his skin as his eyes swung over to Joey, also grinning, also displaying the same row of shark-sharp teeth. To his horror, the children blinked, and when their eyes slid open again, they shone gold, from edge to edge.

'Are you OK, Jim?' Joey asked.

'Um, I, er . . . I'm not sure I feel very well.'

'Don't worry about that,' Chloe-Lee soothed. 'Just write what we tell you to, and then you can go home and have a rest. How does that sound?'

'That sounds great.' Jim swallowed.

'Good lad,' Joey said.

So, the forms were signed off. The children expressed the desire to never see their parents again, even if they showed up (which they never did), and they skipped off to explore Elrick Park with their new carer, Martha Garstang.

Eventually she adopted them, giving them her

surname, and Jim remained their social-work contact – but to his immense relief, he was rarely asked to go anywhere near them.

Just as well, he told his boyfriend as they lay there in the dark, feet entwined beneath the sheets, because, well, all that happened over ten years ago now, and yet last time he was up there they still had those tattoos.

Worse still, they hadn't aged a day.

2

JENNY

In Jenny's defence, the demon caught her at a low point. Several low points, actually.

For starters, she didn't even want to be at Kai's Halloween party, except she'd fallen out with her auntie's boyfriend again and had nowhere else to sleep that night. Kai's taste in music was predictably rubbish, all bleepy-bloopy Scene Kid crap composed on Game Boys. By the time she arrived the booze was already out, and it also seemed everyone else had received a memo she hadn't: it was fancy dress. She glanced down at her black skinny jeans and oversized hoodie and reflected that if she'd dressed up as anything, it was 'Caspian Sanderson's girlfriend'. It was his hoodie, after all. She should probably think about giving it back at some point.

As if none of this was bad enough, as soon as the party

host saw her his face broke into what she could only describe as a 'leer', and he swaggered forward, skinny legs encased in jeans so tight he looked like a stork, top half covered in a red and brown striped jumper several sizes too big for him.

'Oh,' he gloated. 'Turned up after all, did we?'

There was a long label peeking out from the hem of his top, so she reached for it, reading it before answering.

'I'm still not going to shag you, Generic Slasher Villain. And definitely not in your nan's bed.'

'Yeah, yeah.' He grinned, leaning in as though closer proximity to the overpowering smell of his aftershave was going to make her change her mind.

Ugh. Why were teenage boys the worst?

She sidestepped Kai's advances and made a quick turn into the living room. She knew it was the living room because as a kid, Jenny had come here all the time. Before puberty and hormones and arrogance got involved, she'd actually kind of liked Kai Hodges.

But Kai's nan had just moved into a residential village, and the house wasn't due on the market for another week. At school, Jenny had heard him telling people this party was 'What she would have wanted – bit of a goer in her day, my nan.'

Which seemed unlikely, somehow. Kai's nan was their Sunday school teacher.

Still, there was something reassuring about the geography of the flat. It reminded her of being that innocent, Sunday-school-going kid, before she realized her family wasn't even religious and just liked the free childcare. Before her dad got sick of playing happy families and pissed off, never to be heard from again. Before her mum stopped trusting people, all people, even her own daughter.

Careful, she warned herself. *No one wants to be the sober, crying girl.*

Jenny was only here tonight because she needed a distraction from all that. Idly, she wondered what her old Sunday school teacher would think about having a living room full of slutty cats and last-minute zombies.

Already, the party felt like a mistake. What she had wanted was a repeat of the old days, before her life got so complicated. A piss-up with some mates. If she got tipsy enough, she might even use some of her precious remaining credit to text her ex-boyfriend and tell him she was sorry about the other day. Maybe they could talk. Maybe he'd sneak her into his room like he used to, and maybe this time she'd give him what he wanted. Better Caspian than Kai Hodges, after all.

But things had changed. Tonight wouldn't go like that.

For one thing, when she stepped into the living room, she was surprised to find Caspian already there. He was dressed in something that could either have been a vampire's cape or one of his bedroom curtains, but even in costume, her eyes found him immediately.

Weird, she thought, *he doesn't even like Kai*.

As her eyes adjusted to the dim lighting, she frowned. It was definitely Caspian, his long, lean silhouette folded into a corner with a can of Carling in one hand and in the other—

Hang on.

Why did he have his arm around Amber Coombs?

Neither of them noticed her. They gazed at each other, a tiny smile playing on Caspian's face. Amber laughed, her hand pressed on Caspian's chest as though she needed to stabilize herself against him, fake blood dripping from her chin and into her corseted cleavage. As usual, she was wearing so much eyeliner she was more raccoon than girl. But Caspian wasn't making snide comments about this tonight. No, right now he was watching Amber like she was the most fascinating person he had ever met, as though if someone had yelled 'Jenny's here!' he would have asked 'Jenny who?'

Jenny's heart clenched behind her ribs. He broke up with her less than a week ago. What was he doing? She took a step back and hit the wall. She couldn't take her eyes off them, couldn't stop the flush of heat crawling over her skin, couldn't even find the energy to do what she really wanted, which was to snatch off the hoodie she was wearing – Caspian's hoodie – and *set it on fire*.

As she watched, Amber's face was suddenly very close to Caspian's.

Oh, no. Of all the people – of every human being on the face of the planet – why was he doing this with Amber?

She watched her ex-boyfriend lean in and kiss her ex-best friend.

She sensed tears coming, felt the tell-tale prickle behind her irises, and at the same moment noticed there were other people in the room too, their eyes flicking between her and them. Waiting to see how she'd react.

She sucked in a deep breath, straightened her spine against the wall, and pulled the hoodie off over her head. Underneath she had on a thin cotton band T-shirt; *The Bronx* spelt out in cracked white lettering. She dumped Caspian's hoodie on the orange and brown carpet and walked back out of the living room.

She stormed out of Kai's nan's front door into the cold of the cul-de-sac, blinking back what could only be tears of rage because they sure as hell weren't tears of anything else, thank you very much. Her glasses steamed up, heated by her cheeks. She couldn't see, but that didn't matter. She just needed to get away from the scene burnt into her retinas, of Caspian, and his tongue, and the way it slid, slick, into Amber's mouth.

Which is probably why she marched smack-bang, nose-first, glasses-ouch into the sternum of a demon. Or at least, she assumed that's why he had a pair of tiny prosthetic horns at his hairline.

'Jesus!' she snapped, reeling, rubbing the bridge of her nose where her glasses had dug in on impact.

'Not quite,' the demon grinned.

Other than the horns, he was dressed entirely normally, blue jeans and a faded Beatles T-shirt. She squinted up at him, noticing the way his floppy blond hair fell over the subtle spikes. Possibly a little *too* subtle for this party, as costumes went, but that wasn't Jenny's problem.

'Are you all right?' he asked, a touch belatedly.

'Not really, no,' Jenny replied.

He didn't move, continuing instead to block her escape from the absolute hellscape that was Kai's house party.

'Right, well, it's been a real pleasure meeting you,' she said, 'but I have somewhere to be, so . . .'

'No, you don't,' the boy said, a crease puckering his forehead.

'Um, what?'

'You don't have anywhere to be. I mean, you *are* Jenny Hall, right? As in, "semi-homeless, directionless and angst-ridden with a chip the size of Blackburn on her shoulder" Jenny Hall?'

'And who the hell are you?' retorted semi-homeless, directionless and angst-ridden with a chip the size of Blackburn on her shoulder Jenny Hall.

'Duh,' he said, jabbing his finger up to his forehead. 'I'm a demon. And I'm here to make you a deal.'

Jenny did not have time for this.

'Whatever,' she snapped and tried to walk round him.

The demon's hand shot out to grab her arm, and she felt a familiar flash of blind rage. Before she really considered what she was about to do, she smacked him on the side of his head. Hard.

His face registered surprise, which wasn't unusual. Lads – they never expected her to hit them. Surprise was common, that and a moment of panic that someone might have witnessed their pain at the hands of a five-foot-two emo kid.

Not that she was emo, obviously. She wasn't – it was just people sometimes *said* she was, what with the skinny jeans and the faded green dip-dye in her otherwise mousy hair.

But just because she liked Fall Out Boy and Panic!, that didn't make her emo. She also liked crashing guitars and loud, screaming punks – but no one ever made *that* into an integral part of her personality, did they?

It wasn't like she punched people all the time. Mainly it happened when lads called her emo, or on the couple of occasions someone had tried to slide their hands under her clothes without permission, because apparently girls weren't real, with feelings and boundaries, and therefore didn't mind if their bodily autonomy was violated. Sometimes, Jenny reasoned, a quick jab to the ribs was necessary to show them she existed.

Usually they brazened it out, acted like her puny little fists hadn't caused them to so much as flinch. After all, girls who aren't real can't hurt you, can they? Sometimes they'd get angry at her when she hit them, but mostly they laughed it off, maybe even started flirting again, to prove they were fine.

The boy/demon/whatever responded differently. The surprise on his face lasted only seconds before melting into something else. He smiled, a self-satisfied kind of grin as though he'd at last found the missing piece of some invisible puzzle. He blinked, and there was something wrong with his eyes – the black from his pupils blossomed outwards, ink on tissue, until there was no white left in them. Just a sheen of oily black from edge to edge.

'I found you.'

'Er, what?'

She had to admit, that trick with the eyes was cool, some kind of contact lenses or something, but this wasn't a LARPing kind of party.

She was about to tell him exactly this when he yelled, 'Zilch! I found her!'

'*Don't* call me that,' a voice snapped, and as Jenny watched, some shadows from a neighbour's hedge detached themselves and stepped forward.

'What have you come as?' Jenny asked as the shadows revealed themselves: a girl, as tall as the demon boy, but with an expression on her face as dark as her hair. She, at least, was wearing a proper costume: black leather, skin-tight on her legs, and a matching top that looked more like armour than clothing.

The girl ignored her, turning her sour expression on to the blond boy.

'I think you'll find *I* found her, Luc Pyro.'

Luc – since apparently that was his name – glanced slyly at Jenny. When her eyes met his, he winked.

'Jenny Hall, meet Zillah Sixth Daughter, one of the elite Succubae of All Hell.'

'Uh, hi,' Jenny managed weakly, not entirely sure how to explain that whatever fictional universe they were referencing, she hadn't read it.

Then Luc added in a stagey whisper, 'Don't let her scare you – she's just a necessary evil.'

'Well screw you very much too,' Zillah muttered under her breath.

Evidently, Luc enjoyed winding up the scary leather girl, because his grin widened, and Jenny stared at his mouth. Not because he had a pretty smile (although he did), but because his teeth looked sharp.

It wasn't something Jenny had ever noticed in a person before. A wolf on TV, sure, but not a human. And yet, that's what held her attention. Shiny, white, sharp.

He switched the full beam of his pleasure on her, and next time he spoke his voice dropped lower, intimate. She had to stop herself leaning forward. *All the better to hear him, my dear.*

'Your life doesn't have to be squished into a bin bag in your aunt's living room, you know.'

The shiny jet black of his eyes locked with hers, but it wasn't his gaze that held her still, it was the words dripping from his mouth.

'I can offer you something that this place . . .' here he indicated the cul-de-sac Kai's party had spilt into, 'never will. I'm offering you a chance, Jenny Hall. To regain what you've lost. There's an abyss inside you. An emptiness. You've known that for a long time, haven't you? I can help. Come with me.'

His words rolled through to her bones, tempting. *What if* . . . but something primal told her to stop listening.

She sucked in a breath; Luc blinked, and the spell cracked.

'Are you offering me drugs?'

If he was offering her drugs, she might even apologize for hitting him.

Zillah, who had been watching this conversation with something suspiciously like bored indifference until now, snorted.

Luc shook his head. 'I'm not a drug dealer. I told you – I'm a demon.'

'Don't be a prick,' Jenny sighed. 'I can't deal with this tonight.'

All at once, she was exhausted. She just wanted to go *home* – even if she wasn't sure where that was.

Luc's face fell. 'You don't believe me?'

'Of course not!' Jenny snapped.

Zillah muttered something that sounded a lot like 'Told you so.'

Sick of this whole thing, Jenny moved to walk past Luc the Demon and Zillah Sixth Daughter.

'Wait,' Luc said.

Against her better judgement, she did.

'At least think about it,' he said. 'You can find me at the funfair. You know, if you change your mind.'

'Sure,' Jenny said, laying the sarcasm thickly over her tongue as she walked away. 'Or, you could go shag yourself.'

3

JENNY

She got as far as the Londis on Leeman Road before she realized why what Luc had said bothered her so much. No, not the 'there's an abyss inside you' rubbish, because duh – didn't everyone have one of those? No, what bothered her was: 'Your life doesn't have to be squished into a bin bag in your aunt's living room.'

Just how in the ever-loving piss did he know about that?

Only a handful of people knew she was crashing at her auntie's in the wake of The Fight with her mum. It wasn't that she was ashamed of it or anything. It was just that, saying it out loud, telling people, well, what if that made it real, somehow? Permanent? And as much as she loved her auntie, it was not a situation that could go on for ever. For one thing, it would mean permanently living with Auntie Vee's boyfriend, Charlie.

What Vee saw in Charlie, Jenny could not fathom. What kind of man had a go at a teenage girl because she wanted to get some sleep? It wasn't her fault the TV in his and Vee's room broke, was it?

'Can't even watch telly in me own fucking house!'

God almighty, she was sick of him paddying.

OK, sure, she probably shouldn't have snapped this time. Probably shouldn't have yelled through from the kitchen, 'It's not your house anyway, you useless dildo!'

In hindsight, that hadn't helped the situation.

But the sofa, and her aunt's house, were on the other side of the city now anyway, and Kai's house party was streets away, where no doubt that 'demon' was freaking out someone else, and where Caspian's tongue was probably still halfway down Amber's throat.

Now she hovered on the pavement in front of Londis with only the light through the glass entrance to see by, and everything that hurt her seemed very far away. She pulled her phone out of her front jeans pocket, knowing she had nowhere else to go, no one left to call—

And that's when she called her mum. She felt a pang at the six missed calls from Auntie Vee but ignored them, instead calling the number that *should* have been home.

Her mum didn't answer.

She hadn't picked up the phone to her only daughter for weeks. Just like Jenny ignored her calls in return. Why would tonight be any different?

Out of options, she flipped her phone closed and slid it back in her pocket before walking back to Vee's, pretending her thighs weren't really aching now from all this wandering about. All the lights were off, so she jiggled the Yale lock with her debit card until the mechanism clicked open.

Jenny didn't like to use this secret technique too often, in case Charlie caught wind, but it was handy in a pinch.

Her plan was simple enough: slip inside and go to sleep as normal. Charlie would find her there in the morning, but like a toddler he was better-tempered after a sleep. With any luck he'd be on earlies anyway, so he'd be at work before she even woke up. Problem solved, conflict avoided, and she wouldn't have to apologize for something she wasn't sorry for.

Except, when she quietly closed the front door behind her and stole into the living room, she realized she was mistaken. Not all the lights were off – there was still one on in the kitchen. She walked through the living room to get to it and found Vee in a fluffy dressing gown, drinking tea from a Sports Direct mug.

'You're home, then,' Vee said as Jenny stepped through the doorway.

'Did you wait up for me?' A flare of panic. 'Has something happened?'

Vee sighed and ran her thumb and forefinger against the bridge of her nose.

'My sixteen-year-old niece called my boyfriend a dildo and did a runner,' she replied. 'That's what happened.'

Before Jenny could react, Vee continued.

'You can't keep running off in the night when things don't go your way—'

'Go my way?' Jenny interrupted. 'Is that what we're calling this? Not, you know, Charlie making me feel unwelcome here, again? I don't *love* feeling like that all the time, you know. I don't *love* being homeless and—'

'You're not homeless,' Vee said quickly. 'I love having you here. You know that; I wouldn't have offered if I didn't mean it. I want you to feel at home.'

'I sleep on your sofa and everything I own fits in a bin bag at one end of it,' Jenny pointed out. 'Forgive me if that doesn't feel like a stable home environment.'

Vee pouted. She shook her head, the scraped-back rope of her hair jiggling like a horse's tail flicking flies. These two motions – the pouting, the hair shake – were both signs she was rattled.

'I know none of this is your fault,' Jenny conceded. 'And I am grateful for everything.'

She sank down into a kitchen chair across from Vee.

'I didn't mean to worry you.'

'The thing is, love, it doesn't occur to you I will worry. You seem to think no one cares about you, and if the slightest thing confirms your theory, you just . . . go. Abandon ship.'

Uh-oh.

Why didn't it feel like they were still talking about Charlie being a mardy git?

'I don't—' she began, but Vee cut her off.

'Of all the people in the world, I know my sister isn't perfect,' Vee said.

Ding ding ding! Bingo.

‘I don’t want to talk about Mum. I know I shouldn’t have said that to Charlie, and I’ll apologize, I promise. But The Fight with Mum was different. That wasn’t me “abandoning ship” or whatever. She hates me.’

‘Your mum does not hate you!’

‘You weren’t there. You didn’t hear what she said. What I said.’

‘And neither of you will tell me, so—’

So Vee had spoken to Jenny’s mum, then. Or tried to, at least. Jenny supposed she couldn’t really be mad about that; they were sisters, and Auntie Vee was letting Jenny stay at her house for free. It shouldn’t be a surprise that she was curious about The Fight.

But she’d have to stay curious.

She folded her arms across her chest and deflected. ‘If me being here is causing problems between you and Charlie . . .’

‘Any problems between Charlie and me are exactly that: between us. I told him tonight not to say things like that again, and we’re going to get a new telly at the weekend for the bedroom.’

As though Charlie’s dislike of Jenny was so easy to fix.

‘But,’ Vee continued, ‘I need you to stop baiting him. Calling him names doesn’t help anyone, does it? And frankly, Jen, I’m having enough problems getting the boys to give him a chance. I don’t need them taking inspiration from you.’

‘The boys’ were Vee’s children from her previous relationship: Connor and Tyler, both of whom disliked

Charlie as much as Jenny did.

Then why are you with him, Vee? The question sat on the end of Jenny's tongue, but she wasn't quite brave enough to let it out. For one thing, she suspected she knew the answer: Vee had been there when Jenny's dad left. She'd seen a parade of men stomp in and out of her sister's life since, and she'd watched as Jenny's relationship with her mum deteriorated because of it.

Charlie, for all his (many) faults, was still here. As far as Jenny could tell, that alone didn't make him a role model for the boys, but it stopped her asking that question.

'I'll make more effort,' Jenny promised.

Vee relaxed. The tension under the fluffy dressing gown eased, and her shoulders dropped from their position by her ears.

'Good,' she said, pushing back her chair to stand. Her lips twisted upward at one side.

'Oh, love,' she breathed. 'Whatever happened to that sweet little girl with a smile for the whole world?'

She rinsed out her mug and patted her niece on the head as she passed. She left the light on, but it didn't really matter. Jenny was too stunned to move. Maybe it was meeting that demon, the stuff he said about her being empty, but whatever it was, Vee's passing nostalgia for a cheerful, childhood version of Jenny hit her right in the chest.

Because, the thing is, she knew exactly when that friendly little girl had disappeared. She was six years old, on a camping holiday, with a heavily pregnant Auntie

Vee because her parents were getting divorced.

Ouch.

She hadn't thought about Elrick Park for a very, very long time.

4

LUC | 2 WEEKS AGO

There were worse things than an urgent summons to his father's office, Luc thought as he made his way over, but surely not many.

Seth Pyro's office sat on the top floor of a glossy black cube of a building, ostentatious and completely out of place next to the original Suicides' Forest. It was the headquarters of Seven, Inc., the company of which his father was CEO, and which essentially existed, as far as Luc could tell, to own other companies. Pretty much every business and piece of land in All Hell, for example, and more than a few on Earth too, although that wasn't information Luc was supposed to bandy about willy-nilly. Something to do with 'keeping your mouth shut if you know what's good for you'.

Luc knew what was good for him. Living with the

most powerful demon in all of the Abyss kind of hammered that home. And Seth Pyro was certainly that: powerful. Even if Seven, Inc. hadn't existed, Seth was still the only son of the most famous Fallen Angel of them all, Lucifer the Lightbringer, and as such, largely untouchable.

Shame that kind of prestige somehow didn't seem to pass down the line to Lucifer's grandson. Luc waved at the security demon on shift as he walked through the doors and received a scowl in return. Not that he expected anything else; he might *look* enough like his father that no one would question his presence, but he knew the demons in his father's employ didn't like him. He made a point to smile sweetly in return, which only made things worse. 'Sweet' was rarely a winning strategy in Hell.

Another scowl greeted him at the gilded lifts, where an elevator attendant waved sharp claws over a set of runes carved into the wall. Luc stepped inside as some of the runes lit up, and the lift mechanism growled into life, carrying Luc and the attendant upwards towards the top floor. No words passed between them until Luc got off at the top.

'You've got meat in your teeth,' Luc told the attendant calmly, masking the smile that wanted to emerge as she frantically tried to pick it out with one pointed foreclaw. The lift sank out of sight and Luc allowed himself that victory.

Then he set his shoulders and turned towards his father's office. There would be no victories in there; Seth Pyro would make sure of that.

'You're here,' Seth said flatly as Luc slid into the office.

'You sent for me.'

'Stop dithering by the door and sit down, then.'

Luc bit back the defensive retort that rolled up his throat and instead did exactly as he was told, striding through the room and taking a seat in the polished leather chair across the desk from his father. This office, he thought, was so masculine it practically sweated single malt. He let his eyes rest on the desk, the expanse of varnish and mahogany between them like a metaphor.

And then he waited for his father to tell him what he'd done wrong this time. There had to be something, otherwise he wouldn't be here. That was the worst aspect of having Seth Pyro for a father: spies, everywhere.

Seth regarded him for a long moment, steepling his fingers thoughtfully.

'You know I've always considered you a disappointment, don't you?'

Luc blinked. The shock of that bald statement was a bucket of cold water over his head, and it took him a second to recover. But when he did, his father was watching his face. Looking for the hurt he knew he had inflicted.

'Yes,' Luc said quickly, hiding the worst of it as best he could. 'I do know that.'

'Good. Perhaps you're not a total lackwit, in that case.'

'Is that it?' Normally his father just waited until he got home to remind Luc he was a failure, a disgrace to Lucifer's line.

'Of course not,' Seth snapped, in a tone that suggested he was revising his previous statement regarding the state of Luc's wits. He tugged impatiently at one of his desk drawers, retrieved a package from it and slid it across the desk.

'I wanted you to have this.'

Suspicion wormed through Luc immediately. They did *not* have the kind of relationship that involved gift giving. Once, when Luc was younger, he had asked why they didn't celebrate birthdays like his friends' parents did, and Pyro had told him that birthday celebrations were reserved for children who weren't merely parasites.

Still, his curiosity won out, so he opened the package and pulled out a contraption the likes of which he had never seen. If he didn't know any better, he might think his father had just gifted him *jewellery*, since there were leather straps on either side for tying the thing to his wrist, but he did know better, so he ignored the straps and instead inspected the object held in the middle. It was a flat disc, like a watch face, except there was no way it could tell the time. For one thing, the material didn't appear to be glass, exactly, just something *like* glass, and for another it didn't have numbers, numerals or clock hands. Instead, the glass disc domed slightly over what looked like a near-perfect replica of the night sky.

Not that Luc had ever seen the night sky, since the stars in the Abyss were false, but he'd seen illustrations of constellations before. But whatever was going on inside the disc was no illustration. He peered deeper into the detail. A flash of light caught his eye, and a shooting star crossed the disc.

'What is it?' he asked.

'Very expensive, is what it is, so you'd better not lose it.'

'You're *giving* this to me?'

Seth looked exasperated. 'It certainly looks that way, doesn't it?'

'But why?'

'That device tracks the celestial spheres,' his father said. 'Twist the disc and you'll see what I mean.'

He did, and the image on the disc shifted, until he could see another set of stars, another night sky, overlaid across the top of the one that had already impressed him. The stars, he noted, were almost identical in terms of constellations, but the positions didn't align properly. It was like this second set of stars stalked the first set, shadows always two steps behind.

'I need you to do something for me.'

This was new; normally his father didn't trust him with anything.

'What?'

'It's high time you proved yourself. Your entire existence cannot be pointless for ever – and since you have thus far refused to declare your Demonity, this feels appropriate.'

This was a low blow.

'There is a delicate matter,' Seth continued, 'which must be resolved before the stars in that disc align.'

Another desk drawer, another retrieval, this time a slim manila folder with a name typewritten across the front:

Jennifer Louise Hall. Luc flipped it open and skimmed through the first page of notes, a frown deepening as he did so.

'You want me to go to the surface, to find a girl?'

'I do.'

'But that's—'

'Breaking the Sacred Agreement? Yes, that's rather why I need you to be discreet.'

It made sense, suddenly. If one of Seth Pyro's many agents got caught doing something like this, they'd be hauled up in front of the Celestial Council before they could blink, and no doubt it would be a long, drawn-out affair to get them back. And Pyro *would* try to get one of his usual agents back, because he valued their skills, their loyalty.

As for Luc?

'What happens if I get caught?'

'I would strongly advise against that.'

Because Seth wouldn't expend any energy at all on retrieving his only son from the clutches of the Celestial Council. A slow, burning anger rose to the surface of Luc's body. His hands shook with it, so he laid the device back on the desk, covering a grainy photograph of the human girl. *Fig 1: answers to 'Jenny'*.

'What if I say no?' he asked quietly.

His father seemed to consider this seriously for a moment. 'Well,' he said, drawing the word out, 'then you would be of absolutely no use to me, would you? No powers, no apparent intelligence to speak of, certainly no respect among the demons here. I should need to *find* a use for you. In the Legions, perhaps?'

Luc's skin felt tight and his eyes widened in horror.

'You wouldn't,' he whispered, even though he knew his father absolutely would.

Seth didn't reply, waiting him out instead.

The demons of the Legions were not administrators. They didn't exist to *assign* humans to punishments, they were the punishers. They weren't *designers*, working out how to refresh torture pits every few centuries for maximum hurt – they *were* the hurt. The demons of the Legions meted their punishments out by hand, and they revelled in it. The things they did to human souls were abhorrent. Vile. Sanctioned under the Sacred Agreement, yes, but not *moral*. Not right, and yet they *enjoyed* it.

And demons like that weren't born. They were made, right there in the Legions, brainwashed and transmuted into the worst kinds of monsters.

Luc felt sick. For the first time, he realized exactly how deep his father's loathing ran. Sending him to the Legions was not just a death sentence – demons of that ilk lived short, violent, brutish lives – it would *destroy* him first.

'What's so special about this girl?' he managed to choke. She had to be the second coming, surely, for his father to threaten him with the Legions in service of catching her.

'Absolutely nothing,' Seth sniffed, as though he didn't know his son was in turmoil. 'She is a nobody, a non-entity, and that is why the Council will barely note her disappearance. I could have chosen any one of the several billion crawling across the surface, but this one happened to be in the right place at the right time.'

Luc wondered if this girl would agree with that assessment. His gaze fell on the shelves behind his father's desk. Books, ledgers, lever arch files – and one shelf filled exclusively with empty soft drinks cans. He knew they were empty because all the tabs had been popped; all but one, anyway. He also knew they weren't actually designed to hold fizzy drinks. He glanced back at the file on the desk and confirmed what he'd already guessed: the single full can contained the girl's soul. Luc was supposed to use this as bait. A pit opened up in his stomach. He'd always found the soul-contracts distasteful, which wasn't a popular view among demonkind. It wasn't that he had any particular love for humanity – he hadn't even met a human while they were still alive – but he didn't feel the need to add to their torment. He didn't want *this*. But it was him or her, wasn't it? His eye fell again on that grainy image. *Answers to 'Jenny'*. Jenny, or the Legions.

'I'll do it,' he said. 'On one condition.'

'Oh?' Pyro narrowed his eyes. 'In a strong position to be making conditions, are you?'

'I need a Succubus.'

'You can't trust a Succubus,' Seth said, irritated.

'They're my best chance at getting past the twins, Dad. If you want this girl before the stars align, I need a Succubus.'

And apparently Seth Pyro did want the girl before

then, because within twenty minutes Zillah arrived, scowling just like everyone else in All Hell did.

'Good luck,' his father told him as Luc strapped the star tracker to his wrist. 'And remember, Luc, you *must* get her here before those stars align.'

5

JENNY

Jenny got to school in the nick of time, breathless from the quickest walk she'd been able to muster that wasn't a cringey jog. You'd think it was impossible to oversleep when your bedroom doubled as a living room, but it turned out you could. And oversleeping at Vee's house meant missing the optimal grooming window. There was only one bathroom, and five people to get ready for the day. She didn't even get in to brush her teeth until the whole room reeked of Lynx Africa and unwashed armpits, and she was already running late.

Her foundation was sticky on her face and her glasses were all steamed up as she swung into an empty seat in the Year Eleven registration room, so she fanned herself with her planner to dry the sweat. She considered, briefly, taking off the baggy navy jumper that had the school's logo embroidered across the left breast, but that was bound to smudge her make-up, so she didn't bother. Anyway, she'd had to grab one of Connor's polo shirts from the laundry basket this morning, and there was some kind of yellow stain on it she didn't want anyone seeing.

Mr Parker wasn't there to take the register yet, so Jenny leant on the back two legs of her chair and tried to cool down before anyone noticed her dishevelled state.

Fate had other plans. Someone landed in the seat next to her. Not fate, then. Amber bloody Coombs. Also known as the Incredible Boyfriend-Stealing Slagbag.

'Hey . . .' Amber said, in that affected sing-song voice that always did Jenny's head in.

Someone must have told her Jenny was at the party last night. There was no other earthly reason Amber would be here right now, sitting next to her. Once upon a time, sure, because back then it was Amber's seat and if anyone else dared to sit there, she'd have had something to say, but now . . .

'Are you lost?' Jenny asked, forcing her face into stillness to hide her feelings.

Amber pouted. 'No.'

'Well, get that way.'

She didn't. Instead, a slow smile spread across her pink and white complexion, blooming under the constellation of freckles she tried to hide with sticks of too-pale concealer.

'I bumped into Caspian at Kai's party last night,' she said. Her voice was sickly sweet.

I bet you did, Jenny thought.

She said, 'Oh.'

'He mentioned you two broke up last week. I was sorry to hear that.'

'What do you want, Amber?'

'He found his hoodie – it's the weirdest thing. He said he'd lent it to you, so how it got into the living room at Kai's nan's house, I have no idea.'

She unzipped her schoolbag and pulled the hoodie out.

'Anyway, he said I could wear it if I wanted.'

She wasn't even being subtle. She wanted a rise out of Jenny – but *why*?

'I'm sure it looks great on you,' Jenny lied, trying not to remember the night Caspian first gave it to her to wear, seated under Scarborough Bridge just far enough away from the rest of their group for it to feel intimate. She'd told Caspian things that night that she'd told no one else, and she'd let him kiss her afterwards. It was wetter than she'd expected, and when he snaked his tongue into her mouth, she'd had to fight the urge to gag, but still.

That night was special, and now Amber had Caspian's hoodie instead.

'Thank you,' Amber squealed. 'I knew you'd be happy for me – for us. After all, it's not like you two were serious, was it?'

'Was it not?' This was news to Jenny. It had felt pretty serious. Four months out of her life she wasn't getting back.

'You know, I mean . . .' Amber chewed her lip before

continuing. Jenny watched the pink flesh disappear between white teeth. 'I'm just saying, it's not like you had sex or anything.'

'Wow. Told you that, did he?'

Amber's eyebrows lifted, her perfect rosebud mouth opened, but then Mr Parker strolled in. The lads near the front started whooping as though welcoming a homecoming hero, and Amber snapped her mouth shut again, turning towards the front.

But if Jenny thought that was the end of it, she was sadly mistaken.

'I hope you're not upset he told me,' Amber whispered as Mr Parker called out names for the register.

Jenny ignored her.

'I know you wouldn't understand, because Caspian's the only boyfriend you've ever had, but when you meet someone new, you'll tell them things, too. It's like, how it starts.'

'You went after my ex-boyfriend by chatting shit about me behind my back, then?' Jenny snapped.

Amber's eyes widened, and Jenny could read the triumph in them. How had this horrible specimen of a so-called human ever been her best mate?

'I didn't *go after* anyone, thank you very much,' Amber replied.

From the front, Mr Parker glanced up. 'Everything OK over there, girls?'

Both Amber and Jenny ignored him, glaring at each other now.

'Oh no? It hasn't even been a week since we split up, and you've already jumped on him!'

'Split up? He dumped you, Jenny. I know he did because he told me he was going to. I didn't have to jump on him – he came to me of his own free will, because he needed someone to talk to. And since I already know what you're like, it only made sense that he came to me.'

Jenny's ears rang. She could see Amber's lips moving, and somewhere she was conscious of the words spilling from them – but nothing else. Was Mr Parker still asking them to calm down? How many of their classmates had swivelled round to watch the show? She scraped back her chair and stood up, backed away from the desk as though Amber was made of poison. Because she was.

'What else did he tell you?'

The words came from her, but she hadn't consciously spoken them. A rolling heat washed through her, steaming the edges of her glasses until she could only see Amber, who was also on her feet now.

'He told me you were sad because you fell out with your mum and had to go live with your auntie.' Amber's triumph peaked. 'And honestly? I'm not even surprised. Not even your own parents want you.'

It was like Jenny's body and mind were on separate wavelengths. In her head, just a black tangle of rage, wordless. In her body, the heat that had been building found an outlet as she took two steps towards her one-time best friend and punched her.

6

LUC

At Luc's expensive private school, he had taken a class called Earthly Cultures. It was a mandatory class, with a shrewish, sour teacher called Madam Alecto. She would hunch at the front of the classroom, scowling in completely uncalled-for rage, jabbing at the blackboard with a long piece of yellow chalk.

Madam Alecto *hated* Earth, and all who lived there. Humans, she spat, were usurpers. Lower than a pit viper's belly. Selfish, craven creatures, nothing like demons. Demons, by contrast, were unfairly punished. Oppressed. Damned to live in an endless Abyss while the truly vile creatures of Earth proliferated under the sun.

In Luc's current position, which was standing inside a damp-smelling ticket booth for a haunted house attraction at a ramshackle funfair, he had a pretty good view of this

Earthly sky, and he had news for Madam Alecto: they weren't proliferating under the sun. More like 'under heavy cloud cover'.

Ah, if only his old teacher could see him now.

You could always tell when Madam Alecto was really animated about some facet of humanity, because the end of that stick of chalk would bang against the blackboard hard enough to crumble, tiny plumes of sulphur-yellow powder falling to her feet.

In particular, Madam Alecto liked to point out that humans were gullible, and that they were cowards. Gullible, because how else could you explain all the demonic pacts over the years? And cowards, because they were uniformly, utterly terrified of anything even remotely demonic. The Sacred Agreement had banned (most) demons from walking on Earth without explicit approval, and this was a shame, Madam Alecto said, because the only good human was a human *soiling themselves from fear*. Hence all the creative and dastardly punishments for the human souls condemned to All Hell after death, Luc supposed.

Not for the first time, he wondered *why* so many of his peers felt the need to hurt humans. He wouldn't call himself an expert, exactly, but from the limited time he'd so far spent on Earth he already knew Madam Alecto's teachings were seriously outdated.

For example, in Luc's experience, humans were not afraid of the demonic. If they were, people wouldn't keep asking him if he was wearing false teeth. Far from inflicting terror on them with his obsidian demonic eyeballs, he discovered groups of teenagers wearing black clothes and loads of eyeliner crowded round the booth where he worked, clamouring with questions about where he got his contact lenses, and did he ever like, have any problems with conjunctivitis?

Obviously, they all thought he was in 'costume' for his job at Hugo's House of Horrible Haunts. A place where, by all accounts, humans went inside *in the hopes of being scared*. Which . . . kind of destroyed Madam Alecto's theory of fear, no?

All in all, he wasn't sure that class was worth the money his father had paid for his education.

Unfortunately, thinking about his father soured Luc's mood. Every day that Luc spent here, selling tickets to a crappy haunted house, was another day he had failed in the mission his father had set for him, and another day closer to the sealing of Luc's fate. Maybe humans weren't afraid of demons, but Luc was – or at least, he was afraid of what Seth planned to do to him if he failed.

For probably the fiftieth time that day, he pulled back the sleeve of his uniform and twisted the glass disc on his wrist. Was he imagining it, or were those secondary stars moving quicker now?

But what could he do? Jenny had refused his offer. She wasn't as gullible as Madam Alecto had suggested she would be. And she wasn't scared of him. No one was.

And that was the thing, wasn't it? Humans round here weren't unafraid of demons because they'd discovered the right protection charms, or because they were confident their prayers would always be answered. No, these people weren't afraid of demons because they didn't even believe in them.

A young human couple approached the booth. Two men, one of them hanging off the other's arm and giggling nervously.

'It won't be too scary, will it?' this one asked his boyfriend.

'Nah,' the other replied, shooting him an affectionate grin. 'It'll be a laugh.'

Luc scowled at them and let his eyes blossom black as he handed over their tickets and gave them their change. The nervous man squeaked, but his boyfriend just laughed, and said, 'Great trick.'

So, now Luc's main problem was this: how was he supposed to persuade a cynical, homeless nobody that demons not only existed but that she should absolutely follow one through a portal into All Hell?

He knew what his father would expect him to do.

Lie to her.

7

JENNY

Jenny supposed she should be grateful that Amber smacked her right back, twice as hard, because this was the only thing that prevented the school from calling the police and excluding her on the spot.

She knew this because Raffo (Ms Rafferty, really, but no one called the Deputy Head that) was explaining it to her, while Jenny held an ice pack wrapped in blue paper towels to her jaw. It was sore now.

She was in Raffo's office, a large room for a Deputy Headteacher's office in a bog-standard comprehensive. Beyond the desk set-up there was a round, green rug, several potted plants with wide leaves, and even a sofa, which is where Jenny was currently sitting. Raffo crouched in front of her, 'getting down to her level'.

'I'm sure you're aware your actions today fell short of

our expectations for students at Lawton. You and Amber have been separated from each other and the rest of the student population until we can be sure you're no longer a danger to each other or to anyone else.'

Was this Jenny's cue to fall to her knees and apologize?

'By rights, we should at least consider suspension, if not long-term exclusion.'

Jesus Christ. What did these people want from her?

'Suspend me then,' Jenny said. 'I'm not asking for special treatment.'

And in some ways, it would be a relief. A couple of weeks off school, no more daily pretence. She could ask Allie or Tahmina to meet her somewhere to hand off homework tasks – they weren't exactly friends, but they were nice girls who didn't live that far from Vee's and were both more interested in getting good grades than boyfriends and associated drama.

Apparently, Raffo had other ideas.

'I'll need to speak to your parents, of course, so in the meantime, you'll be working in the library with Ms Carlson.'

Not the isolation room, Jenny realized. Presumably because Amber was already in there and they didn't want a rematch on their hands.

But, more importantly:

'You can't call my parents.'

From the shifty expression on Raffo's face, she guessed they'd already tried. She could imagine what kind of response they got from her mother – if she'd even answered the phone. As for her dad, well, Jenny suspected any number the school held for him was long out of date.

'We can call your aunt,' Raffo suggested. 'I understand that's where you're staying?'

Jenny nodded. Poor Vee – she was working a double today, and now this. Guilt washed through her; maybe Amber had a point. Even her parents didn't want her, so why should anyone else? All she ever did was cause trouble.

These thoughts racketed through her brain, keeping her quiet as Raffo left a message on her aunt's voicemail.

'You go on ahead to the library now,' Raffo said.

'I'm sorry, Raf . . . I mean, Ms Rafferty,' she said.

The Deputy Head shot her a quick smile and handed her school bag to her.

'This is the first time I've ever seen you in my office, Jenny, so I know this is out of character. You're a good girl, and it sounds like things are rough at home right now. Remember, we're here to help you, if we can.'

Jenny struggled not to roll her eyes.

How were *teachers* going to help her, when clearly they didn't even understand her? See, she wasn't a good girl. Not really. Not when her only emotions were anger and sadness, except for that tiny moment when her fist connected with Amber's perfect skin. She'd felt a flare of something else then, and if she was completely honest with herself, she wanted to feel it again. She'd been pretending to be good for as long as she could remember, but right now she wasn't sure why she bothered.

Because she wasn't a good girl, Jenny didn't head straight down the corridor towards the library. Instead, she hung a right and pushed open the door towards the PE changing sheds. There was no one in there this morning, no one to see as she slipped behind them and through the gap in the hedge that by tacit agreement no student ever told the teachers about.

What was the point of hanging around here, pretending she was something she wasn't? No. Instead she was headed back to the house, where if she was lucky Vee would have forgotten her phone, and Jenny could erase that voicemail before her aunt could find out what a violent, angry little madam was living under her roof.

Although, she was forced to remind herself, the bruise on her jaw might be a bit of a giveaway. It throbbed now, and even though she couldn't see it, she could imagine it: an unholy purple and green bloom, like alien algae crawling beneath the surface of her skin. She could imagine, too, the horror on Vee's face, the slick triumph on Charlie's . . . the boys would probably think it was cool, but that was why Vee wouldn't like it.

Even worse, Jenny realized as she walked the familiar path towards Vee's house, Charlie might be home at this time of day. He was on bloody earlies, wasn't he? If he wasn't home already, it wouldn't be long. The thought of him, sweating in his work gear on the sofa Jenny would need to sleep on later, made her nauseous. Only the hope of deleting that voicemail kept her going in that direction.

Just as she'd feared, Charlie's car was pulled up on the

kerb. At least the door was unlocked, so she didn't have to knock and wait like a visitor. Thank Christ for small mercies. She closed it quietly behind her out of habit more than politeness, then stepped into the living room, which was empty. Maybe he was asleep. That wouldn't be so bad.

She took her bag off and was just about to go searching for some concealer for her bruise when she heard the voices coming from the other side of the open kitchen door. Charlie and Vee – apparently arguing about something. So Vee *was* home. *Uh-oh*.

Feeling like a criminal, Jenny made herself as quiet as possible so she could hear them better.

'. . . I only asked how long she's going to be here for!' Charlie said, and Jenny's spine straightened.

'And I can't answer that, can I? What do you want me to do – chuck her out on the street?'

'No.' The sound of something landing on the kitchen table. 'No! Obviously not! As if you think I'd suggest that, Vee. I'm just saying, it's relentless. I work hard – really bloody hard. When I come home I just want to chill out in front of the telly, but the whole time she's there, waiting for us all to leave.'

'Well, she needs to sleep. She's at school—'

'I know that. I know! But she's moody, and rude, and now apparently violent, and for God's sake you said it was just for a few weeks. It's been months! What happens come Christmas? We have to put up with that mopey cow ruining the day for everyone?'

It was very warm in the house. Jenny's glasses were all foggy, and sweat prickled uncomfortably in her armpits, across her back. She waited for Auntie Vee to defend her, to snap at Charlie that, of course, Jenny was welcome there for Christmas. That she was welcome as long as she liked and anyway, who the hell was he calling a mopey cow?

Auntie Vee said nothing. The silence crystallized, and Jenny realized Vee wasn't going to disagree. About any of it. And at any moment, one of them was bound to come into the living room and find her there, and then they'd know she overheard everything and then, and then . . . and then what?

What if it was the perfect opportunity for her to admit she hated having Jenny there, and that maybe it was time she left? And Charlie's smug face would be over her shoulder, watching in barely contained delight as Jenny picked up her bin bag of clothes and . . .

Nah. Not happening. No, ta.

If she was leaving, she was doing it on her own terms.

She was wearing plain ballet flats, black skinny jeans, a stained polo shirt, and her school jumper. She had her bright pink phone in one front jeans pocket, and £3.62 in the other.

Those were the things she took with her when she crept back across the living room and slid out of the front door, as quietly as she'd come in.

8

MARTHA OF ELRICK PARK

Martha Garstang was a short woman, plump, with the right sort of ruddy cheeks and green aprons for a life like the one she led now. Now she lived in the country air, in a modern wood-framed cottage, amidst a glorious forest.

'Some people have all the luck,' guests sometimes told her, admiring her home, but it wasn't really a matter of luck. She hadn't stumbled aimlessly into this life, no – she deserved it. She'd made a bargain to get where she was, and worked hard every day besides! And she wasn't a passive beneficiary but a guardian: in her role as Site Manager at Elrick Park she was guardian of the forest, and she was also the official guardian of two beautiful children. *Children!* Who would ever have thought it, eh? Everything she could ever have wanted, painted bright on the canvas of life.

Oh, fine, so they weren't ordinary children. When she'd told her benefactor she'd always dreamt of being a mother, her eyes sparkling over the very nice two-for-one cocktail he bought for her, she hadn't expected . . . *this*. But still.

Her life at the park was very different to the life she once lived, but she didn't need to worry about that any more. Why would she want to think back on that time, when she had so much to enjoy in the here and now? Things like rushing through acres of forest on a golf buggy or sitting in a sentry box doing crosswords.

Crosswords! Old ladies did crosswords, didn't they? Martha was not an old lady. Not yet anyway. But she liked crosswords. She liked the simple things. She liked the fact she had time to do crosswords, and to sit in the sentry box, basking in the solitude even at times of day or night when the chances of a customer rolling up to the gate were very slim indeed. She liked to sit there quite a lot, actually, to the extent that a casual observer might reasonably conclude she was perhaps avoiding something. Someone. A pair of someones.

But that wasn't true. She just enjoyed her own company, that was all – and the children were more than capable of looking after themselves. She enjoyed being on her own in the sentry box, which was only a small space, really, and sometimes her muscles spasmed if she sat for too long, but if she managed to get properly absorbed in her crosswords then she could stop some of the thoughts that . . .

Anyway, the point was that Martha wasn't old, despite

the crosswords, and sometimes she felt almost guilty about this fact. Only sometimes, usually when she wasn't doing a crossword, and her thoughts weren't focused on seven down or sixteen across, when she let herself remember that she hadn't been young when she arrived at Elrick Park, and ten whole years had passed since that day, a span of time that should rightly have left some mark on her face, no? A dark patch here, a newly sprouted hair there? A wrinkle or two? And yet, if anything, when Martha looked in the mirror these days, she was sometimes struck by the notion she might actually appear *younger* than she once had. Ha! Imagine! Perhaps the forest was keeping her young. And that wasn't a disconcerting thought, not even remotely.

Anyway, staring in the mirror might be all right for some women, but not for Martha. Martha was busy. Busy managing the Park, which meant keeping the paths clear of nature's debris, cleaning the guest lodges after visitors left. (Whether they officially checked out or – more commonly – just slipped off in the night. Honestly, the rudeness of some people.) She'd even had to work out how to build a website to advertise, which seemed a little ridiculous – surely Seven, Inc. had the resources to hire some young web designer? As it was, Martha barely knew what WYSIWYG stood for.

But a website was necessary, because the suits at Seven, Inc. wanted Elrick Park to attract young people – stag and hen parties, that kind of thing. It struck Martha as a little odd, because most of their competitors focused on the 'family friendly' market, but she wasn't the boss, was she? What did little old Martha know about things like market segmentation and user-centred design? But sometimes she really did think the suits at Seven, Inc. needed to spend more time at Elrick Park if they wanted to ever understand the additional pressures Martha faced owing to their decision to focus on the young, carefree market.

The rebellious market, that's what it was – if not by name. Martha would know! She was the one dealing with missing reservations and purposefully ignored check-out deadlines. It *certainly* didn't help that by virtue of the Park's . . . interesting geography, there were certain rules guests needed to abide by if they wished to stay. Not difficult rules, and not too many to remember: one, stay on the paths away from the trees, and two, do not, under any circumstances, leave your allotted guest house after dusk.

It wasn't too much to ask, was it, that guests followed two teeny-tiny little ground rules? Unusual, perhaps, but if people wanted to be like everyone else they could go to Center Parcs, couldn't they?

Maybe the rules would be OK, for a pleasant family with responsible adults and well-behaved children, the kind you saw in the adverts for other holiday parks. The kind they had once been able to attract here, too. But Martha got the rebellious market now, didn't she? The ones who didn't like rules. Sometimes she sighed over this fact as she slopped another bucket of meaty gloop down the purpose-built drain near the middle of the forest.

Still, on the bright side, they weren't rules any guest

broke twice. And, fortunately, the payment policy ensured all guests paid for their stay in full, in advance, so even the groups who disappeared into the forest at night didn't leave marks on her budget.

All in all, it was challenging work, but enjoyable, mostly. And she could always retreat to her sentry box when things got too much.

Even more than the job, though, Martha enjoyed the lifestyle it afforded her. What other job would allow her to live on the edge of a 400-acre forest, and treat the whole thing like it was her own personal garden? What other job would gift that option to her two adopted children too, so they could run and play and climb trees to their hearts' content?

Not that they were the kind of children who ran, or played, or climbed trees. But still.

And if there were certain elements of the job, the Park itself, that didn't exactly make sense, well – that lifestyle, the children, outweighed them. For example – and Martha did not claim to be a geographer by any means – if they were as far north and as far west as they most definitely were, then surely there was no room on the coast for a 400-acre forest.

She'd checked a map once, to confirm this. According to the map, her sentry box should rightly be somewhere in the Irish Sea.

But that couldn't be right. Her own eyes, her ears, and the feel of the ground beneath her feet told her otherwise, and so she chose to ignore the mystery. Mysteries were just life's little way of adding spice to things – it wouldn't do to solve all of them, would it?

Much like the car left behind by the last lot of rule-breakers: the mystery of where its occupants had gone might once have stayed with her for days, but now she thought about it just long enough to decide which one of the twins' turn it was to dispose of it in case the police came, and then it was gone. Locked in a compartmentalized filing system in the deepest recesses of her clever human brain.

Sometimes it was hard, of course. Sometimes her humanity called out – *this isn't right, Martha* – but that was easy to quell. A comfy chair. A flask of tea. A crossword or two.

Anyway, aside from that small instance of guest misbehaviour, the week so far had been a total success, and things were quiet now they'd reached off-season.

She could perhaps look forward to a week of tranquillity, here in the sentry box with her crosswords and a flask of tea.

But sometimes life doesn't work out the way you might hope, does it?

9

JENNY

It was strange, being at the fair in daylight.

It wasn't a high-quality fair at the best of times, largely because it wasn't a static part of the city's landscape. It was a travelling fair, which meant the machinery was scuffed from years of being loaded on and off trucks, and it relied on the glamour of nightfall to cover its inadequacies. Without the velvet dark for camouflage, the lights were less dazzling, the music coming from each ride more obviously outdated.

Jenny pushed the rickety metal gate open and stepped inside.

The sky was grey and clouded, adding to the dreariness of the fair. Even the smells of the place were dampened by daylight – stale popcorn, yesterday's hot dogs.

It wasn't hard to find Luc. Compared to the jaded

reluctance apparent in most of the workers, some of whom pushed brooms over rubber floor panels, some of whom hid behind carousel ponies with rollies in their mouths, Luc stood out like a shiny gem on a piece of costume jewellery.

She found him outside a wooden structure with a painted sign in purple and black that said, HUGO'S HOUSE OF HORRIBLE HAUNTS. When he saw her coming towards him, his grin lit up his entire face. So, apparently *someone* was pleased to see her.

'Glad you could make it,' he told her when she was in earshot. He sounded suspiciously like he meant it.

Then he caught sight of her face, the bruise blossoming along one side of her jaw.

'What happened?' he asked, his eyes (which were ordinary eyes, not polished obsidian stones) widening.

'I don't want to talk about it,' Jenny said, on autopilot.

'No?' Luc cocked an eyebrow.

He didn't need to ask the rest of the question, but she heard it anyway: *So why are you here?*

It was a fair question. *God*, she thought irritably, *I'm such an idiot.*

The honest answer, obviously, was that she had absolutely nowhere else to be, and even though his performance at Kai's party was weird as hell, Luc at least wanted to spend time with her. For what purpose, she wasn't sure, but . . .

I found you.

That's what he'd said, like he'd been looking for her.

Like she mattered. Like she was wanted.

She swallowed, realizing she hadn't answered him. But instead of pushing for a response, Luc glanced around the fair and inclined his head towards a battered, much-loved dodgems set-up.

'Fancy a bang?' he asked, completely deadpan.

Jenny snorted, feeling colour flood her face. Oh, good, apparently she could still feel embarrassment. That was useful to know.

'You know you're not supposed to bash the cars,' she choked out.

'Why not? They're called *bumper* cars.'

'Dodgems,' Jenny insisted, 'as in, *dodge them*.'

Luc's eyebrow rose.

'Still . . . want a go?'

'Sure,' Jenny agreed, and to her surprise she realized she did. It was better than explaining her bruise, or that she was now much more 'homeless' than the 'semi-homeless' he'd accused her of outside Kai's nan's house.

The stocky man loitering outside the ticket box rolled his eyes when Luc asked for two cars, but he didn't refuse. Instead, he gave Jenny a pointed look as he helped her into her car.

'Hope you know what you're getting yourself into with him,' he muttered in a gravelly voice.

'I do,' she lied, gripping the steering wheel of her car, and pinning what she hoped was a steely gaze in Luc's direction.

He grinned in return, flicking his blond hair out of his

eyes. With a jolt, Jenny realized he was still wearing those tiny horns by his hairline. She hadn't noticed because his fringe more or less covered them. It must be part of the whole haunted house thing, she decided.

The ride operator slipped back into his booth and Jenny felt the surge of electricity enter her car. She watched as lights danced up the pole attached to the back of Luc's car, white and orange. The rest of the cars had been pushed out of the way around the edges, like a sullen crowd watching a face-off between Jenny and Luc.

A horn sounded, and Jenny's car moved. She twisted the wheel, and something light fluttered in her stomach. *Ah, yeah – this is what* fun *feels like.* She remembered. What with the whole 'falling out with Mum and moving in with Vee and getting dumped' situation, she'd forgotten.

She caught sight of Luc's car coming at her in her peripheral vision, a determination on his face that made her laugh, and she urged the car faster, spinning the wheel, so the front of his car only clipped the back of hers.

'Hey!' she yelled, spinning her wheel to avoid a collision with a stationary car and zipping away in the other direction.

He was on her tail in an instant, gaining on her, his mouth wide, revealing those sharp teeth. She shivered, not in fear but with a conviction that he would not catch her. More spinning of the wheel, more strategic turns to stop him bumping her car. They circled each other like animals, and when Luc made a misstep, accidentally ramming into one of the parked cars, Jenny threw her head back and barked out a laugh that felt so *free* she could barely focus on sweeping herself once more out of Luc's way.

Their time ended too soon. As soon as the power from the car faded, Jenny launched herself up from the seat and jumped out, giddy. Adrenalin coursed through her, bubbling up in her throat and escaping as laughter. She felt wild, suddenly. This was what she'd needed when she'd gone to Kai's party, this abandonment of real life, of real problems. There were no problems at the fair, and the chase wasn't over just because their time on the dodgems was.

'You can't catch me!' she yelled, bouncing past the dodgems operator, and throwing a 'Thank you!' in her wake.

Where could she go next? The answer presented itself when the helter skelter rose in her eyeline, a sorbet-yellow tower with its slide twisted around the outside. There was a spiral staircase running from the bottom, next to a neat pile of oversized welcome mats. She grabbed one as she went, hauling herself up the steps before the attendant could even run back over from where he'd been chatting up one of the candyfloss girls.

She heard voices behind her, then footsteps on the metal stairs, and she knew it was Luc, still in pursuit.

A bubble of gleeful panic rose in her throat as she reached the top of the enormous slide. She tossed the mat down on the lip, and for a moment she looked up. From this vantage, she could see the light of her home city spread out before her – streetlights just now winking into life as evening darkened the sky. She could see the architecture of the city, too – the jagged stone lines of the tower, the museum, Tudor buildings jostling with Victorian and modern architecture. The Minster stood in the distance, tall and patient. This was *her* city, her hometown, and right in that moment at the top of the helter skelter she understood for a second what it felt like to *feel* where you were from, roots anchoring her there.

But then she heard Luc's steps behind her, and she launched herself down the slide, her fingers gripping the edges of the rough-woven mat as she whooshed round, round, spiralling down.

She landed at the bottom with a dull thud and quickly stood up to return the mat to the scowling attendant.

'That was incredible,' she told him, and something in her face must have persuaded him she meant it, because his irritation melted.

'Always a good view when we set up here,' he acknowledged.

She heard another thud behind her and realized she should have kept running if she wanted to lose Luc, but she waited for him to bring his mat back, too. His eyes sparkled, she noticed, his cheeks flushed, and his hair tousled enough that the tiny horns were out.

'You win. Are you hungry?' Luc asked, and she realized she was.

He was good company. Over the next couple of hours, they wandered through the fair together, watching the place come alive as darkness settled overhead. The air was frosty, shining with the lights from various booths. The carnival atmosphere increased, and Jenny watched as queues of mums with young kids appeared by the teacup rides. The scent of popcorn intensified. Noisy machines chimed and kicked into gear.

Luc bought them both hot dogs, staring in barely disguised disgust as Jenny squeezed viscous red ketchup over the top. They ate them as they meandered through the fair in companionable silence. It had been a long time, Jenny realized, since she'd felt so comfortable in another person's company.

Which was especially weird given that he was still, basically, a total stranger. A total stranger with wolf-sharp teeth and spiky bumps by his hair even though Halloween was over. Even if it was a uniform for his job, it was a little weird.

But, still, she couldn't make herself care. It didn't matter who he was, just that he was here, where he'd told her to find him, and he seemed pleased to have her with him.

'I got into a fight with a girl at school,' she heard herself say.

It was like an offering, this information, and he seemed to understand this because he didn't rush in to respond, instead letting the words float in the air with them as they walked.

'Why?' he asked, eventually.

'She stole my boyfriend.' That wasn't the whole truth, exactly, but it was the easiest version of it to say out loud.

‘Fair enough,’ Luc said, and the lack of judgement in his tone loosened Jenny’s shoulders. She hadn’t realized she’d been worried about his reaction.

He stopped walking and raised a hand to her chin, avoiding the bruise but tilting her head so he could see it better.

‘I hope you hit her harder than you hit me the other night,’ he said.

As much as she told herself she wasn’t proud of her occasional violent outbursts, Jenny couldn’t help the warm bloom that swelled in her chest as she thought about this.

‘I’m pretty sure my jaw hurts less than her nose does,’ Jenny admitted.

Luc dropped his hand and nodded approvingly. ‘Good – maybe next time she’ll think a bit more carefully before she steals someone’s boyfriend.’

Jenny smiled at that. Out of the corner of her eye she caught him fiddling with something on his wrist; she couldn’t tell if it was a watch or a bracelet, but either way, she didn’t want to lose his attention to it.

‘I’m not really that bothered about Caspian,’ she said.

Luc snorted. ‘Caspian? What kind of name is that?’

‘The kind of name where your parents are rich,’ Jenny replied, fighting and failing to keep the giggle out of her mouth. Come to think of it, Caspian *was* a pretty funny name, wasn’t it?

‘Although,’ Luc said wryly, ‘I’m not sure I should judge him too harshly. My full name is Lucifer.’

'Bugger *off*,' Jenny said, almost choking on her last bite of hot dog.

'Can't, it's true! I'm named after my grandfather.'

The wheels turned in Jenny's head. Even she knew who Lucifer was – the angel who challenged God in the Bible. The one that 'fell' and became the leader of all the demons in hell.

'So, you want me to believe this demon thing?' she said evenly.

'If you don't believe me, why are you here?' Luc shot back.

Which was a reasonable question, she supposed.

'I don't have anywhere else to go.'

When he didn't respond right away, she asked, 'How did you find me? *If* you're really a demon, I mean.'

'Zillah,' Luc said succinctly.

Ah yes, the scary girl who liked leather.

'She's a demon too?'

'You couldn't tell?' Luc's lips quirked.

'So, your father's Lucifer?'

'Grandfather. My father is called Seth. Seth Pyro. And he's a total arsehole, honestly.'

'Hey, we have that in common! My dad is also a complete bumcrack of a human.'

'My father's not human.'

'Mine barely is.'

Luc opened his mouth as though to reply, but then his eyes snagged on a candyfloss stall.

'You know, I've been working here for days and not

tried that stuff yet.'

Jenny laughed. 'Well, don't let me stop you.'

'Want some?'

She shook her head, conscious that he'd already paid for hot dogs, and technically got her free entry on the rides.

He returned with two sticks anyway, thrusting one into her hand.

She watched out of the corner of her eye as he stuck his face into the sticky mass of sugar.

'Oh!' he said, his eyes bright. 'It's . . . *weird*!'

Apparently, that was high praise. They found a bench out of the way and sat down, and Jenny let a mouthful of pink and blue candyfloss melt on her tongue. After a while, the silence grew around them, and Jenny realized Luc was once again waiting for her to come to him.

'I don't believe in demons, obviously,' she said. 'And if I was sensible, I'd probably run far, far away from someone claiming to be one. Like, did you drop too much acid or something? I hear that messes you up.'

He didn't reply, just waited for her to go on. She could feel his eyes on her as he stuffed more candyfloss into his mouth.

'You said there's an . . . emptiness in me,' she said, hating the way her voice wobbled. 'I don't know how you knew that, but you're right, there is. I don't *feel* like I think I'm supposed to. I don't get excited about things the way other people seem to, and I don't *trust* people. My auntie says I abandon ship when things get hard, and she's probably right. Just like Amber's probably right that there's something wrong with me, and no one wants me because of it.'

Still nothing. Jenny chewed the inside of her lip before getting to the point.

'There's something broken in me, and you *knew.* I've spent so long feeling like this. Like, if I could just figure out which bit's missing, and fix it, then I can feel. I can be happy. And . . . maybe a bit nicer to be around, as well.'

She wasn't sure he was going to respond until he sucked in a breath.

'I know what's wrong with you,' he said. 'You don't have a soul.'

Whatever she'd expected him to say, it wasn't that. Her wrists felt funny, and her heart raced in her chest. Who the *hell* said things like that to someone? She was so close to hitting him again.

'Souls don't exist. Neither do demons. I don't know whether this is a cruel prank or a sex-trafficking scam, but you don't get to just tell someone they don't have a soul.'

Luc watched her, his expression thoughtful. He opened his mouth, but before he could speak, a hand shot out from the shadows behind him and cuffed him around the horns.

Zillah stepped out in front of their bench, hands on hips, scowling bleakly.

'*Where* have you been?' she snapped.

'I've been here,' Luc replied, rubbing his head where Zillah's smack had landed. 'Do you mind? We're having a moment here.'

Zillah's eyes narrowed.

'Is she coming with?'

'Uh, hi,' Jenny said, reminding Zillah she was *sitting right there.*

Zillah ignored her.

'That's what we're talking about,' Luc said. 'Chill out, Zilch, what's the rush?'

'Don't *call* me that!' she grimaced. 'And the *rush* is that I don't want to be here any more. This whole plane of existence makes my skin itch.'

Luc rolled his eyes, and for the first time, Zillah swung round to Jenny.

'What's the hold-up?'

'Uh . . .'

'She doesn't believe in demons,' Luc pointed out. 'That's proving to be a barrier.'

Zillah made a low noise in the back of her throat, folded her arms, and regarded Jenny like she was some kind of unknown lab specimen.

'Is that all?' she asked silkily. 'Because I can fix that. I can prove demons exist.'

'Zillah, no—'

But Jenny's interest shot up. 'Can you?'

It was one thing to believe Luc might be a scam artist making up some weird stuff about hell and her soul, but Zillah was so much more authentic. It was hard to believe a girl like her would ever feel the need to lie about who she was.

So if *she* was also in on this whole demon thing, did

that mean . . .

'Stand up, and I'll show you.'

She did as Zillah suggested. Luc protested again, but Jenny ignored him. He wanted her to believe him, didn't he? And, the logical part of her brain reminded her, Zillah couldn't possibly live up to her promise here. It was going to be some kind of sleight-of-hand street magician rubbish. Had to be. There was no harm in going along with it, was there?

Zillah moved slowly, so as not to startle her, and laid both of her long, warm hands across Jenny's cheeks and jaw. She was gentle enough that even the bruise didn't hurt, but the action turned Jenny's face up until she gazed into Zillah's eyes. They were purple, which wasn't a colour she'd ever seen in eyes before. She was close enough to see all the shimmers and ridges in Zillah's irises – like a set of matching amethysts. For an absurd moment she wanted to take her glasses off, like the lenses were too much of a barrier between her and this leather-clad goddess—

Then Zillah blinked, and her pupils ballooned, swallowing her irises until the whole of her eyes were fathomlessly black.

Cold splintered in Jenny's stomach, but she couldn't step away, couldn't so much as close her eyes against the twin black lagoons.

Zillah's lips quirked up, and she dropped one side of Jenny's face so she could take hold of a jumper-covered wrist instead. Jenny's mouth went dry. Her breath paused in her throat. Blood thundered in her ears.

She was trapped here, in this moment, with a creature so utterly magnetic the rest of the fair fell completely away. Jenny's body fought with her head, determined to stay close to this beautiful girl, to bask in any light she was willing to share.

The only sensation left in the world was the feeling of Zillah's fingertips as they slid slow, slow, down on to the cuff of her school jumper. Despite herself, Jenny's hand opened like a flower, and she felt the barest tips of Zillah's nails skate across the heart of her palm. Their skin brushed. The pads of their fingers pressed together. Jenny's eyes ached, but she couldn't blink, couldn't tear herself away.

Her hand tingled as Zillah interlaced their fingers. Something bloomed inside her wrist, a sensation she knew but couldn't place, something that made her knees feel soft and her teeth ache. She opened her mouth, and –

Zillah was in her head.

It was impossible to explain. She just knew that the girl with the enchanting eyes was *in* her thoughts, sorting through them like she was searching for something. All the follicles on Jenny's skin reacted to the sensation, and a voice screamed at her to break contact. She couldn't.

Instead, she could only wait until Zillah found what she'd come for. Jenny felt like a rack of CDs at a car boot sale, with Zillah's fingers flipping through them, pausing here, lingering there, but ultimately moving on each time. She hesitated over the memory of The Fight with Jenny's mum, her lips curling upwards even as Jenny flinched, but ultimately she left that alone too. And then, triumph lit up her eyes as she found a memory she wanted, coaxed it out of hiding. It didn't need to come far, since Jenny had been reminded of it recently. The summer Jenny stopped feeling.

Elrick Park.

They used to go on holiday all together – Jenny, Mum, Dad, Vee and even little Connor, usually somewhere like Butlin's or Haven.

But that year was different. That year, Mum and Dad weren't there.

That year it was just Auntie Vee, Connor and her. Well, and the baby in Auntie Vee's belly that would soon become Tyler. And they weren't at Butlin's, or Haven, they were at a new (significantly cheaper) holiday park Auntie Vee found in the paper called Elrick Park.

Jenny didn't much like Elrick Park. There was no swimming pool, for a start, and no friendly grown-ups in red jackets to come and take her on fun activities. Just Connor, who was too little to do much, and Auntie Vee, who was too full of baby to do much either.

There was a big forest, and Jenny spent time in there pretending she could talk to the trees by touching them, but only until she got shouted at by the lady who ran the place. She said *stay on the paths and don't touch the trees* and made Jenny cry.

After that, Jenny stuck close to Auntie Vee.

One day the three of them went for a picnic, and Connor was a big baby, wailing that he didn't want to eat his sandwiches because he didn't like fish paste, even though he had fish paste sandwiches yesterday and he liked them then, and he waddled off at a speed that made Auntie Vee huff as she hauled herself up off the blanket.

And then Jenny was on her own, glaring at her own sandwiches like they'd told her a bad story, and when she looked up there was a man on the picnic blanket, holding out a shiny can of pop with a happy yellow label.

She didn't see him arrive, but there he was, crouched down even though it strained the fabric of his posh suit at the knees. It was the same colour as the ash from the wood stove in their cottage, the man's suit, and his shoes were dark red, like dried blood. His tie matched his shoes, as did a neat pocket square.

He held out the can and said something to her in a low, calm voice like when Daddy read her bedtime stories. He hadn't done that for a while, though.

She didn't really understand what the man said to her, because she was too focused on the can. Jenny wasn't allowed pop at home, Mummy said it might rot her teeth and then she'd be sorry, but she'd had some at Connor's birthday party and really liked it, and before she knew it her greedy little fingers clasped around the can, which was almost too big for her to hold, and the man in the suit smiled wide, his teeth wolf-sharp.

'Open it,' he purred. 'It's a special drink, for good girls. You're a good girl, aren't you?'

And maybe she was and maybe she wasn't, but she opened the can and lifted it to her mouth, and something happened, something uncoiled inside her and swam up through her and no matter how much she drank, the can got heavier and she couldn't stop drinking, and she wanted to cry but the man was still there, and when she saw his face her heart stuttered in her chest.

No, not the little girl's heart, because *she* didn't recognize him, but *Jenny* did, and her heart screamed a warning at her the only way it knew how, by almost stopping.

Because it was Luc's face.

She snatched her hand away from Zillah, and ran.

10

JENNY

She ran like her feet were on fire. Her heart pounded, her pulse rocketed, adrenalin spiked through her nervous system. She was no longer human, instead a being made wholly of panic, of instinct.

She let her feet guide her, her cheap ballet flats slapping against the concrete pavement as she raced away from the fair. She was in a part of the city she didn't spend much time in any more, not since she was a kid, but it was as familiar to her as an old friend and she made a sharp right at a junction without pausing, launching herself towards the only place she could think of that might offer sanctuary.

Sunday school. Cheap biscuits and colouring in. That's what it was in her memories – an encapsulation of simple childhood pleasures. She'd never really paid attention to the stories themselves, instead just enjoying the way no one shouted there, not like at home. Jenny wasn't religious, but she associated church with peace.

God only knew how much she needed that right now.

It was an old church, nothing like the grandeur of the Minster she'd seen from the helter skelter, but still full of history and intricate stonework. She raced through the wrought-iron gates into the graveyard and flew up the deep stone steps towards the main doors set into a tall, rounded archway. One of them was ajar, inviting parishioners to join Evensong. Somewhere above, a bell chimed.

As soon as she was inside, Jenny stopped, heart hammering behind her ribs. She tasted blood. She pressed her back against the exposed stone wall next to the door and struggled to contain her breath. Here she was. House of God. Sanctuary.

The church was big enough that the sparse congregation towards the front didn't seem to notice her entry. This was, after all, evening prayer on an ordinary weeknight, not exactly the headline act. The vicar stood behind a brass lectern shaped like an eagle, the bird's wings acting as a rest for the Bible. He was grey-haired but didn't seem old enough for it, and he intoned slowly, clearly, as Jenny stepped forward and grabbed a hymn book from a pile on a table by the aisle. Just like she had after Kai's nan brought them downstairs after Sunday school.

She found an empty pew and took a seat.

'The sacrifices of God are a broken spirit,' the vicar was saying. 'A broken and contrite heart, the Lord could never despise.'

Well, Jenny's heart had broken a hundred times over, hadn't it? So according to the fella with the holy book at the front, God couldn't possibly despise Jenny, because her heart was in tatters and her spirit, soul, whatever – well, her soul was definitely in trouble. *If I even have one*, a little voice whispered. A hot tear splashed on to her cheek, and she dashed it away quickly.

Because that's what went into the can that day at Elrick Park, wasn't it? She hadn't known then, when it happened, because how could she? She was *six*. But now . . . ten years later, she suddenly had a very clear idea about why Luc thought there was a void inside her. He put it there, the day he took her soul and stuffed it in a yellow can of pop.

Help me, then, she prayed internally. *Tell me what I'm supposed to do now I know demons are real.*

But there was no answer, except the sound of the vicar's voice as he continued with his work. She didn't understand most of it, except for things like 'confess our sins' and 'obedience', neither of which were exactly Jenny's strong suit.

Although she hadn't been inside a church since she was about seven, this felt comfortably familiar. The thin cushion on the pew slid when she moved, and she remembered the way young Kai had wiggled on purpose to make it do just that. The kneeling bench on the floor in front of her was covered with faded green and yellow tapestry, and she remembered how much trouble they got in if they put their feet up on it. Even the hymnal in her hands was familiar, the leather binding warm to the touch, the paper inside worn and well-thumbed from the thousands of reverent hands that had flipped its pages in search of hymns to sing for their Lord God.

There were a fair few in here about souls, she noticed. 'Awake, my soul, and with the sun.' 'Hark, hark my soul!' Some others too, about how God was the light of the soul or how He made them shine. Nothing useful to Jenny's current predicament, though. None she remembered singing, either. It was all 'Morning has broken' and that kind of thing when Jenny used to sing here.

Tears itched her eyes. Why weren't things simple any more? Why did she have to live like this instead? Pursued by literal demons, while the rest of her life was on fire? Where was God's divine love when she needed it?

Is it because I stopped coming here? she asked silently. All of this – falling out with Amber, losing Caspian, the fight with her mum and – then – the rest of her family. Demons coming after her. Was it all because she stopped coming to church, stopped being a good little Christian girl?

Her rage simmered. What kind of God would let all this happen just because she had better things to do than sit in a draughty old building and sing? Like, didn't He have better things to do as well? Better things than punishing teenagers. It wasn't Jenny's fault her mum stopped sending her to Sunday school when her dad left!

Why wasn't God curing cancer or stopping all the wars going on around the world? Why was He so bothered about whether people were singing pretty songs to Him, or where insignificant old Jenny Hall spent her Sunday mornings?

Surely, Jenny thought, if God was real (and wow, that was a much more complicated 'if' now she knew demons existed), He would be more concerned about whether a person was good-hearted and wanted the best for the world around them than whether or not they went to a church, a mosque, a synagogue or whatever, so many times a week? Wouldn't He care more about being kind, about loving thy neighbour and not murdering each other?

It just didn't make sense any other way.

'Almighty and most merciful Father,' the vicar said, 'we have erred and strayed from your ways like lost sheep.'

Merciful? Jenny almost laughed out loud. If God had caused the stuff that had happened to her, as a punishment for her 'sins', or to get her to beg His forgiveness, he had seriously misjudged her. She was only here for protection from demons – demons who only existed because He or some other God must have made them. It was like running into Frankenstein's lab to hide from Frankenstein's monster.

At the front of the church, the vicar recited the Lord's Prayer. Didn't that happen near the end of the service? Where had the time gone? She didn't know how long she'd be allowed to stay after the service ended. She could only hope Zillah's tracking abilities didn't extend to consecrated ground.

'Our Father, who art in Heaven, hallowed be thy name . . .'

The vicar got as far as 'Thy will be done, on Earth as it is in Heaven' when someone sat down next to her.

Luc.

'What are you doing here?' she squeaked.

'I came to find you,' he replied. 'Oh, you mean why am I *here*, here?'

'Yeah.' She swallowed. 'Why aren't you on fire?'

Luc smirked. 'Church of England, innit.'

Jenny shot him a scandalized look, and the demon struggled to keep in his laughter.

'I'm joking,' he said. 'Churches are places where sinners come to atone, and who's a bigger sinner than a demon? We can come inside churches, it's just that most of us don't like it. You'll notice Zillah didn't join me.'

When Jenny didn't reply, just stared at him with frightened eyes, he continued.

'I never minded churches. I like the architecture. One of the many reasons I'm a disappointment to my old man.'

Before Jenny could respond, Luc grabbed the hymn book from where she'd dropped it and flipped through it. She panicked at his closeness, wriggling further away on the bench to keep space between them.

'It wasn't me, you know.'

'What do you mean?'

'I didn't take your soul. My dad did. Our shared face is about the only thing we have in common, and he hates to be reminded of it, so . . . yeah. I didn't steal your soul, but my father did, and *I know where it is*.'

Despite herself, Jenny's curiosity perked up.

'That's why I'm here – it's hard to explain to you, because you don't understand our world, but the simplest way I can explain it is that my dad is evil.'

Jenny's eyebrow hiked up her face. 'You don't say.'

Luc winced. 'Yes. I mean, duh, obviously, he steals kids' souls with fizzy drinks, but I mean, even by demonic standards. He's obsessed with power and status; his whole personality boils down to the fact that he's Lucifer's only son.'

'What has this got to do with my soul?'

'He shouldn't have taken it, Jenny. That's against the rules. We're allowed to make contracts with humans, but not with children! And we're not supposed to just take their souls, you know? There's a whole process. An agreement, between our people and the celestial lot. My dad broke that when he took your soul.'

She eyed him suspiciously. He sounded sincere, but on what grounds was she supposed to trust him? It was like a switch had flicked – one minute he was making snarky jokes about the Church of England and the next he was all 'my father is evil but I want to help', and was she just supposed to believe him? He was still a demon.

She swallowed. She was in a church, talking to a demon.

She opened her mouth to interrogate him further, but Luc flinched, and Jenny realized someone was standing at the end of their pew, watching them. The vicar. He wore an unreadable expression, his eyes flicking between them as though he hadn't quite decided what to think. The rest of the congregation had left. She'd been so caught up in her conversation she hadn't noticed.

'Are you two quite all right back here?' the vicar asked, his voice warm and reassuring, and also just a little bit suspicious.

'Sorry, Reverend,' Luc replied, turning his sharp-toothed smile on the priest. 'We got caught up, discussing . . . the soul.'

'Hmm,' the vicar said. His eyes slid back to Jenny, and he widened them at her, a question. She didn't need to be a mind reader to understand it: *Do you need me to intervene?* This was her chance. All she had to do was tell the vicar Luc was bothering her and . . . and what? Sure, she could get rid of Luc, but then she'd have to explain herself.

Father, I have no soul and I must pray.

Yeah, maybe not.

'We enjoyed the sermon,' she lied. 'We'll be on our way now.' She tugged the arm of Luc's T-shirt. 'Will you walk me home? We can continue our discussion.'

'Of course,' Luc replied, and Jenny smiled wide even as she internally thought, *I still don't trust you.*

After a moment's hesitation, the vicar nodded. 'Peace be with you,' he murmured as they sidled past him out of the pew.

'And also with you,' Jenny replied as they left. Old habits, and all that.

Outside on the steps, Luc sucked in a deep lungful of air. The sky was decidedly darker now, stars glittering in the velvet blue above. Jenny followed him down the steps and across the flagstones to the iron gate, where a shadow flickered: Zillah.

'You took your time,' she snapped, ignoring Jenny completely.

'Yeah, well, we're all good now. Jenny's coming with us.'

'I don't think I agreed to that, exactly,' she pointed out quickly.

Luc huffed. 'Jenny. Please. I can take you to your soul.'

'And it's not like you've got anywhere pressing to be now, is it?' Zillah crooned.

Which, unfortunately, was a good point.

'Will it fix me?' she asked impulsively, turning to Luc and skewering him with a gaze so direct he took a step back.

'Fix you?' Luc frowned.

'The void inside me where my soul should be. Will filling it fix me?' It wasn't exactly what she meant to say. But she couldn't tell him what she did mean, couldn't say those words out loud . . .

Apparently, though, Zillah could. She'd seen the inside of Jenny's mind, after all.

'She thinks she's unlovable,' the Succubus drawled lazily. 'Inherently damaged in a way that everyone else can sense.'

Jenny's face blazed in mortification. When Zillah said it, it sounded pathetic. But she wasn't wrong, was she? And if Jenny wanted to fix it, then maybe she'd need to take one hell of a risk.

'Well?' she asked Luc.

'I guess so,' he replied, which wasn't exactly comforting. 'I mean, I'm not an expert but it's a part of you, right? So, if something's missing, it only makes sense that you'll feel better when you get it back.'

Jenny swallowed. That's what she'd hoped he'd say – although, ideally, she'd have liked more conviction on his part.

'OK then. So, where do we go?'

For a moment, Luc looked conflicted. Then he shot her one of his confident grins and despite herself, her stomach somersaulted.

'I shall escort you to it myself. It's by the Lake of Lament.'

'And where is that, exactly?'

Zillah grinned unpleasantly. 'Right in the heart of All Hell.'

'But to get there,' Luc put in quickly, 'we have to go to Elrick Park first.'

Oh, goody. Jenny pushed down a sigh and followed the two demons into the night.

11

JENNY

It was as Jenny watched two demons fighting about how to use a train ticket machine in the station that it properly hit her what she was doing. She was *leaving*. Not 'running away', exactly, because where would she be running *from*, but she was leaving this city. She was making choices and doing things.

Sure, she was doing those things with a pair of supernatural creatures she genuinely hadn't considered to be real from a realm she hadn't thought existed up until a few short hours ago, but like, it was still a positive step for her.

'No, Zilch, I think it's pretty clear that we're meant to feed it before we get the tickets out.'

'Yes, I know that – and *stop* calling me that or I will *gut you*, you phallic object. I mean, we have to tell it where we want to go.'

'How? Telepathy?'

'I don't *think* that will work . . .'

'Oh, for goodness' sake,' Jenny sighed, shouldering the useless pair of them out of the way. She held her hand out for Luc's credit card, which was black, obviously. She tapped 'E' and 'L' into the options menu and scrolled until she found Elrick Station. For a brief moment her fingers hovered over the 'return' button, but she firmly selected three single tickets instead. No matter what happened next, she wasn't coming back. She had nothing to come back to.

The train was a battered, five-carriage affair empty enough that it was easy to find a table seat for the three of them. Zillah slid in first and immediately stared out of the window, squarely ignoring both Jenny and Luc. Apparently 'aloof and bitchy' was her whole thing. Fine with Jenny – she could still feel Zillah's demon powers slipping around inside her mind, and shivered thinking about it.

Luc sat next to Zillah, leaving Jenny to scooch in opposite him.

'I don't get it,' Luc said, frowning down at the row of orange and yellow tickets spread out in front of him on the plastic tabletop. 'The train doesn't just go where we want it to?'

Jenny rolled her eyes. She didn't really want to explain the intricacies of the British rail system, but she did her best, describing the changes they'd have to make.

'It's not like our destination is exactly a travel hub,' she pointed out. 'People go to Elrick Park to get away from it all, you know.'

Zillah, who was apparently listening even if she was trying not to, snorted.

'It *is* a travel hub,' she corrected. 'But only for one very specific destination.'

'Right.'

Jenny ignored the prickly feeling under her skin that reminded her what she'd agreed to by coming with these two, and swept up the tickets from the table. Somehow, she didn't quite trust Luc to take care of them.

The train pulled out of the station and they settled into silence. Zillah maintained a stony glare out of the window, and Luc leant back against the seat with his arms crossed, his eyes closed.

Otherwise, the carriage was empty, and before long the steady thrum of the engine, the wheels on the track carried up through the body of the train, even the light patter of rain that thankfully only started when they were already inside – all of these sounds combined into a calming beat in Jenny's head.

This is good, her mind whispered in time to the beat. *This is good, this is good.*

It *was* good. Wasn't it? She was free now. Independent. No longer beholden to the guilt that lived with her every moment she was awake, reminding her she was basically just another mouth to feed for her auntie; a duty, not a beloved niece. Well, no more. So what, she had less than a fiver to her name? So what, she had no idea what her plan was apart from getting her soul back? It was a plan, at least, a purpose – she hadn't had one of those in a long time.

What had she said to Luc before? That if she could just figure out what was broken inside her, she could be happy. Well, she'd identified what was broken – she was missing a piece. And now she was going to get it back. She wriggled in her seat.

Luc's eyes flickered open. They'd blossomed black as he rested them; Jenny watched as the black rolled inwards like smoke, revealing the irises beneath. How had she ever thought contact lenses caused that? He winked at her, and she caught her breath. His face – it was *so much* like the demon in her memory, the one who took her soul away.

It was also distractingly good-looking, when his gaze was all soft like that . . . she broke eye contact as a blush swept up over her face. Was that some kind of demon thing he was doing, to embarrass her?

The train picked up speed as it carried them out of the city, away from its medieval architecture and cobbled streets and out into the country.

Her phone buzzed in her pocket. She pulled it out and stared at it in surprise. Vee.

Well, duh. She didn't know Jenny had been eavesdropping, did she? She watched her auntie's name on the screen as the phone vibrated in her hand, but she didn't answer it. Eventually it stopped ringing, and she flipped it open, switched it off. Pushed it into the middle of the plastic table and watched it as though it might burst into flame.

'You OK?' Luc asked her, one eyebrow raised.

'Yeah,' she half-lied in reply. She hoped Vee wasn't too worried. She probably wasn't; she was probably relieved.

'Luc?'

'Uh-huh?'

'What does your dad want my soul for?' *And why would you help me get it back?* But she didn't want to ask that second question in front of Zillah. Hard to trust a girl who could crawl into her brain.

She could swear Zillah's shoulders tensed out of the corner of her eye, but the Succubus was still gazing fixedly out of the window, giving no indication she'd even heard Jenny's question.

Luc shrugged. 'Honestly, I'm not sure.'

Jenny frowned. 'But what do you *think* he wants it for?'

'I'm sure he has a plan,' Luc replied. 'He's always up to something dodgy. Maybe he wanted to see what would happen to a soul separated from a person for a long time? Or maybe he was planning to come back and bargain with you for it in the future.'

The thought of that made her shiver.

'. . . but it doesn't matter anyway, because in a few hours you'll have it back.'

Jenny couldn't help shooting a grin at him then, and he returned it, kicking her gently under the table until she giggled.

'I'm bored,' Zillah snapped, interrupting their playfulness. She stretched. 'Who does a girl have to infatuate around here to grab a snack?'

Before Luc could give his thoughts on the matter, the

carriage doors whooshed open, and a trolley rattled through. The young man pushing it seemed tired, his uniform rumpled as though he'd been called on to this shift at short notice. Jenny wondered if they were the only passengers on the train. She could only imagine how pissed off she'd be if she had to push that trolley all the way through the train for no pay-off.

'Any drinks or snacks?' he asked as he neared.

'I've got this,' Zillah said, leaning forward across the table.

Instinctively, Jenny shrank back. The demon girl shot a perfect white smile at the trolley attendant, an action that transformed her in seconds from a surly, unapproachable supermodel type to a winsome, friendly girl-next-door.

'What have you got for me?' she asked, her voice pitched just on the border between 'innocent' and 'sultry'.

It made the hairs stand up on the back of Jenny's neck.

As she watched, the young man's posture straightened. 'Sandwiches,' he managed to choke out. 'Crisps, chocolate, biscuits. Um . . . a couple of bottles of orange.'

It was like he couldn't see Jenny, or Luc for that matter. His entire attention fixed on Zillah, on the strand of hair she was curling around one finger, on the length of her neck when she tilted her chin up.

The Succubus's eyes bloomed like they had at the fair, and as though on autopilot the trolley attendant unloaded a pile of snack food on the table. The train rocked, and a pack of shortbread slid on to Jenny's lap. She resisted the urge to flinch.

‘That’ll be thirty-eight pounds,’ the young man said, and Jenny could barely breathe as she saw Zillah’s head tilt, just slightly, as she considered this information.

‘I don’t have thirty-eight pounds,’ she replied evenly.

Jenny felt her cheeks burn. She stared down at the shortbread wrapper in her lap as though it was the most interesting thing she’d ever seen. What was going to happen now? Would they get kicked off early? Would the police get involved? Surely not – they hadn’t even officially stolen anything – yet.

She slammed the shortbread back on the table. Luc’s mouth twitched; she felt the blood heat in her face.

‘That’s OK,’ the young man said, as though Jenny and her shortbread weren’t even there.

What was going on?

His eyes were glassy, and he didn’t take them off Zillah even as he slid his hand into his pocket, reaching for his wallet.

‘I’ve got this,’ he said.

He slid out a debit card, slotting it into the card machine on his own trolley.

Jenny’s eyes widened as she watched him tap in the four-digit PIN, and she swallowed as he tore off a receipt before handing it straight over to Zillah, for all the world as though she’d been the one making the payment all along.

‘Enjoy your snacks,’ he said, eyes still glassy, smiling shyly in Zillah’s direction. Then he moved along, rattling his much-depleted trolley on into the next carriage.

Once the electric doors had snicked closed behind him, Zillah reached forward and danced her fingers across the mountain of pre-packaged fare before selecting a packet of salt and vinegar crisps.

'What if he comes back?' Jenny squeaked. 'Or tells someone?'

Luc reached forward and plucked a bar of chocolate from the pile.

'Who's he going to tell?' he asked. 'He *willingly* put his hand in his pocket and paid for this stuff. Zillah didn't even touch him; you and I certainly didn't. Even if he did tell someone – what exactly is he going to say?'

Jenny swallowed down the illogical rebuttals sitting on her tongue. He was right, she knew that. Even though she'd felt the sweeping power of Zillah's influence on the trolley attendant, she couldn't exactly describe it now. It wasn't a tangible kind of theft – it was a subtler scam than that. A confidence trick: Zillah was confident he would pay for their snacks, and therefore he did.

'There's no trail this way,' Zillah told her. 'I could have distracted him while Luc pocketed stuff, but he'd be more likely to suspect that and call the police, don't you think? This way the company that owns that trolley doesn't have any losses to account for, there's no reason for them to check their closed-circuit surveillance systems, and we . . .' she flicked a small biscuit pack, sending it skittering towards Jenny across the table, 'get off scot-free.'

All of this made perfect sense. It was just . . .

'But it's not like a victimless crime, is it?' A small flame of morality burnt in Jenny, just bright enough that she couldn't quite ignore it. 'That poor man's going to figure out he was robbed.'

'No.' Zillah shook her head. 'He is going to feel *amazing* for the next eight to twelve hours. Like, floating-on-air great. It's like . . . a drug for humans – that's how we got away with it so often, back before all the *regulations*.' She grimaced. Then added, 'He loved it, don't you worry about him.'

'Must have been a different type of magic than you used on me, then,' Jenny grumbled. 'What happens when it wears off?'

Zillah shrugged. 'I wasn't influencing you, I was just looking for something. And he'll feel like he's caught a virus, nothing serious. Achy limbs, headache. He'll remember paying for our snacks, but he won't really remember why he did it. Worst-case scenario, he'll feel a bit stupid, but he won't connect what I did with why he feels like he has the mother of all hangovers.' She stretched. 'Why would he? Demons aren't *real*, remember. And as for victimless crimes – that's not really my area of interest if I'm honest.'

Jenny had a lot of questions, but this was as much as Zillah had ever said to her in one go, and she didn't want to push her luck. Instead, she ate a croissant and the shortbread, and drank some orange juice. The sugar made her feel a little better about the whole situation.

Only a little, though.

12

FERRIER OF THE ACHERON

Damn all the Celestials.

The Ferrier reached up and tugged the hood more firmly over their head as the barge drew nearer to shore.

They didn't speak to the newly dead souls as they boarded; there was no point, the dead never understood the Ferrier anyway. Instead, they held out a hand for the passage fees, and as the new souls stepped past, each one pressed a large, silver disc into the Ferrier's waiting palm.

It was all a bit pointless now, this 'coin for the Ferryman' BS. Hardly anyone's loved ones buried them properly any more, with a coin on each eye so they could be sure to pay the fare. Sometimes they rocked up with photo albums they'd been buried with, or stuffed toys from their childhoods, or other such rubbish, but what were they meant to do with those?

So, the demons had changed the system. The silver discs were 'tokens', not real coins, and the souls only had to hand them over to tally their numbers.

There was a bin by the shore for the sentimental crap. No property on the barge, that was the rule.

The Acheron was as wide and impassive as ever when the Ferrier was ready for their first return journey. Its surface was flat and unbroken, no winds in All Hell to cause a ripple, no insects to skim its surface. Until, that is, the Ferrier's barge pole skewered it, and drove the boat forward into the mists.

In this direction, the Ferrier stood at the back of the boat, overlooking the salmagundi of humanity seated on the wooden benches. The Ferrier kept their gaze on the centre of the milky-white mist that rolled over the Acheron, knowing that on the other side was their goal: getting rid of this cargo.

Of course, that only meant they could return to pick up more, but such was this existence.

A commotion broke out among the passengers, and the Ferrier sighed, irritated, before lowering their gaze to see what was going on.

'I did see something!' yelled the semi-lucent soul of an old man. He must have died of some internal disease, because his skin was unblemished, although lined, and when he stood up to gesture towards the water his limbs seemed strong enough.

'You did not,' a middle-aged female soul snapped. 'Stop trying to scare us – as if being dead isn't bad enough.'

This wasn't something the Ferrier needed to concern themself with, they decided. Worst-case scenario, the old soul would fall into the river, but that was unlikely. There wasn't exactly much current to make him sway.

The Ferrier lifted their head again, and as they did so, they saw the creature the old soul had spotted in the river. A large, white fish with long, trailing fins. It was covered in wounds: missing scales, a tear in one fin, an eye ruptured. Clearly it had found its way out of the Styx and decided to rest up here where there were no greybirds to peck at it.

Unfortunately, that was against the rules.

With another sigh, the Ferrier slipped a hand inside their cloak and drew out a net. They cast it over the side and watched as the fish struggled to break free of its bonds.

Don't struggle too hard, little fishie, the Ferrier thought. *You'll only cause yourself more damage than you can handle.*

The other souls watched as the Ferrier hauled the catch out of the river. The white fish flopped pathetically at the bottom of the boat, but it knew it was caught, and soon fell still.

'Is it dead?' someone asked, a hint of distaste in their haughty voice.

'Can't be dead twice,' the Ferrier said, but they could tell from the way the souls reared back in fright that they hadn't understood at all.

They made it to the other side without further incident. A MINOS agent waited by the jetty, her uniform so black it sucked in any light nearby. Her hair coiled severely on top of her head, under a triangular cap. She stood straight, tall, and when all of the new souls had disembarked, she saluted the Ferrier sharply before taking a quantity of yellow cans from a box by her feet. She handed them out; as each passenger 'drank' from their can, their glowing forms decanted into the vessel, falling neatly back into the storage box.

'Wait,' the Ferrier called to her. 'There's one more.'

They bent to untangle the fish from the net, and the MINOS agent wrinkled her nose. Still, she reached out and grasped the creature by its tail. She regarded it with cool detachment before clicking her fingers. Another yellow can fizzed into existence in her waiting palm, and she unceremoniously stuffed the glowing fish into the aluminium receptacle. Once it was inside, the lid sealed, safe for travel. And that glowing fish would travel, the Ferrier knew. All the way back to the Styx, where its eternal punishment would resume. On one hand, it was a brave soul to have attempted escape. On the other, well, the Ferrier only felt limited sympathy. In some ways, weren't they all trapped? All abiding by the Sacred Agreement that created this Hell in the first place?

'Did you hear about Pyro's kid?' the MINOS agent asked, in much the same tone an office worker might use in the tearoom.

Despite not really caring what their boss's kid got up to, the Ferrier at least recognized the attempt at friendly gossip, and summonsed up some false curiosity.

'What about him?'

'Disappeared through a Hellmouth.'

'The one at Hekla?'

'Nah.' She jerked her head directly across the river from where they were currently. 'Elrick.'

'Huh.'

'Reckon he's up to something?'

'The kid?'

'Nah, Pyro.'

'Probably.' The head of Seven, Inc. was always up to something, as far as the Ferrier was concerned. And those in their positions, mere cogs in the immensity of the Seven, Inc. machine, would likely never know the details. Pyro cared about power, not his people.

Not for the first time, the Ferrier thought it a shame it was Lucifer chained to the mountain, and not his son.

The MINOS agent nodded sharply, glad her gossip had been appropriately received, then picked up her box of yellow cans and set off towards the MINOS processing tower, barely visible in the distance.

Finding the fish in the Acheron would no doubt be the most exciting part of this shift, the Ferrier thought as they folded up the net and slid it back inside their cloak. The rest of today's journeys would be as unbroken as the surface of the river. The Ferrier could stand to be confident about this, given experience. These shifts, and in fact their entire monotonous existence, ran on a current as sluggish as the Acheron's.

No one knew how many Ferriers there were, working the Acheron. Not even the Ferrier knew, although they'd spent enough time working for Acheron Crossings (a Seven, Inc. property) to have heard some of the more preposterous rumours from other demons. That there was only one Ferrier, for example. That was patently absurd. Admittedly, they'd never met any of the others, and the way their shifts were staggered meant there was never any crossover, but that only proved that all Ferriers took their duties seriously: arrive on time, ferry the souls and use discretion, because it wouldn't do to gossip about new arrivals.

What they did know, after many aeons of loyal service to the role, was that each new soul they ferried across the river was luckier by multitudes than the last. All Hell was not a kind place to be a fresh soul condemned, and eternity lasts a long while.

Every day the souls put off their arrival was one less day of agony and torture.

The Ferrier should know. The Ferrier had been in All Hell since the beginning.

So, yes, damn all the Celestials – they were the ones that condemned them to this Abyss, were they not?

But when the Ferrier considered their employers, those that kept them in this eternal tedium, another thought couldn't help wriggling to the surface of their mind, much like that fish struggling in the net:

Damn all the demons, too.

13

JENNY

As soon as she stepped off the train at Elrick Station, nostalgia threatened to wash Jenny right off her feet. Elrick itself was a tiny village, almost a hamlet, with only a corner shop that doubled up as a post office to serve the residents and holidaymakers heading to Elrick Park.

The station was built from sandstone, and as the three of them headed outside, Jenny couldn't help herself: she reached out to trail her fingertips across the rough surface of the stone. It was cold, familiar. Mere hours ago, Jenny had sat in a church at Evensong, praying for the safe return of her soul. Now she was more than a hundred miles away, and the velvet dark of a November night draped the sky overhead.

'It doesn't matter how many times you check that weird watch,' she told Luc, who covered his wrist back up immediately, 'we'll still have missed the last bus to the park.'

'And it doesn't matter how often you use that tone with me,' Luc grumbled, 'it's still unhelpful and annoying.'

She didn't think she actually had used that tone before; he was just being a dick. Well, he was a demon, wasn't he?

Zillah huffed out a noise that sounded to Jenny's ears like the definition of 'annoyed', but apart from kicking a loose stone so hard it skittered out of sight into the road, she didn't say anything else as Luc set off down the narrow road.

'When we get there,' she heard him say to Zillah, 'we need to be stealthy, all right? I know *you* can do what you want, but I'd rather stay under the radar.'

'Whatever,' Zillah said back.

But Jenny wasn't really interested in the logistics. She was getting her soul back. She thought about all the things in her life that might have been different if Luc's father hadn't taken it when he did: maybe she wouldn't have been such a surly little girl, chasing away first her dad's affection and then her mum's. Maybe she'd have had more friends, invitations to sleepovers and shopping trips, instead of spending so long in her room reading Choose Your Own Adventure books. So many things might have been different. And soon, she'd get to know what it felt like to have those options. To be . . . like everyone else.

Now that Zillah had been in her mind, it was easier to identify the raw edges of the place that should have a soul in it. She couldn't have explained exactly *where* this was, maybe in her mind? Her heart? By her kidneys? It didn't seem to have a specific place like that, but she could feel it all the same. It was just . . . there. An empty space, closed over with scar tissue that kept a thick barrier between the space and the rest of her.

It was hard to know how long they walked; her phone was still switched off in her pocket and she'd never owned a watch. Given how defensive Luc got when she mentioned his, she didn't think he'd let her borrow it. The darkness was like a blanket, anyway, blocking out her perception of time. She'd only ever travelled between Elrick Station and Elrick Park via bus, and that had been ten years ago anyway.

Remembering that switched-off phone gave her pause. A wave of guilt rolled over her; it was getting late, now. Would Vee be worrying? Then again, she hadn't exactly defended Jenny, had she? Maybe she'd be relieved when Jenny didn't come home. Yeah, that felt more likely. No one wanted her around, except for (apparently) the demon boy walking in front of her, having a low, murmured conversation with a Succubus.

In fact, everything about this place brought a dark cloud over her. Sure, being here made her think about Vee, because last time she was here was that holiday when Vee was pregnant. But that summer was significant because it was the summer her parents divorced, too. Her stomach clenched. People got divorced, obviously, and she even remembered them doing that 'we still love you but we don't love each other' thing when she got home.

Which turned out, ultimately, not to be true, didn't it? After all, her dad had faded from her life after the divorce. Oh, he tried at first, swinging by in his new, sporty car to pick her up from school for his weekends with her. He had a flat in the city centre, only small, but there was a box room for her to stay in, and she remembered trips out to Flamingo Land, to the coast where her paternal grandparents lived, to the outlet store on the outskirts of town.

But she also remembered the Fridays he didn't turn up. Watching the playground empty out until she was the only one left and her teacher asked if they should call her mother.

'But Daddy's meant to be picking me up.'

Shifty looks, because they'd already called him and couldn't get through. So her mum would come get her, and hold her while she cried, and later that night she'd get a frantic, apologetic phone call from her dad because he'd 'been so tied up with work, honey, I just forgot'.

He didn't forget, though. He just didn't want to see her any more. A fact confirmed when she was nine, and met her soon-to-be stepsister, whose bedroom was now in the little box room that had, up until then, been Jenny's second bedroom.

On some level, she'd known then that she'd been replaced with a better version, and it hadn't really been a surprise when he stopped calling as much. By the time she was eleven, she didn't see him at all – by then it was just Jenny and her mum against the world.

Until that also went to pot. But she didn't really want

to think about The Fight. She could think about her dad without (much) anger now, because it was years ago. The Fight, though, that was new and fresh, the edges still bleeding.

The idea her mum didn't love her either made her chest hurt.

Eventually, the road smoothed beneath her feet. Following Luc's lead, they rounded a corner and Jenny saw a tall fence, an iron sign with the words ELRICK PARK wrought into the frame. To the right of this, a sentry box stood next to a red and white striped mechanical barrier. She had an instinct that the sentry box was green in daylight, even though now it was the same shiny black that Luc and Zillah's eyes sometimes shone.

There was a dull, yellow light in the booth, and as they drew closer Jenny was surprised to see a figure sitting in the chair behind the security window. It was a woman, hunched over and definitely not focused on the road. Why would she be? Like Luc had said, most guests probably didn't rock up when it was already past ten at night.

Luc cursed just loudly enough for Jenny to hear, before whispering something to Zillah. She nodded and stepped forward, towards the booth. Luc dropped back, and Jenny felt a gentle pressure on her arm as he pulled her back a couple of steps.

'Let Zilch handle this,' he murmured. 'I'm trying to keep a low profile.'

'Why?'

She glanced up at his face and there was something

there she couldn't quite read. Embarrassment? Guilt? After a moment, he leant in so he could speak directly into her ear.

'I'm not really supposed to be here – the Earthly plane, I mean.'

Jenny frowned. 'So, how did you end up here, then?'

'Zillah. She can come and go as she pleases – it's a contractual thing. When we came in, she set up a distraction, for me.'

'What kind of distraction?'

Luc pulled a face. 'I didn't like to ask.'

Zillah stepped towards the sentry box and tapped her fingernails on the plastic of the window. In the stillness of the night, the sound carried, a woodpecker in spring, and Jenny winced.

The woman inside the booth jumped like a gun had gone off.

For a moment, the woman stared at Zillah. Jenny sympathized – in the dark, the demon girl could easily pass as a black-haired spectre, and since she really was a supernatural being that shouldn't exist . . . well, the woman's reaction was hardly surprising.

But, instead of screaming or rubbing her eyes, she seemed to deflate. She laid down the pen that had been in her hand and slowly pushed open the security window at the side of the sentry box.

'Can I help you, love?' she asked, her voice gruff but not otherwise concerned.

'Oh, I *hope* so,' Zillah purred, leaning closer to the

window. Her hands were on the lip, the balls of her feet rocking her forward, into the woman's personal space. Her voice dropped, low, intimate, and Jenny swallowed back an unpleasant sensation that tried to roll up her throat.

It was impossible to hear what Zillah was saying, her voice no more than a purr carried to where Jenny and Luc waited, but Jenny could imagine the words, the soft coaxing, the gentle encouragement. *Let me in. Give me everything I want.*

She clenched her teeth and waited for the barrier to open. For Zillah's uncanny power to do its magic.

Except, the woman inside the sentry box didn't move. She didn't seem to be breathing, her eyes fixed on Zillah's face.

Triumphant, Zillah stepped back.

Then the woman in the booth did something unexpected. She barked out a laugh.

'Nice try. Do you have a reservation?'

'Excuse me?' Zillah's spine straightened, and although Jenny could only see the cascade of glossy hair at the back of her head, it wasn't hard to imagine Zillah was showing her teeth.

'A reservation,' the woman repeated, apparently completely unmoved. 'Do you have one?'

'I don't think you understand,' Zillah said, allowing a small spark of warning to filter into her tone.

The woman in the booth sniffed. 'Email confirmation?'

'No.' The word left Zillah's throat as a growl.

'Voucher code?' The woman's mouth twitched. *Is she*

enjoying *this?* Jenny wondered.

'Are you being purposefully obstructive?' Zillah snapped. 'You have no idea what this place is, do you? What *I* am? How much *danger* you're in, sitting so close to that forest.'

'No,' Luc murmured next to Jenny, 'don't do this, Zilch.'

'Oh, I know exactly how much danger I'm in,' the woman replied, cheerfully, and Jenny had the feeling she meant *none*.

'Open the barrier,' Zillah demanded tightly.

Jenny rolled her eyes and took an automatic step forward to intervene. She never could stand people who were rude to customer service workers. But Luc pulled her back.

'We're flying under the radar, remember? She can still pull this back. She's just *affected*, right now. It's the Hellmouth, calling to her. It's making her impatient. Can you feel it?'

Jenny shook her head, but even as she did so she felt . . . *something*. Whether it was the 'Hellmouth' or not she couldn't say, but as she lifted her eyes up and over the sentry box, across the empty car park to the shadowy treeline, there was definitely . . . something. It swirled in the empty space where her soul should be, like smoke, and she couldn't tell if it was a warning or a welcome.

The woman in the sentry box hadn't responded to the demand to lift the barrier, and neither did she seem to be in any hurry to do so.

Zillah's influence had failed.

After another moment of reflection, the woman sniffed loudly, leant back, and folded her arms across her broad chest.

'No reservation, then?'

'I am *warning* you,' Zillah growled.

At Jenny's side, Luc made a muffled sound in the back of his throat.

'Stop it,' he muttered so only Jenny could hear.

But Zillah clearly wasn't planning to stop it. All the hairs along Jenny's forearms spiked. The forest hunkered, malevolent, a wide black grin in the dark just barely covering its teeth.

Oh yeah, she could *feel* the thing Luc was talking about, all right. Just, it didn't feel exactly pleasant to her. Why Zillah was impatient to get to it was anyone's bloody guess.

She was so distracted by the dark pull of the forest that she missed whatever the woman said in reply to Zillah, so what happened next made her jump.

It was a blur of sound and motion. Zillah shrieked into the booth. Even from this distance Jenny could see the spittle leaving Zillah's mouth. Then the demon girl spun around, and Jenny flinched: Zillah's face was a mask of pure rage, her lips drawn back to unsheathe her teeth. She backed up, almost to where Luc's hand still held Jenny still, and then she took a running jump at the space above the barrier.

'Oh, shit,' Luc muttered, and Jenny blinked, not sure

she could trust her own eyes as a haze formed right where Zillah's body was aimed. It was like liquid, maybe oil, iridescent in the moonlight.

Zillah hit it with the full force of a pissed-off demon and the momentum bounced her straight back on to the road behind her. She landed flat on her back and her head made an audible crack as it hit the tarmac. She stayed down.

For a long moment no one reacted, and then the woman reached forward to pick up a brick-like walkie-talkie. Before she pressed the call button she leant out of the window and gazed down at Zillah.

'If you don't have a reservation,' she said, 'you'll need to see the twins.'

14

JENNY

All at once, Luc's plan to 'fly under the radar' vanished and he dropped Jenny's arm, stepping forward and waving to catch the woman's attention.

'No, no, no,' Luc said quickly, stepping over the still body of his friend.

The woman's face froze, and any colour left in it from the chill temperature drained down her neck and out of sight. Her jaw slackened and she stared at Luc as though he might be there to kill her, or worse.

'I . . .' Her voice was practically a squeak. 'I'm so sorry, sir, I didn't know . . .'

Luc paused.

'What?'

'I said I'm sorry. If I knew you were here, I'd never have . . .'

'Oh.' As Jenny joined him, Luc's shoulders sagged. 'I'm not him,' he said, sounding defeated.

'You're . . . you're not?'

He shook his head and Jenny realized belatedly what had just happened: the same thing that happened to her when Zillah showed her the face of the man who took her soul.

'I'm his son,' Luc clarified.

The woman in the booth visibly relaxed, even as she rolled her chair back, putting more space between herself and Luc.

'You'll still need to see the twins,' she pointed out.

Luc had stepped back and was now holding a hand out to Zillah, who was rubbing the back of her head and pointedly ignoring his offer of help.

'I'd rather not,' Luc tried again. 'Is there no way—'

'They're the guardians of the Hellmouth,' the woman said, a flicker of authority entering her voice. 'You know how it is.'

Luc visibly deflated. 'It was worth a try.'

The woman hit a button. The mechanical barrier creaked in protest as it inched its way upwards, and she got up from her seat and exited the booth via a door behind her chair.

'I suppose you ought to follow me, then,' she said. She set off across the car park before throwing another comment over her shoulder: 'I'm Martha, by the way.'

'The *mother*,' Zillah grunted in recognition.

'At least that explains why your . . . charms didn't work

on her,' Luc pointed out.

Zillah growled and stomped ahead, leaving Luc to wait for Jenny to catch up before they too walked past the barrier and into Elrick Park.

To Jenny's surprise, about halfway across the tarmac of the empty car park, she felt Luc's hand grip hers, giving it a squeeze. He grinned at her, his teeth practically glowing in the dark.

'You feeling OK?'

'Better than Zillah, I think,' she replied. Luc laughed and dropped her hand, which she immediately folded into her other arm, holding them both across her chest.

'It's only her pride,' he pointed out. 'She'll get over it.'

Jenny made a noncommittal sound and repeated Luc's question in her own head: *was* she feeling OK? It was a lot to take in, the whole demons and magic influences thing. Once more she remembered how it felt to have Zillah in her mind, and swallowed as fresh goosebumps skittered over her skin. Then she remembered the way that haze above the barrier knocked Zillah flat on her arse, and suppressed a smile.

So, maybe not *all* demon magic was horrible.

Was it demon magic, though? Because Martha was human. She had to be, or else Zillah wouldn't have even tried that infatuation thing on her – but it hadn't worked. Why? Clearly, Martha belonged here, and she wasn't fazed at the prospect of an angry demon.

Luc fazed her, though. Luc's *face*. Evidently Seth Pyro's reputation preceded him.

'Luc?'

'Uh-huh?'

'I just wanted to say that I really appreciate what you're doing for me, here. I'm a total stranger, just some human, and yet, you – you sneaked illegally on to Earth to find me, and I—'

'Don't,' Luc interrupted. She could hardly make out his face. 'Don't thank me.'

'But . . .'

'Seriously. Don't.'

His face, already shadowed in the dark, tensed. His eyes blossomed to black, and all at once she wished they weren't standing quite so close. Was he angry, for some reason? All she'd said was thank you. She nodded, pressing her lips together. Apparently, he didn't want her gratitude.

Luc blinked, then turned away, leaving her to trail along behind, confused. He blew hot and cold more than a faulty tap; was that just demonic? Or was it because he could also tell she was broken, and he couldn't always hide his reaction to her?

There was a building where the car park met the forest – a squat A-frame wooden cottage. Jenny thought that was where they were headed until Martha took a sharp turn on to a path that led . . . *Oh, Christ.* Of course she was going to lead them right into the creature's mouth.

Jenny sucked in a deep, steadying breath and felt Luc's hand again, this time on her elbow. She jerked away from him, still stung by his attitude. Martha called out over her shoulder again, 'Make sure the human stays on the path –

it's bad enough we're here in the dark, we don't want to lose anyone. I hate it when they insist on running around out here, but they wanted to *commune*, they said. Something about an eclipse, and apparently they can't do that in the cabin, where there's heating and electric light, oh no, must commune in the bloody woods at night . . . oh, make sure she doesn't touch the trees, either.'

Jenny swallowed. *Wow, déjà vu, much?*

The path had been marked out with sandstone, like the train station back in the village, and as the forest swallowed the light from the moon she was glad of the brightness in the stone. She almost wished she'd let Luc take hold of her arm after all. The trees flanked the path at a polite distance. Hadn't she thought she could speak to these trees, once?

Maybe she could.

Ugh, why was she thinking about sentient trees? It was this place! She shuddered as they passed under a carved wooden archway with a series of angular, stylized letters pared into the columns at regular intervals: *selva oscura*.

As with most things she was coming across these past couple of days, this meant knack all to Jenny. Maybe that was the Latin name for the type of trees around here, she decided. They were certainly different to trees in normal forests; a variety of colours ranging from 'deathly pale' through 'rotting mushroom' to 'black mould', their bark had a weird, glistening quality that made Jenny feel like if she touched their trunks they'd be warm and sweaty under the pads of her fingers. So, she definitely wasn't going to do that. She felt a bit sick just imagining it.

Had they always been like that? she wondered. Maybe that was why Martha didn't want anyone touching them, maybe they were diseased. Bit weird for a holiday park, mind.

They followed Martha along the path to a fork, then along to the left, where the path got narrower. This time, when she felt Luc's hand on her shoulder, she let him nudge her in front of him, relieved she didn't have to be at the back any more. There was something primal inside her that kept suggesting she might get picked off from the herd.

'I don't think I like this,' she whispered.

'I've got you,' Luc whispered back, and for some reason this actually made her feel better.

It was somehow even colder here in the forest and Jenny fought against rolling waves that shivered over her skin. She could barely see beyond her outstretched fingers, except the pale sandstone and just ahead of her, Zillah's heavy black boots.

Then the boots stopped walking, and Jenny gasped as she came to a stop, narrowly avoiding slamming into the demon girl's spine. No doubt her mood hadn't yet improved, Jenny thought, so that wouldn't have been a clever idea.

She peered over Zillah's shoulder. Martha had brought them to a clearing, and she could see this because there was a small pool of light emanating from a flat-topped rock in the middle of it.

Zillah stepped off the path towards the clearing; Jenny made to follow her, but Luc put a hand on her shoulder and stepped around her, shaking his head.

'Better not,' he warned. 'Stay on the path where I know you're safe.'

Oh. Great.

She tried to find a snarky response, something to show she was *fine*, not remotely freaked out by this whole shebang, but nothing came to her, mainly because she was, indeed, remotely freaked out. Freaked out up-close, too.

Instead, she watched as everyone else walked over to the rock. When she strained her eyes, she could just make out some of the objects strewn across its surface. Candles, obviously, tall pillar-style ones like they had in the church. They were well used, too, thick globs of wax melted down the sides of them, fusing them to the rock.

The other items were a little harder to see, the flickering of the candle flames throwing them in and out of shadow. Pinecones, she recognized first, and shiny pebbles. Crystals, maybe? There were other items too – small, twig-like things it took her a moment to recognize as bird bones. *Oh, gross.*

It was an altar, she realized, but something of a haphazard one. And then – she almost jumped when she realized why Luc, Zillah and Martha were walking towards it. Her gaze travelled down to the base of the rock where two small children sat cross-legged, facing each other. They each had a thick wodge of playing cards in their hands, even though the light from the candles barely reached them.

Martha held a hand up to stop Luc or Zillah interrupting their game until it came to a natural end. Jenny had to squint, but she could see that they were dressed in old-fashioned clothes: linen, or rough cotton maybe. The girl had long blonde hair loose down her back, while the boy's darker hair was cropped close to his ears. Both wore wreaths on their heads, like little crowns or halos. They were like miniature pagan deities.

Eventually, the boy threw his empty hands up, an apparent sign of defeat, and Martha clapped her hands to get their attention.

'Chloe-Lee, Joey,' she said. 'These . . . people would like to speak with you.'

Two small faces swung towards them, patched with dappled moonlight.

Joey got up first, his face slipping into surprise when he saw Luc.

'Ah, young Lucifer!' he announced, sounding very much not like a child at all as far as Jenny was concerned.

'Good evening, Joey,' Luc said in reply – and he sounded more formal too, talking to this child.

'And Zillah Sixth Daughter. What a delight.'

'Mm.' Zillah didn't sound exactly convinced.

'And who is *this* charming creature?' Joey held a hand out towards Jenny.

'No one,' Luc said quickly.

Now, why did that send a bolt right through Jenny's guts?

'My name's Jenny Hall,' she told the little boy. 'I'm no one.'

'No, you're not,' Joey told her, taking her hand. He

flipped it over and his eyes scanned the lines of her palm.

'Ah! You've been here before, I see.'

Chloe-Lee joined her brother and bent her head over Jenny's palm too. Then a look passed between them.

'You must stay for tea, seeing as you're an old friend.'

'Uh, no,' Luc said. 'I mean, we'd love to, but we don't really have time. We're just passing through, and . . .'

'Odd,' Joey mused, 'that you should be passing through without the correct papers, though. Especially with such a delightful, not to mention *living* human in tow. No, we insist, Master Lightbringer. Tea, and then perhaps a story, don't you agree?'

'Damn it,' Luc muttered under his breath.

The twins and Martha collected up the trappings of the altar and led the way back out of the forest. As soon as they were clear of the trees, Luc dropped back and murmured conspiratorially at Jenny.

'Would you mind doing me a favour?'

'Depends what it is,' Jenny replied.

'Just . . . when they ask what you're doing here – and they will, nosey buggers – would you mind *not* mentioning the whole deal with your soul?'

'Um, what am I supposed to say, then?'

'I dunno. Could you maybe act like I've charmed you into it?'

She felt her eyebrows hike up her face. 'You *charmed* me into it?'

His face stilled, transformed back to the stone-faced

demon who didn't want her thanks. 'You know what? Forget I asked.'

'No, wait . . .'

But he pulled forward, leaving Jenny trailing behind everyone else. But she was sure she could feel someone watching her anyway. Some*thing*, still in the forest.

She shivered.

15

JENNY

The kitchen of the A-frame cottage had rustic wooden units and a coal-black range. The roof rose to a sharp apex. As soon as they were inside, Martha came into her own, bustling them into seats around a wide, farmhouse-style table. Luc bundled in next to her, and Zillah was pressed into an overstuffed armchair by the wall. The twins took their seats on a pair of mismatched stools opposite the bench, then Martha disappeared back out the door.

'She finds this kind of thing very uncomfortable,' Chloe-Lee said, noticing Jenny's gaze as it followed her mother out of the room.

'Always has,' Joey agreed, pouring tea from a large teapot on the table into three cups.

Jenny could have sworn that teapot wasn't there before.

She blinked but didn't object when Joey pressed a mug into her hands. It looked exactly how she took it: as orange as He-Man and not a sprinkle of sugar in sight.

'How did you know how I . . . You know what? Never mind. Thank you.'

She sipped her tea (which was perfect) and waited for something to happen. Nothing did. The minutes stretched, and the atmosphere tensed around them. Luc had his arms folded, pointedly ignoring the black tea in front of him, even when Chloe-Lee pushed a small pot of honey towards him. Zillah was drinking hers happily enough; Jenny could smell the ginger from where she sat.

The twins seemed unperturbed by the awkwardness and appeared to be communicating with each other by means of peeking at the tea leaves in each other's cups.

Luc fiddled with something under the table (probably that bloody watch), until finally, he snapped.

'Can we get this over with?'

'Get *what* over with, young Lucifer? Do you not like the tea?' Joey's tone was light, but Jenny heard something else in it, under the surface, which made her spine straighten.

'Come on,' Luc sighed. 'We all know this isn't about tea.'

Jenny shrugged. 'I don't. I don't understand any of this.'

Luc shot her a Look, but it was too late to take it back, and Chloe-Lee was already nodding eagerly, leaning forward.

'Exactly that, exactly that!' she said, as though Jenny had hit upon some salient point.

‘I didn’t trick her, if that’s what you’re worried about,’ Luc said.

If Jenny didn’t know any better, she’d think he was . . . nervous. She hadn’t really noticed before, what with the surrealness of being served tea by two of the most formal children she’d ever met in her life. But he definitely was; as soon as she sensed it, she couldn’t stop, it rolled off him in waves.

But it didn’t seem to be the twins causing it – he was staring past them, over their shoulders, as though the idea of gazing at them directly was too much.

So, who – or what *– are they?* Jenny wondered.

As though he could hear her thoughts, Joey shot her a reassuring smile. Except it wasn’t reassuring, because it felt an awful lot like he’d just heard her thoughts.

‘All right, young—’ Chloe-Lee began.

‘Stop calling me that,’ Luc grunted. Then hastily added, ‘Please.’

‘As you wish. Luc, then. Well, Luc, as you know, we are the guardians of the portal here at Elrick Park. It’s a duty we take seriously, because the Sacred Agreement makes clear the rules regarding traversing the planes, and the portal is one of only a few such passing places.’

Jenny had a feeling this information was for her benefit; Luc clenched and unclenched his jaw like he wanted to interrupt, and Zillah stifled an ill-concealed yawn. This wasn’t new information to either of them.

‘. . . And,’ Joey picked up when Chloe-Lee stopped, a habit they seemed to have that was vaguely unnerving, 'one of the cardinal rules of the Agreement is that all demonkind – with the exception of special cases like the lovely Sixth Daughter, here – must apply for a permit if they wish to pass through the portal and spend time on the Earthly plane.'

Chloe-Lee coughed delicately. 'Which you did not do, young . . . I mean, Luc.'

'How did you manage to get past us in the first place?' Joey asked. He didn't sound angry, just curious, but out of the corner of her eye Jenny thought Luc flinched anyway.

'You were busy with something else,' he said.

'Busy?'

This time Jenny definitely wasn't imagining the way Luc's eyes slid towards her, just for a second.

'Cleaning up a mess,' Luc said.

From the overstuffed armchair, Zillah huffed out an irritated breath. 'Luc, just be straight with them. When we came through the portal the first time, you were jet-washing blood and feathers off the path nearest the portal.'

The Succubus caught Jenny's shocked gaze and stared her down.

'They're not really little kids, in case you hadn't guessed. And this isn't really a holiday park. More of a Venus flytrap for dumb humans who don't know how to follow simple rules.'

The twins had the good grace to blush.

'But . . . feathers?' Jenny wasn't sure she understood.

'The harpies can get . . . rather animated,' Chloe-Lee said weakly. 'So, we were distracted, and you managed to slip through. Hmm. That is something to consider in future, don't you think, Joey?'

'Yeah, yeah, yeah,' Zillah broke in, 'but, like, can I just point out that I don't know why I'm here? Like you said, I'm a special exception. So . . .'

'You're entirely right, of course,' Chloe-Lee nodded.

'Although,' Joey pointed out, 'you were attempting to aid Luc's attempt to remain hidden, with a living human in tow, on your way back to All Hell, were you not? You could have simply announced yourself as Lilith's sixth daughter and you'd have been waved through.'

Zillah shrugged, cool and unconcerned. 'Luc's the direct grandson of Lucifer himself. I live in a hierarchical society. Do you really think little old me has the power to say *no* to Luc Pyro?'

Luc scowled, and Zillah smiled sweetly at him. The twins shared a moment of silence, which to Jenny looked an awful lot like communication, only silent. Which, again, was unsettling.

'You make a good point,' Joey conceded reluctantly. 'In that case, you are free to go.'

Luc's eyes narrowed. 'You're not . . . leaving me here?'

The Succubus shrugged. 'Not my circus, amigo. I agreed to help you find the kid, and we found her. I'm out.'

She pushed the armchair back noisily and stood up, stretching luxuriously.

'Nice meeting you,' she deadpanned towards Jenny, who didn't believe her for a second. And then she was out the door without a backward glance.

Luc muttered something inaudible, although Jenny thought she might have caught the word 'bitch' in there somewhere. She finished her tea, and caught her attention wandering around the kitchen. It was so . . . ordinary, which was odd considering the situation she was in. Cosy, and warm, with yellow gingham curtains and a windowsill packed with plants. Mint, she recognized, and thyme . . . and then something that made the breath hitch in her chest.

She stood up without really knowing she'd done it and crossed to the sink, reaching out for the familiar item even as she felt a hand on her shoulder.

It was a can. The same size and shape as a thousand other cans of pop, sure, but this one had a yellow label, and the white letters spelling out *Seven, Inc.* It was . . .

'It's not yours.' Luc's voice was warm in her ear. 'I'm sorry, I forgot to warn you about that. It's Martha's soul, Jenny, not yours.'

And that void inside her, the one she'd felt earlier, oh, it *ached*. Tears sprang to her eyes, and she turned into him, pressing her face against his chest. *Demons have heartbeats, then*, she thought distantly. She felt him hesitate, and then his arms closed around her. Her throat was full and tight as she tried to stop herself bursting into noisy, humiliating tears. What good would that do?

'It's all right,' she heard Luc say. 'I've got you.'

She drew in a shuddering breath.

Deep breath, and then she stepped away to face the twins, who were staring at the pair of them with undisguised curiosity.

'You should let him go, too,' she told them. 'And you should let me go into Hell with him. Because he's right, he didn't trick me. I'm here of my own free will, and I want to go with Luc.'

'To get your soul back?' Chloe-Lee asked, her voice soft and quiet.

Damn. Luc had explicitly asked her not to mention that . . . well, too late. The cat was out of the bag now, wasn't it?

'That's right,' she said. Just behind her, Luc sucked in a sharp breath.

There was a long silence, and then as one, the twins stood up.

'We have no wish to stand in the way of free will,' Chloe-Lee said.

'But we do have a duty to protect the Sacred Agreement,' Joey pointed out.

'We must insist that you both stay here – at least for tonight,' Chloe-Lee continued.

'As our guests,' Joey stressed.

Luc made to speak, but Joey cut him off.

'We really must insist, Luc.'

'Then there's nothing else for it,' the demon boy replied, but he didn't sound happy.

'Don't sound so glum!' Chloe-Lee said, a wide smile breaking on to her face. 'This is a holiday park! Some people would pay a premium for a night in one of our cabins.'

16

LUC

S*hit, shit, shit!*

It wasn't supposed to be like this.

Luc paced across the floor of the guest chalet, urgently trying to marshal his thoughts. His dad was going to kill him. No question about it, and even if he didn't do it personally (because when did Seth Pyro ever do anything personally?), the Legions would do it for him.

A flicker of genuine fear sparked up Luc's spine. He didn't want to die a soldier. A *torturer.* He didn't want to die at all.

But there was no getting round it, he had failed. Even Zillah knew that – look how quickly she'd cut and run when it suited her!

For once, his dad was right. You really couldn't trust a Succubus.

Couldn't trust a human, either, apparently, although the only unusual thing about that was Luc's own surprise that she'd blown it like that. Although, wait, that wasn't fair. Jenny hadn't known that was Martha's soul in the can. She'd only just accepted what happened to her own; was it any surprise seeing one of those cans affected her like that?

And why did the twins just keep it on the windowsill in the kitchen? He wished – well, he wished he'd never heard the name 'Jenny Hall', but even as the thought crossed his mind, he dismissed it.

None of this was Jenny's fault.

It was his. All of it – including that weird protective urge that came over him earlier, the one that made him wrap his arms around her in the kitchen, the one that made him nudge her in front of him in the woods. Maybe his dad was right. He was too *soft*.

At least his room was nice. Chalet, whatever. They'd separated him and Jenny, obviously, no doubt interrogating her at this exact moment to get as much dirt on all the promises he'd made her as possible.

Oh, Luc was many things, but stupid wasn't (always) one of them. He knew exactly why they'd had to insist on an overnight stay here. They needed time to convene the Celestial Council, didn't they, so they could grass him in.

The entire thing was hopeless.

But what if he could show his dad he was loyal? No doubt the twins would visit him when they were done with Jenny; if he kept his dad's name out of it, would Pyro take his silence into account when deciding what to do with him?

As though on cue, someone knocked on the door. Before Luc could call out, the handle turned, and Joey stepped inside.

'Everything all right, dear boy?'

'No.'

'Come, now, we don't have to be enemies. Sit down, let's talk.'

He considered refusing, but what was the point? Joey took possession of a chair by the window, so Luc was left with the bed.

'Talk, then,' he muttered.

'Oh, that attitude!' Joey sighed, shaking his head. His eyes gleamed gold, the only indication that he was genuinely affected by Luc's impertinence. 'You broke the Agreement. I don't know why you're getting so bent out of shape when my sister and I are merely doing our jobs.'

'Stop it.' Annoyance floated under Luc's skin, making him feel like he was outside of himself. 'Stop with this performance. The human isn't here, now. Stop saying Chloe-Lee's your sister – stop calling yourselves "Chloe-Lee" and "Joey", for Hell's sake! And stop acting so high and mighty, like you've never searched the terms of the Agreement and found a loophole that suits you better than reality.'

'What precisely do you mean by that?' Joey asked.

'I mean this entire charade that you're just innocent kids who happened to be placed with an appropriate mother figure by the state. You're always making little jokes about who my grandfather is, but don't forget my father too. He helped you; he found a human you could manipulate into giving up her old life . . .'

'Martha was deeply unhappy in her old life!' Joey snapped.

'And Jenny is unhappy now,' Luc retorted. 'She wants her soul back, and I know where it is. I can help her get it.'

'It's not the same at all and you know it! Martha was overworked, and, and . . . underappreciated, and she wanted a family! She wanted us!'

'She wanted children. Are you really going to sit there and try to tell me that's what she got? You happily went along with it when my father took her soul, and handed it over to you and your "sister" for safekeeping. But I show up on a mission to make a human girl's life actively better and I'm the bad guy?'

Silence fell as Joey digested Luc's tirade. He drew himself up in his chair and blinked the gold emotions out of his eyes so he could gaze levelly at Luc, stroking his feather tattoo with one hand as he did so.

'If that's true, Luc, that you want to truly help Jenny – then tell me, why didn't you just steal her soul from your father yourself and bring it to her? Why exactly do you need her to come through the portal with you? Hmm?'

Luc swallowed. Time to put all those years watching his father lie for a living to good use.

'My father would have noticed it missing. This way she

can open the can immediately and there won't be anything he can do.'

'Except she'll be in Hell. Outside the Council's jurisdiction. That seems like an incredibly dangerous situation to put a young woman in.'

Luc didn't reply.

'And,' Joey continued, 'it's interesting to me that you would do all this – involving a Succubus in the plan, no less – for a human girl you'd never met.'

A low growl formed in the back of Luc's throat, but he swallowed it back.

'Here's the thing, young Lucifer. I don't trust you. Chloe-Lee doesn't trust you. I mean, of course she doesn't; as you say, she's not really my sister. So, I can confidently speak for both of us when I say that we will do everything in our power to stop you taking that girl into Hell.' A brief pause. 'Now, do you have enough clean towels for your stay with us?'

'Leave me alone.'

'Gladly. I do hope when we speak in the morning you will be better rested and sweeter tempered.'

Joey stood up and crossed to the door. Hesitated.

'If we find out this is some scheme involving the coming eclipse, and you lied about it, there will be significant consequences, Luc. Don't doubt that, not even for a second.'

The door closed behind him, and Luc heard a lock click. He reached over to the bedside table where an old-fashioned corded phone was plugged in and launched it at the door. It crashed satisfyingly against the wood and landed on the carpet with a thunk.

The twins were always talking in riddles. What was all that about an eclipse? He glanced down at his wrist guiltily, but his hoodie sleeve was still covering the star tracker. They couldn't know he had that, right? Frustrated, Luc flopped back on the mattress, which was pleasantly squishy – a fact that did nothing to assuage the roiling emotions running through him. He wondered whether Jenny was OK. Maybe he shouldn't have broken that phone; would he have been able to find her room number and talk to her, if he hadn't?

But what would he even say to her, if he could?

You'd lie to her again. He winced and pulled a pillow up underneath his head. Yep, there was no getting round it, really: Joey was right about that. He was a liar, just like his father raised him to be.

He'd been taught from school it was OK to lie to humans, though, because they were the enemy. Selfish parasites, sucking up resources that should by rights have been for demonkind to enjoy.

Was that true, though? He'd only been on Earth for a short time, and sure, he'd seen some selfishness and bad behaviour, even in the confines of the funfair. But was it any worse than the way demons were with each other? Did it really stack up that humans were the problem, here?

Or was he only doubting himself because when Jenny buried her head in his chest earlier on, his entire body had screamed at him to protect her? *She's not special.* He mentally slapped the thought away as soon as it entered his head, even though his dad had said it: she wasn't some chosen, magical creature prophesied to journey through All Hell. She was just . . . there, when Pyro needed a kid to mess with. She wasn't special. Not at all.

So why did he want to walk back into his dad's office and punch him square in the nose for ever saying something so ridiculous?

He groaned, a long, low, desperate sound. What exactly had she done to him? And when had she done it? He sat up, mind rolling as he tried to figure it out. When did *this* start?

Was it when he introduced himself to her, and she hit him? She hadn't hurt him, not really, but thinking about it now, he knew it was significant. It was like some defensive, spiky part of her had reached out and found the defensive, spiky part of Luc. He'd seen something in her, recognized it – and then when she turned up at the fair with a huge bruise blossoming across a quarter of her face . . . he wanted to protect her then, too. Wanted to take her mind off everything that hurt her. That's why he'd suggested dodgems and chased her through the fair like children playing tag.

He'd wanted to see her laugh, he realized.

And when she had . . . the pride he felt, watching her light up, watching her defences slowly dissolve as she explained herself to him.

I don't have anywhere else to go.

So, she came to him. His heart thumped painfully in his

chest – so hard, in fact, that he didn't hear the first stone on the window.

When the second one came, followed rapidly by a third, he jumped off the bed and peered outside.

'What the Hell are you still doing here?' he muttered when he saw Zillah grinning all her sharp teeth at him.

'All right?' she asked, once he'd managed to wrangle the window open just wide enough for her to crawl through.

The Succubus landed on the floor with a bump not dissimilar to the one the bedside phone had made, but she righted herself elegantly enough. She was like a cat, Luc thought, not for the first time, somehow always capable of convincingly pretending 'I meant to do that'.

'Oh yeah,' Luc replied, layering sarcasm thick on his tongue. 'Just, you know, chilling out in this locked room while the twins plot my celestial downfall.'

'Yeah . . .' Zillah scrunched her face up. 'Little shits, aren't they?'

Which just about summed it up, in Luc's opinion.

'What are you doing here? I thought you'd be halfway back to Dis by now.'

'Thought about it,' Zillah shrugged. 'Oh, and the look on your face when I said I was just gonna bounce. I'm sorry, but that was worth it.'

'You're a dick.'

'And you wouldn't have me any other way.'

'You haven't answered my question.'

'True.' She walked past him and did a little jump up on to the bed, occupying the space Luc had just vacated.

'Hey, this bed's all right, you know? That is one thing about the Earthly plane I have to give credit for. Why are Hellish mattresses so horrendous?'

'It's the straw,' Luc said. 'Pokes out through the sheets.'

'Yeah. Ooh, and we don't get this channel in the Abyss.' She snatched up a remote control from the bedside table and flicked on a television Luc had barely registered the existence of. Some women were currently arguing about something, and Zillah was entranced immediately.

'Zillah. Zil. Zilch. I thought this whole plane of existence made your skin itch?'

'Oh, it does,' she grinned. 'But, like, I couldn't just abandon you here, could I? Not when what you're doing with the girl is so important. You understand that, right?' She was still watching the TV, but Luc got the distinct impression he had her full attention.

'Uh . . .'

'So, that's a no.' Eye-rolls, another thing the Succubae excelled at.

'Hang on,' Luc said, sitting down in the chair Joey had interrogated him from. 'Why do you care?'

The smile that crept up Zillah's face was slow and knowing.

'You're so sweet, did you know that? And maybe that's the problem. Maybe the Board would take you more seriously if you had . . . power. As it is, I can see they're not keeping you in the loop.'

Luc stared at her. The power thing was an old wound, and a stark reminder of exactly why he was here in the first place. And it wasn't like he hadn't tried to find his power. Every rumour about stirring tea widdershins with an eagle's beak, every old wives' tale about petting Cerberus's middle head while wearing a nettle shirt . . . he'd tried it all. Nothing worked. If he had a power at all, the elusive little bugger would have to come out in its own time.

But he also knew bait when he heard it. He wasn't getting dragged into that.

'What loop?' he asked, instead.

Zillah beamed at him. 'There you go. Clever boy.'

'Zilch, stop patronizing me and just say what you came here to say, all right?'

'I will when you stop it with that nickname.'

'I thought you liked it.'

'No, Luc. I do not like Lucifer's entitled, bratty grandson reminding me constantly that your family considers mine to be worthless. Nothings.'

'I don't! Bloody Hell, Zil, I would never—'

'Because we're not worthless. I'm not worthless.'

'Zillah, I swear to the chains binding my grandfather, I have never thought of you like that. If my dad does, it's because he's so far up his own arse all he can see is his own stomach lining. Come on, I came to you for help finding Jenny because you're the best.'

Zillah's face went very still as he said this.

'I mean, I am the best.' A flash of her normal confidence. 'And I'll stop being cryptic now. I spoke to my mother before agreeing to this job.'

'And?'

'And she said this is bigger than your dad's ego or my dislike of Earth. There's an eclipse coming, did you know?'

'Joey mentioned something about it, but I didn't know what he was talking about.'

'Well, this one's a big deal. It's not just the moon crossing in front of the sun, it's . . . an alignment. For a few minutes, the celestial spheres are going to overlap – not just like here, with the Hellmouth, but everywhere.'

Luc stared at her, aware of a creeping sensation in his guts, and the hairs crawling on his arms. His wrist felt hot where the star tracker met his skin. Or not 'star tracker', apparently, but 'celestial sphere tracker'.

'What does that mean?'

'Maybe nothing. Maybe your dad's wrong. But when he called a secret meeting of the Board, a bunch of top-flight MINOS bigshots, and half the generals in the Legions . . . he said it might mean we could break Lucifer's chains. Wake him up. Tip the balance firmly in our favour, use Lucifer's Light to bust open a way out of the Abyss.'

Every atom in Luc's body vibrated as Zillah explained this. His head felt full, too full, like all this information was squeezing against his skull and clamouring to get out. He could explode with the pressure of it.

'And they need Jenny for this?' Even to his own ears, his voice sounded very far away.

Zillah nodded. 'A living creature with no soul. It's in the Agreement – no one else can climb the mountain. It's a chance to get out of All Hell for good.'

He could be the reason the demons got out of All Hell. The enormity of this made his heart swell, his stomach flip. This was more than just escaping a life in the Legions, this was world-altering, life-changing – for every demon in existence, not just for him.

Even as the thoughts swelled inside him, though, so did something else. Suspicion.

'And my dad's behind this, is he?'

'Yep. Apparently he's been planning it for years. Researching the Agreement, finding a way to take a soul from a living human without it eventually killing them.'

Luc's memory conjured up a bookcase filled with used soul vessels, all yellow with white writing on them. How many humans had Pyro destroyed before realizing the trick was to take a soul from a child?

'And then what happens to Jenny?' he heard himself ask. 'After she's broken the chains, I mean?'

Zillah shrugged. Evidently this wasn't of major concern to her.

'No idea. Maybe she gets her soul back and gets on with her life.' The Succubus tilted her head to one side as she considered this. 'Although, that life might be a bit different, when we've released All Hell.'

17

JENNY

The chalet assigned to Jenny was a small, anonymous room that felt familiar in the same way a chain hotel feels familiar. No matter where you are, the bedding is the same, the furniture is the same . . . and, in fact, it was laid out much like a chain hotel too. Double bed, a desk with a TV on the wall above it, even a kettle and tray of tea bags.

There were two doors: one that led off into the bathroom, and the other, outside.

She'd been here for some time now. She couldn't say precisely how long because . . . well, so she'd had a nap, all right? Turned out it was bloody *exhausting*, all this traipsing cross-country in search of her soul. Besides, the bed was so soft and squishy, and Chloe-Lee had done everything she could to make her feel at home – *do you have enough towels?* As though she needed more than two, at a push. *Is there a tea you like to drink on the tray? I can bring you another type if you like. What about biscuits?*

She'd even shown Jenny one of the drawers, filled with soft cotton pyjamas. That's what she was wearing now, a matching set in mint green. Chloe-Lee had whisked her school clothes away and promised to return them, 'freshly laundered and pressed'. It was only when she considered going in search of Luc, pyjamas be damned, that she realized Chloe-Lee had also taken her shoes with her, so that plan was out.

Her eyes flicked over to the bathroom door. On the other hand . . . imagine, a shower, with no smelly pre-teen boys banging on the door for her to hurry up!

'Lead us not into temptation,' she muttered, but it was too much. She got off the bed and walked into the bathroom.

The shower, it had to be said, was excellent. Whether the plumbing had been upgraded since her last stay as a child, or whether it was just the relief of this being all for her right now, she couldn't say. She stood under the hot water far longer than she really needed to, eyes closed, letting the spray land on her upturned face.

Afterwards, she put her glasses back on and combed her wet hair with her fingers, tying it into a loose plait to keep it out of her face, looping a hair elastic she'd had around her wrist for the past God knows how long over the end of the braid. She put the pyjamas back on and crawled under the duvet, which was like a cross between marshmallows and clouds, and picked up the TV remote. If she was to be so cruelly trapped here, she might as well enjoy it.

She got through two whole episodes of *The Simpsons* before Chloe-Lee returned, bearing an armful of school-uniform-shaped gifts.

'There was a most peculiar stain on the shirt,' she trilled as she laid them on a chair by the window, 'but Martha managed to get it out with some genius concoction involving bicarbonate of soda. The woman is truly a marvel. As for the shoes . . . well, I wanted to give them a polish, but alas, they're not much the better for it.'

'Don't worry about it,' she said. 'They're not real leather.'

'Forgive me if I'm overstepping politeness here,' Chloe-Lee said, 'but I must ask – are you experiencing some kind of hardship, at home?'

You sound like Raffo, Jenny thought. But this wasn't an overanxious Deputy Head, it was a creepy ten-year-old. Was that better? Or worse?

'I don't think it takes a genius to work that out,' Jenny said.

'And . . . Master Lucifer. I take it he has made some promise to you, about improving your life by collecting your soul from its current owner?'

'*I'm* its current owner,' Jenny said quickly.

'Well . . . legally speaking . . .'

'I was *six* when Luc's dad stole it,' she pointed out. 'I don't know much about this Sacred Agreement you all keep banging on about, but where I'm from, six-year-olds can't legally consent to something like this.'

'That is true,' Chloe-Lee acquiesced. 'And perhaps . . . well. We would never wish to stand in the way of true free will, so if it transpires all is above board then we will wave you off at the portal ourselves, but . . . there could be another way, you know.'

'What do you mean?'

'Luc did not come here through the correct channels. We have a duty to bring that to the attention of the Celestial Council; only they can decide what's to be done with him.'

Something odd happened in Jenny's chest as she said that. The idea of anything 'being done with' Luc didn't feel . . . good.

'But while the Council is convened, perhaps we could request they also investigate that other matter.'

'My soul, you mean?'

Chloe-Lee nodded. 'They cannot reject a direct request from a living human. The complication, of course, is that normally that living human must be in possession of their soul when the request is made, but perhaps they might be willing to be flexible, under the circumstances.'

'But what if they're not?' Jenny asked. 'Then I'd be in the same boat I'm in now, except Luc's dad would know I was coming, and he'd lock my soul away somewhere I couldn't get to it.'

Chloe-Lee blinked as she considered this, and for a brief second her eyes shone gold. But it was gone again just as quickly.

'I would just ask you to consider it carefully, that's all,' the little girl said softly. 'If the Council choose to make an example of Luc, then I'm afraid you might not have other options.'

She made as though to leave, but paused at the door. 'You could, of course, simply go home.'

'Without my soul?'

Chloe-Lee inclined her head.

'I can't do that,' Jenny said firmly. 'I . . . get the impression you wouldn't understand.'

'That may be,' Chloe-Lee murmured. 'I merely presented the option.' Then she added, 'I won't lock this door after me. You have free will, after all. However, as a guest at Elrick Park it is important that I impart our two rules: please do not leave the cabin, now. Dusk has long since passed, and the paths can be treacherous in the dark. Also, do not touch the trees, if you can possibly avoid it.'

Jenny waited for her to leave, and then another couple of minutes (just to be sure) before she clambered out of bed and got dressed in her school uniform. Her clothes were so clean they almost looked new, and just as promised, Martha's trick with the bicarb had entirely eliminated the stain from the polo shirt, and all in all they were warm, soft, and smelt divine.

The shoes, despite Chloe-Lee's attentions, still looked like they cost a fiver from the market, which was mainly because they did.

Once dressed, she slipped her phone back in her

pocket and the small collection of coins that represented all her worldly wealth in the other, then walked to the front door of her chalet, and left.

Chloe-Lee hadn't lied about the dark. For some reason it was even more oppressive now, and without a cavalcade of demons and demon-adjacent creatures (she wasn't entirely sure what the twins *were*, but she knew they weren't exactly like Zillah and Luc) to guide her, she struggled to see one step in front of the other. Even the moon had gone into hiding behind some inconvenient clouds. The plan, obviously, was to find Luc, and see what he had to say about all this. One thing she knew for certain: she wasn't giving up now. Not when she'd come all this way.

Of course, in theory finding Luc was easy, but in practice – she had absolutely no idea whether his chalet was close to hers, and it wasn't like she knew where she was in the first place. Still, she kept putting one foot in front of the other until she came to one of those sandstone paths . . . and something moved in the corner of her eye.

She whipped her head round towards it until she identified it again; something human-shaped (which didn't exactly narrow things down) was on the path to her left, and seemed to be headed towards the forest, as though they weren't even afraid of it.

Luc?

Surely he wasn't going to abandon her here?

She took off after them, only resisting calling out in case it was one of the twins, who no doubt would ship her straight back to bed, or chastise her for already breaking one of the rules.

As she drew slightly nearer, careful of her steps despite the dark, she realized it wasn't Luc. It wasn't the twins either. It was Martha.

The Site Manager of Elrick Park was walking the sandstone path as though she didn't want anyone to see her, which was a) peculiar, given she was literally the boss around here and b) highly suspicious.

And whatever she was doing, she was so focused on her task she didn't seem to notice she was being followed. She didn't look back, and when she reached a smaller tributary of the main path that veered straight into the heart of the forest, she didn't hesitate.

Jenny did. The vibrations in this place were most definitely *off* at night, she decided. No wonder one of the rules was *stay away from the trees*.

Martha picked up her pace, forcing Jenny to do the same, following the narrow, winding sandstone path until she lost all sense of direction. If the path disappeared now, she thought uncomfortably, she'd be lost in here. In the dark, the ghostly trees seemed to loom inwards, reaching over her as though drawn by the warmth of her humanity.

Stop scaring yourself, she scolded her own imagination.

Paths didn't just disappear, any more than trees leant in because of someone's bloody body heat. No, paths were bedded into the ground until they ended at their destination, and this one was no exception. She followed at a distance, so she saw the end of the path as soon as Martha stopped.

There was light here, she realized, but it had a different quality to the candles on the twins' rocky altar. Something glowed at the end of the path – risking her stealth, Jenny crept forward to get a better view of where Martha had led them.

The path ended at a stone archway. On either side of it, more of the *selva oscura* trees grew – but at a slight distance, their silhouettes in the gloom reminding Jenny of strangers in crowds, gathered around a tragedy but not wanting to get too close.

The glowing emanated from the middle of the archway. She couldn't see it properly – Martha's back was blocking most of the light – but what she could see was . . . *beautiful.* A kaleidoscope of colours filled the archway, a series of interconnected segments shifting and dancing around each other. It was like stained glass, if stained glass were made of liquid and could move.

Jenny gasped, realizing too late how close she was now to Martha, how her feet had carried her forward towards the arch. The older woman spun round, but Jenny was quicker: diving off the safety of the path to duck behind one of the trees, cringing away from its bulk even as she hid in its shadow, only just remembering Chloe-Lee's warning about touching them. She squeezed her eyes tight and waited to see if she'd been caught, but nothing happened.

Martha's attention was on the archway again. From this

slight sideways vantage, Jenny could just make out the curve of her jaw. She was gazing into the prismatic glow, seeing things in it that Jenny could only imagine.

Then, as though she'd been waiting for a sign, Martha sucked in a deep breath and screamed, right into the centre of the kaleidoscope.

18

JENNY

Jenny expected the sound of Martha's scream to shudder through the trees, but to her surprise the archway acted like a vacuum, sucking Martha's anguished cry towards it, inside it, gone.

The woman screamed for a long time. It didn't seem like the first time she'd come here for this purpose. Jenny's heart pinched in sympathy, even though she was more than a little afraid of Martha Garstang.

She knew why she felt sympathy though – they were the same, Jenny and Martha. One way or another, both of them had voids where their souls should be. Although, at least Martha knew where hers was. Was that some comfort, she wondered, or did it make everything worse?

When she finished screaming, Martha was breathless,

hoarse, but she managed to speak in the direction of the archway anyway.

'I can't do this any more,' she told it. 'Can you hear me? I can't *do this any more*.'

She sighed, her shoulders slumped, and she reached out, using the stone structure of the arch to support herself. Jenny wasn't sure if she was expecting an answer, but none came. After a few moments, Martha turned away from the glimmering archway. Jenny slunk further into the dark so that Martha didn't see her as she passed, but it wouldn't have mattered: Elrick Park's Site Manager wasn't paying attention to anything any more. Her whole body was . . . diminished, somehow, as though the visceral shriek she'd loosed into the void had taken part of her with it.

Jenny waited until she was out of sight, then stepped out on to the path and walked towards the archway. It glowed invitingly, waiting for her. Close up, she could see the detail of it – the stone wasn't yellow, like the sandstone paths running like veins through the forest, but a marbled white. It reminded her of cathedral ruins, a once-grand edifice reduced only to this. There were words carved into the stone at even intervals, in the same angular style as the ones she'd seen before, in the wooden archway.

LASCIATE OGNE SPERANZA, VOI CH'INTRATE, they said. As though she had the faintest clue what that meant. Latin, or something, she guessed.

The colours inside the archway were hypnotic, undulating like tides, melding into each other rhythmically, although she couldn't exactly identify the pattern. There was something natural about it, the interconnected slices reminding her of the rings inside a tree, individual sections that at the same time were linked, inextricable, with every other piece of the whole.

She swayed as a sleepy sort of vertigo took hold of her, so that she blinked, noticing as she did the way the colours landed on the front of her school jumper, staining her in pools of incandescent light. She was still dizzy, enough that she stumbled sideways and had to reach out to steady herself against one of the trees. As she did, her bare fingertips brushed the bark.

JENNY, the tree whispered in her mind.

'What the—?' she said out loud, snatching her hand away and stepping smartly away from both the archway and the tree.

This time, her head stayed silent.

She glanced around, suspicious, but she was still alone. Tentative, she walked towards the tree again and sent one outstretched forefinger towards the bark.

HELLO JENNY, the tree said.

'Uh . . . hello?'

YOU DON'T REMEMBER US.

This wasn't a question, but even as the words sounded in her head, she knew they weren't true.

'Yeah, I think I do, actually,' she said. Or at least, there was something, some tickly sensation at the back of her memories. A little girl, alone in the trees. Tracing her fingers over the bark. Voices, in her head.

'I thought I imagined you,' she admitted.

YOU DID NOT.

How had she ended up alone here in the woods, back then? She'd been here with a heavily pregnant Vee, of course, who also had Connor to look after and her own broken heart to tend to. Maybe it wasn't so surprising that six-year-old Jenny had managed to wriggle away and sneak off by herself.

She remembered hopscotching her way along the sandstone path, deeper into the forest, until she'd realized the canopy of trees above was too thick for the sun to sink through, and she was all in darkness.

She'd been frightened. She'd stumbled, off the path, and one little hand had grabbed an outstretched tree limb for support.

The trees spoke to her then. They helped her find her way back to the path, to the sparser edge of the woods.

Then a woman had come along and shouted at her, warning her to stay on the paths and away from the trees. It must have been Martha, a thought which brought her up short. All this time, Martha had been yelling at people to stay away from the trees.

'What are you?' she asked, out loud, because it felt too strange to talk to the trees only in her head.

As soon as she asked the question, something throbbed inside her head, and an image flowered before her eyes; a peculiar sensation, like her head was a cinema and the trees were able to somehow project film on to a screen she didn't know existed.

In the image, a figure. Human – at least she thought so.

It was hard to tell – his outline was blurry and he seemed to shine slightly, a pale, silvery light that emanated outwards through his skin.

He was standing in some sort of temporary office, a box made out of chipboard. In the middle of the room was a plain white desk and sat at the desk was a demon, who was fiddling with an empty yellow can. She could see she was a demon because she had head spikes like Luc, except hers were more prominent, more like horns than the subtle barbs by Luc's hairline. She wore an all-black uniform that read vaguely military to Jenny, and the glowing man stood in front of her desk, wringing his hands.

'Forest,' the demon grunted.

'Excuse me?'

Her tone wasn't unkind. More . . . detached. Clearly, she did this kind of thing a lot.

'You're for the forest. MINOS Agent 3004 will show you where to go.'

Then the image shifted, another scene but the same glowing man, but this time he was in a forest not unlike the one Jenny was standing in. The only difference was that the sky looked wrong, too black, and the pinpricks of light she thought might be stars flickered like candles. The man was walking towards a clearing, guided by another demon in that same black uniform.

The glowing man stood where he was told, glancing around nervously at the trees on either side of him. Then, as Jenny watched, an expression of pure agony cracked his face apart. He struggled, but his feet sank into the soft earth, rooting him in place as his skin cracked, his clothes split apart and he transformed, agonizingly, into a tree.

'You . . . you were human? All of you?' She swallowed. Even from here there seemed to be so many.

WE ARE MANY, the trees told her in agreement. BUT ONLY SMALL IN NUMBER BY THIS HELLMOUTH.

She tried to imagine what that meant, how many of these trees must exist on the other side of the portal, but she couldn't picture it.

She opened her mouth to ask another question, and someone tapped her on the shoulder. She flinched, breaking contact with the tree, and spun around, panicked.

'So that's both the rules you've broken, then.' Zillah smirked at her.

'What are you still doing here?' Jenny shot back.

'*Jeez*, why is no one just pleased to see me tonight?' Zillah rolled her eyes. 'Come on, let's go jailbreak the blond one.'

'Jailbreak?' But Zillah was already walking back up the path, and in a sudden fear of getting left behind, Jenny raced after her.

'*Some of us* haven't got free will, so they locked him in,' Zillah said. 'Forgot about the window, though; turns out attention to detail is not the twins' strong suit. I said I'd come find you first, before I cause the big distraction.'

'I mean, they're only kids— Wait, what distraction?'

'They're not really kids. You know that, right?'

'What are they, then?'

But Zillah ignored her. 'As for the distraction, it's probably best you don't know the details. Just . . . think blood and feathers, like last time.'

'Oh. That wasn't really the harpies, was it?'

'They were real harpy feathers,' Zillah said, which was evidently not an answer.

'But you're not going to actually hurt anyone, are you?'

'Like I said, details. But no, if it makes you feel any better, I'm not going to hurt anyone. Tonight.'

Somehow, as with most things to do with Zillah, it did not make Jenny feel any better.

'Have a nice chat with the trees?' Zillah asked, breaking into Jenny's thoughts with a fairly obvious change in direction.

'Uh, sort of, I think?'

'What are they like?' There was a note of genuine curiosity in Zillah's tone that caught Jenny's attention.

'Have you never spoken to them yourself?'

The Succubus shook her head. 'They don't talk to us.'

Which seemed fair enough, given what Jenny had seen in the vision from the trees.

'Maybe if they weren't condemned to living in tree bodies, they'd feel chattier,' she said mildly.

'Yeah,' Zillah sniffed. 'But their hearts were weighed and found heavier than a feather, so, what are you gonna do?'

'What does that even mean?'

Zillah shrugged. 'Ask the twins. Come on, will you?'

When they reached the main path out of the forest,

Zillah zigzagged her way confidently through a collection of chalets with dark windows until they finally arrived at one with lights on. Lights on, and a curtain twitcher inside. Luc's face lit up when he saw Jenny trailing in Zillah's wake, and she had to fight the urge to blush to the roots of her hair at the sight of his smile.

You are ridiculous, she told herself firmly.

Zillah helped him climb out of the window.

'You two wait out here until you get my sign.' She turned to Jenny. 'I need your jumper.'

'Excuse me?'

Zillah held a hand out and gestured impatiently. 'Jumper. Give. I need to make it look like the girls have got to you, so no one wonders why your room's empty.'

'And by girls, you mean . . .' But she started pulling her jumper sleeves off her arms anyway.

'The girls. Harpies.'

'Right. Fine. Of course.' She handed over the jumper and tried not to shiver as soon as the cool night air touched her skin.

'What's this sign you're going to give us?' Luc asked Zillah.

'Oh, you'll know it when you hear it.' In the dark, her teeth shone like deadly moons.

And then she was gone. She didn't even say goodbye, just took off into the night.

'She's always doing that,' Luc sighed. Then they lapsed into silence. It wasn't uncomfortable, not really, but neither was it nice. It was almost tangible, like a void between them that left Jenny horribly aware of Luc's body heat, the closeness of his hand, his arm . . . if she just shuffled a tiny step closer the hairs on his forearms would brush against hers—

She coughed, breaking the silence.

'I'm sorry I told them,' she said. 'I got overwhelmed.'

'Not your fault.'

She strained her ears for the sound of Zillah's blood and feathers sign, but there was nothing except her own heartbeat. A breeze rippled over her, and she resisted the urge to rub her arms with her hands. She could do this. She was fine.

Totally. Fine.

A scream pierced the air, and she flinched so hard her back slammed against the wall of the chalet.

'Are you all right?' Luc asked, his warm hand on her cool skin sending a bolt of electricity right through her.

'What is *that*?' she hissed as the scream broadened out, trilling, a cross between a human in despair and a peacock's wail.

'That would be a harpy,' Luc said. 'And, I'm guessing, our sign to get out of here.'

'But she said . . .' It didn't matter, she realized, whatever Zillah had said. This was their sign, and if she wanted her soul back she needed to stop questioning everything a Succubus said or did, and *move*.

She wasn't even surprised this time when Luc took hold of her hand. She gripped his fingers in her own and let him yank her out from behind the chalet and on to the path back towards the woods. Towards the Hellmouth.

She didn't bother asking how Luc knew the way – maybe it was like he said before, he could feel the pull of the kaleidoscope portal, could feel his way home. She let him guide them both, even though he was moving so fast the soles of her cheap shoes couldn't lessen the impact of stone against feet. Even though her glasses were steaming up from the exertion, even though adrenalin was shooting through her system.

Don't think, her brain suggested helpfully. *Don't think about where you're going.*

They'd made it to the mouth of the forest when they heard another of those awful screams, and this time the sound of running feet to go with it. Luc hauled Jenny behind a tree. As soon as her skin made contact, *they* were in her head again.

WHAT IS HAPPENING?

But she didn't have time to explain. And how could she, when Luc's body was crushed up against hers as he craned his head round the tree to check their way was clear? She swallowed thickly.

HE IS A DEMON.

They sounded disapproving, and Jenny jolted at the knowledge they could feel her feelings. They knew how she . . . they knew Luc scrambled her thoughts.

It was a relief when he peeled her away from the bark and set off at a run once more. *Déjà vu* – she'd been here less than an hour ago, but this time she had Luc's hand in hers, and they careened down the path, towards that hypnotic, stained-glass Hellmouth, the portal that would take them straight—

Don't think, don't think—

She couldn't stop it, though. As soon as she stepped into that portal, everything would change. Everything. Was it worth it? She wouldn't know unless she did it. They reached the portal and despite herself, Jenny's feet slid to a dead, instinctive stop. Luc jerked back, their hands still clasped.

'Jenny?'

'I know,' she said. 'We have to.' She stared at the swirling colours, her heart thundering in her chest.

'What does that mean?' She pointed at the Latin inscription in the stone.

Luc sighed. 'Abandon all hope, if you enter here,' he said softly.

Right.

'Right.' She swallowed. Nodded. Another harpy shrieked in the distance. She locked eyes with Luc. 'Right. Well then. I'll do that.'

Deep breath. And then she stepped forward, so fast that now Luc was behind her.

'I'll do that.'

And she did.

19

JENNY

The coloured light inside the archway glowed brighter around them as they crossed the boundary. Whatever substance made the Hellmouth work stretched with her like a membrane, sticky against her face until she took one last step and punctured through.

On the other side, she shook herself free of the weblike colours and looked back, expecting to see the other side of the archway. Instead, she found herself at the mouth of a cave, innocuous against the black stone cliff that sheered up and out of her vision, except that as she took a step backwards it coalesced into something else, like a huge carving of a big cat. She'd just walked out between its bared teeth. Slowly, the cobweb stickiness faded, and Luc grinned at her, no evidence of the stained-glass effect on his skin.

She tried to find the sky, but the treetops obscured her view. It still looked like Elrick Park. And yet something had changed when she stepped through the archway. Her heart thumped under her ribs, a banging drum warning her of danger. With every step she took, her skin tightened over her bones, her mouth dried and her thighs felt weak.

'Come on.'

She followed Luc out of the treeline, where she could see the landscape more clearly. Flatlands swept out around her, carpeted with an insipid yellow grass, grass that was long but limp, level with the ground as though trampled by a thousand weary feet.

The quality of the light was strange; no sunshine lit their way. Not that this seemed to worry Luc. Hundreds of hazy spots of light flickered high above in a deeply unstarlike display. There was something so otherworldly about them, she found her footsteps stopping so she could peer at the stars without tripping over her own feet. The thin, unstable quality of the stars was a puzzle, and there was no moon.

And as she stood there, baffled by the starlight, she sensed the stillness of the air around her, and heard . . . nothing.

'What are you doing now?' Luc's hand found hers again, and just like last time the jolt of skin-to-skin shocked her from her thoughts, and a flush of warmth climbed through her nervous system.

'It's just so strange to me,' she told him. 'Like, it should be familiar, but it isn't. Like a dream.'

Luc snorted and cast a careless glance around them. 'It's bleak, is what it is.'

And it should have been, but somehow it just wasn't. It was too *other* for that. Her whole body found a thousand ways to tell her she didn't belong here, and yet all she wanted to do was slow down, take it all in, explore this alien world.

'What's over there?' she asked, pointing towards a flat horizon marred only by a series of bulky silhouettes.

'Uh-oh,' Luc muttered, gripping her hand tighter. 'Look, I'm flattered you're so interested in where I'm from and everything, but we might want to save the sightseeing for later.'

'OK,' Jenny agreed, even as he tugged her along in his wake, almost too quickly for her to comfortably follow. 'What's wrong?'

'Nothing, yet. Just, uh, you probably don't want to meet those things.'

A low level of instinctual panic lived under her skin in this place, and it flared at his words. She kicked her speed up a notch. Was she imagining those strange shapes were larger now, looming ever closer? In fact, were they moving? She gripped Luc's hand and ran with him, until the ground beneath them canted sharply downwards. She shrieked at the sudden velocity.

Luc's arm slipped around her waist, slowing her momentum, stopping her from tilting into a fall. He didn't remove it, not even when they were walking side by side down the side of the hill. A low, rolling fog furled around their ankles, climbing by degrees up Jenny's calves and to her knees. Luc didn't seem worried, so she tried to match his serenity, but she didn't understand . . .

'Is it safe now?' she whispered.

'Almost.'

His arm squeezed tighter around her as the mist enveloped them entirely, so white and thick she couldn't see her own feet.

'Now we're safe,' she heard Luc's voice assure her. But the fog muffled it, making him sound distant, and she wasn't entirely sure she believed him.

By the time the fog faded again, Jenny's feet hurt. Turned out cheap ballet flats off the market weren't exactly made for hiking across an alien landscape.

Jenny had stayed quiet through the mists, focusing on where to put her feet and the feel of Luc's arm around her waist. She tried to ignore the mist, although it was difficult, the damp of it almost seeping under her skin.

It was a relief when it finally petered out, falling back to thin wisps by her ankles.

'What were those things?' she asked, as though the fog had been the only thing keeping her voice in.

'The Uncommitted?'

'If that's what they're called, yeah.'

For a moment she wasn't sure he'd heard her, and when he finally spoke it was in a careful, considered tone.

'Human souls,' he said. 'Or they were, I guess. Now they're . . . well, in life they were people who couldn't make up their minds. Always chasing after what seemed convenient *right now* rather than having any long-term direction. So, in death, they've been sentenced to exist in that place, and every night a wind blows that feels like blades to keep them sharp.'

Human souls? Surely they wouldn't hurt her or anything, in that case?

'Why didn't you want me to meet them?'

Another careful pause.

'I was worried they'd scare you. They don't act much like people any more, that's all.'

Hmm. What did that mean?

He let go of her waist, now that they could see, and she fought back a bite of disappointment when he didn't go for her hand again. He was a half-step in front of her, and she watched his shoulders, squared and tense. He was worried about something. Apparently, despite the pull of the Hellmouth back in the Park, Luc's return to Hell didn't feel exactly jubilant.

Well, she reflected, he had pretty dangerous cargo with him, didn't he? *And he's doing this anyway. For you.*

He stopped abruptly, and she almost walked into him. She'd been so caught up, she realized with a flush of blood to the face, in staring at Luc's back that she hadn't even noticed they'd almost walked into the waters of an almighty river, mist still frilling at its edges.

'This is the Acheron,' Luc said. 'It runs all the way around the perimeter of the Abyss.'

The Acheron was huge, an impassable divide of brackish water, wide enough that the mists swallowed up whatever was on the other side. But, she noticed, it was also entirely still. Not a duck, not a fish, not a breath of air puckering the surface.

'Hang tight,' Luc said. 'I just need to hail a cab.'

He dropped to a crouch and leant forward, one arm hanging over the bank. Jenny watched him search for something just above the water, and when he found what he wanted he knocked on it, three times. A sound like a drum boomed over the river. Luc stood up and gazed out over the water.

Jenny followed his gaze and watched the loose fog billow like a curtain in the breeze. It moved, rolling across the flat top of the river, parting as something angular and dark emerged from within.

A cloaked figure, standing tall at the prow of a long, narrow barge they were punting across the river.

'The Ferryman,' Jenny said. Even she had heard of him.

'Ferrier,' Luc corrected. 'I don't know that's a man, exactly.'

The barge pulled up against the bank and Jenny was struck by how tall and broad the Ferrier was. They said something to Luc, a low, rumbling sound emanating from inside their deep hood. It was like a cross between a purr and a threat, and like everything else in this place the sound was familiar, but not so much that she could understand the words.

Luc, apparently having understood perfectly, rolled his eyes. He hopped forward, on to the boat, and for a panicked second she thought he might be about to zip across the river without her, leaving her stranded on the side with the Uncommitted.

But then a cloaked hand came into view, and the Ferrier helped her to a wide, wooden seat just behind their helm.

Jenny settled herself on to her seat and tried not to be quite so conscious of the fact Luc was directly behind her. For some reason, knowing he could see her, but she couldn't see him, made her nervous. Was she hallucinating the heat of his eyes on the back of her neck?

What was going on with her? She swallowed, trying to calm herself. She'd been alone with him before, at the fair, and that hadn't felt like this, had it? They'd been like giddy kids then, but now . . . well, this felt charged with something she didn't quite understand. Maybe Hell just did that to a girl.

The Ferrier swung their hood towards Jenny. Determined not to be afraid, she lifted her head. She didn't see a face, but the whole hood shook from side to side and the Ferrier said something to Luc in that curious rumble again. They didn't seem happy.

'You can't refuse to carry a demon on request,' Luc said, in what seemed to be a reply.

The Ferrier spoke again, and this time Jenny realized she could understand them – it was just a case of tuning in, as if to a different radio frequency.

'She's not a demon,' was what the Ferrier said.

'No, but she's with m— Look, I hate to go all *do you know who I am* on you, but seriously. Do you know who I am?'

Jenny cringed. Was she about to be booted off the barge?

'I don't give a toss who you are.' Not the kind of language Jenny would have associated with an undead transporter of souls, but there you are.

Luc spluttered. 'Well, maybe you'll change your tune when you figure it out. Have you ever met your boss before?'

The Ferrier sighed. 'You're Pyro's kid?'

'That's right.'

The Ferrier was silent for a moment, but then they shrugged. 'I transport demons and the dead. That's what it says in my contract with Seven, Inc. She is neither a demon, nor is she dead.'

The Ferrier made an excellent point.

There was a pause. Jenny's stomach tightened and she chewed the inside of her cheek furiously, staring out at the dark water.

What was the plan now?

Luc cleared his throat and recited something in a language Jenny didn't understand. Thankfully, he then helpfully translated it.

'Do not impede her journey fate-ordained.'

'*Fate?* If you say so.' The Ferrier didn't sound remotely convinced, but sighed heavily. They heaved the heavy barge pole in the water, shoving the boat out across the river.

Jenny was fairly sure she heard them mutter, 'I hate poetry.'

Luc either didn't hear this, or chose not to comment.

The barge swept across the water. Even where the pole sank below the surface to propel the boat forward, the river barely registered the motion. As though the water was thick, viscous. *Ew.*

Under the dim gleam from the unearthly, glittering lights overhead it looked black too, giving her the distinct impression the barge was essentially wading through treacle.

And that was the last thought she had before she fainted.

20

FRAN OF THE HOPELESS HEART

Eyes and teeth.

Those were the rules at the Hopeless Heart Motel & Diner, off Route Six towards the Demon City of Dis.

Eyes should be bright, sparkling, and full of enthusiasm as Fran took each customer order down on her pad, as she pinned said orders to the piece of string above the cook's station, and as she dealt with the consistent complaints from her entirely demon clientele.

'I didn't order this!'

'The inside of this pie is stone cold!'

'We've been waiting fifteen minutes!'

But this was all part of the punish— Ahem, the job, so she kept her eyes wide and clear, even as one particularly cruel demon launched a full plate of spaghetti at her head. At the last moment, she swerved sideways, and the dish smashed harmlessly against the wall.

Teeth should be clean, of course, and always prominently on show via a cheerful smile. Fran no longer remembered a time when her cheeks didn't ache from this order, but it was too important to forget. If she faltered in this, let her sunny disposition slip, she would be punished far worse. *Yes*, she reminded herself when things felt especially difficult, *there are worse fates than an eternal waitressing shift in the Second Circle of All Hell.*

Her punishment hadn't always been like this. When she was first condemned, there had been a storm. A tempest, designed to remind her of the hurricane emotions that landed her here in the first place, her passions, her ill-placed devotion. She had been stripped naked and tossed into the heart of the storm, buffeted about by an icy, foul-smelling wind.

He had been there too, of course, her paramour, but the gales kept them apart. That had been the punishment, an eternal torment of knowing her love was close, but never being able to speak to him, or touch him.

Of course, after several centuries of that, the effect lessened rather. They say absence makes the heart grow fonder, but in Fran's case she just started to feel numb to the man who had once held her whole heart in his palm. She suspected he felt the same, because whenever she saw him through breaks in the clouds, cast into sharp relief under whipcracks of lightning, his face had lost that tortured, bovine adoration. Instead, he just looked bored.

That was when the powers that be decided it was time

to change their punishments. Hoicked out of the tumult, she had found herself wearing a knee-length dress of pale blue with a frilly white apron over the top. The fabric of both items was so synthetic she crackled as she walked. Then, there were the shoes.

Fran stopped reminiscing just long enough to widen her smile at the customer currently in front of her. A regular; one of Lilith's get, as far as Fran could glean. *Alyssa Third Daughter*, she thought. Alyssa liked to order ice cream in flavours she knew the Hopeless Heart didn't carry, and when she finally accepted rum and raisin as a replacement she'd wait for it to melt, and flick the liquescent results into Fran's hair as she walked past.

But still, Fran grinned brightly as she took down Alyssa's order for mangosteen, kiwi and yuzu gelato.

'I'll check with the kitchen,' she promised perkily.

She already knew they didn't have it.

She kind of wished they did. It sounded bloody delicious.

Her feet pinched in her uniform shoes, so as she leant in through the hatch to the kitchen she let her arms on the counter take the weight of her, just for a moment.

'Tony? We got any mangosteen, kiwi and yuzu gelato?'

The cook didn't even pause from his task, chopping onions.

'No. We've got vanilla, French vanilla and rum and raisin. Same as every day, Fran. Same as we've had for the past four hundred years, Fran. Vanilla, French vanilla and rum and raisin.'

Ah well. Always worth a shot. Tony was only grumpy because today his shift coincided with Cleo's. Right now, the other waitress was beaming vacantly at a table of rowdy young demons all clamouring to tell Cleo exactly how they wanted their steaks cooked. Or rather, barely cooked.

Fran waited another few moments before going back to give Alyssa the bad news. She glanced down at her shoes. They were clogs, which was incongruous alongside the 1950s-esque pinafore dress that made up the rest of the uniform, but Fran knew better than to point this out to the uniforms office at Seven, Inc., which owned the Hopeless Heart.

They were uncomfortable by design, hard to stand in for longer than a few minutes – Fran had to wear them for ten demonic hours at a time. They were white and shiny, because they were made of glazed porcelain.

They were just another sign of Fran's incarceration. Much like the slender length of silver chain wrapped around her ankle. The other end of it disappeared under a series of specially designed cracks in the diner floor, between the black and white tiles. She didn't know exactly what she was chained to, down there, just that the chain was unbreakable, and kept her from straying too far beyond the boundaries of the diner.

Once upon a time, Fran had been the daughter of a very wealthy old man, and then the wife of another very wealthy old man. She'd had servants to bring her every whim on bronze platters. If that had been enough for her, would she have escaped this fate? It was a question she tried to avoid, but one that often haunted her at night, in the bare motel room she shared with some of the other waitresses.

If she hadn't chased love, would she be in Heaven now?

Was Heaven even real? It was hard to imagine, some days. When something as pure and innocent as love had condemned her here, to this fate, well, maybe that was a sign there was nothing else, after all. Cleo liked to say that where she was from, they believed there were only forty-two crimes, but seeing how many souls walked past on their way to the MINOS processing tower, that couldn't possibly be right.

Not that it mattered, anyway. Fran wasn't in Heaven, she was here, serving a rotating cast of the near thirteen million demons who all believed she deserved this fate.

She fixed a cheery grin on her face, trying not to wince as another blister made itself known on her heel. She marched back to Alyssa's table, her feet automatically taking her via the route permitted by the silver chain and the cracks in the floor.

'I'm afraid we don't have mangosteen, kiwi and yuzu gelato,' she beamed. 'How about rum and raisin, instead?'

21

JENNY

When Jenny came round from whatever caused her to black out in a boat over a treacle river, she was, perhaps understandably, disorientated. She opened her eyes, and overhead an endless cavern swept upwards, the only respite from the dark in the distant glow of those reedy, wavering stars.

As her consciousness returned more clearly, she remembered where she was and why. Her head was on something firm but not wooden, and she realized she must have tumbled backwards . . . on to Luc. A wave of embarrassment crawled over her, and she tried to bolt upright but he moved, his arms blocking her escape.

'Wait,' he said softly, 'don't rush it.'

Which was probably a sensible suggestion, given the way her head swam, but even so she felt the red creep of a warning in her gut when Luc's fingertips trailed across her cheek. A path of lightning across her skin. She held her breath, her pulse picking up. Luc was already there, meeting her gaze with eyes that flooded black. His tongue grazed his bottom lip; Jenny's lungs hurt. His face tilted down. Closer . . .

She sat up abruptly, ignoring the fuzz that descended before her eyes. In front of her, the Ferrier stood tall, the excess fabric of their hood making it impossible to know if they'd seen what just transpired.

'We have arrived,' the Ferrier intoned.

'Thanks,' Jenny mumbled as she scrambled out of the boat.

'No worries.' Luc shot her one of his devastating grins.

Jenny gestured at the boat's captain. 'I was talking to them.'

'Oh.' Luc sounded surprised, then glanced at the Ferrier. 'Yeah, thanks for the ride.'

As they walked away, the Ferrier rumbled at them.

'Wait.'

They gestured towards Jenny with a flick of their hood. She stepped closer, curious, as one of their hands dipped inside their cloak. Something clinked, and when they withdrew their hand it held a flat, silver disc about the size of Jenny's palm.

'For you,' the Ferrier rumbled.

'What is it?' It was heavy and cold in her hand, engraved with an intricate series of symbols and images that didn't mean anything to her.

‘A gift.’

Luc huffed impatiently behind her. ‘She doesn’t need that.’

The Ferrier ignored him entirely.

‘It is a passage token,’ they told her.

‘She doesn’t *need* it,’ Luc repeated. ‘She’s with me.’

‘For now, she is.’

A shiver thrilled through Jenny, but she slid the silver disc into the back pocket of her jeans.

‘Thank you,’ she said.

The Ferrier inclined their hood, low, almost a bow. It was so formal, and respectful, that Jenny couldn’t stop herself returning the gesture.

‘Fine, whatever,’ Luc sighed. ‘Can we go now?’

Jenny followed him, but before they rounded a corner she waved at the Ferrier. They were still by the shore, watching. They raised a hand in acknowledgement, then plunged their barge pole into the water, moving the boat into the mists.

This side of the Acheron was mist-less, which was a relief. The grass underfoot was still that insipid yellow colour, and Luc led her along a path that seemed to have been cut into the grass by thousands of feet over the passage of time. Before long, the path opened out to a meadow, where the grasses showed hints of green, and were as high as Jenny’s knees. They were still headed downwards, but this time at a much gentler gradient. What was he thinking? she wondered. What had he been *doing* back in the boat? She could almost swear he’d been about to kiss her, even though that made *no* sense. He was a *demon*. A stupidly *handsome* demon, but a demon all the same. There was no way he would ever . . .

'I want to show you something,' Luc said, as the silence stretched between them.

'Sure.'

He nodded, and changed direction. Jenny followed, wading through the grasses as they reached her waist. Here and there she saw wildflowers, too, shocks of reds and purples that seemed even more vibrant because of their location.

'What is this place?'

'The Fields of Limbo,' Luc told her. 'The only decent picnic spot this side of a Hellmouth.'

'Is that what you're going to show me?' Jenny teased. 'A picnic?'

'Not quite,' Luc smirked.

'Isn't Limbo where they send unbaptized babies?' Jenny asked, as an old memory from some half-forgotten RE lesson came into focus.

'Sometimes,' Luc agreed. 'There's a castle not far from here with a creche and a nursery.'

'Oh, *very* civilized,' Jenny shot back, layering the sarcasm thick on her tongue. 'And do their parents get to visit, in between their torture sessions?'

'Depends on their sin,' Luc replied evenly. 'But I don't know why you're mad at me – I didn't write the Sacred Agreement that put all this in place.'

Which frankly only caused more questions to fly

through her head like a flock of starlings, but before she could ask any, Luc reached out and took her hand. Her fingers flexed automatically around his, and now the starlings migrated to her chest.

'Look,' he said, so she did.

Luc had led her to the edge of the meadow, which was also the edge of a cliff. At her feet, the tall grasses fell away sharply into a sweeping rock face so high it made her knees weak. Something primal warned her to step back, but Luc's hand kept her anchored to the spot.

Beyond the cliffs, the landscape was so peculiar it took her a moment to understand what she was seeing. At the foot of the cliff beneath them the terrain was all crags and rocks, mud-soaked pathways with the occasional patch of yellow grass or a clump of those not-really trees. There were buildings dotted around too; some of them might be cottages while others were too big, too industrial for that. All of them emitted smoke from their chimneys though, a fug of grey that hung over their roofs.

But the smoke, the houses, the craggy terrain – all of that was fine. Ordinary, almost. What was odd was that as far as Jenny could tell, the ground tilted inwards, away from where she stood. And if she peered close enough, she thought she could just make out another stripe of landscape beyond that, before that too tilted downwards and out of sight.

It was like a funnel, she realized. The geography of the Abyss, always leading down, further into Hell.

'How far down do we need to go?' she asked.

'As far as it goes,' Luc said. 'We're going to a place called the Lake of Lament. It's in the Ninth Circle, right in the heart of the Abyss.'

'That's where your dad's office is?'

Luc cleared his throat.

'Uh, it's where your soul is.'

Which was an odd way of putting it. 'Yeah, that's what I meant.'

He dropped her hand and folded his arms across his chest, as though feeling a chill that wasn't there. Out of the corner of her eye she saw him glance down at that strange watch he wore, only partially revealed by the cuff of his hoodie.

'It's a long way,' he sniffed. 'And I don't want you to exhaust yourself before we arrive.'

Why did he do that? she wondered. Like, one moment he'd be holding her hand and talking to her all soft and low, and the next he'd drop her like a hot coal. It was disconcerting.

Then again, he was doing her a favour, wasn't he? It wasn't like they were *friends*. It wasn't like he actually liked her.

'I'm fine,' she told him quickly, determined not to slow him down. 'We can go as fast as you like – I can keep up, I promise.'

'I know you can,' Luc assured her. 'But still I'd feel better if we had a rest soon. It's a lot for you, all of this. And for me too, honestly.' He wasn't looking at her; conspicuously so, in fact.

'OK.'

Why wasn't he meeting her eyes?

'There's a place not too far from here,' he said. 'A restaurant.'

'A restaurant? Here?'

'Well, down there.' He gestured at the rocky landscape at the foot of the cliff. 'I think you'll like it.'

And just like that, decision made, apparently they were going to a restaurant.

22

JENNY

Jenny's feet slipped on the crumbling rocks as Luc guided her down the cliff towards the next layer of Hell.

'Welcome to the Second Circle,' he said when she was finally back on firm ground.

'I'm honoured,' she replied dryly.

Honestly, how much walking was involved in this endeavour? As far as Jenny could tell, the Second Circle of Hell was basically a hiking trail through some of the most boring scenery imaginable. Even if you were into hiking, there was no way anyone could enjoy this. The landscape was flat and dull, all dried-out mud without even much of the yellow grass she'd got used to on the upper level. The road was rocky and treacherous, and so dry that sandy dust settled on the vicious edges of the stones, camouflaging them from view and making every step a dice with serious injury.

Not that Luc seemed bothered. She kept back from him by a couple of paces, all the better to emulate his sure footsteps, my dear.

'You doing all right back there?' he asked over his shoulder.

'Oh yeah, just fine,' she heard herself grumble. 'Not like I needed my ankles intact or anything.'

Luc fired a glance back at her, and something in it almost made her stumble.

'I can always carry you, if you like.'

Her stomach dipped. 'You're all right,' she sniffed, more to cover her genuine reaction than anything else. 'I'm not sure you could manage it.'

Luc raised one arm, flexed. 'You're not exactly a heavy burden, sweetheart. Not for a demon.'

For a moment, her head conjured up an image of being swept up into Luc's arms, like a tiny heroine in a Regency romance novel or something. *Uh-oh*. She had to change the subject. Sharpish.

'Are you part-goat, or something? I cannot understand any other reason you're so good at navigating this awful place.'

'I suppose those cloven-hoof rumours have to come from somewhere.' He said it mildly enough, but still, Jenny was sure his shoulders tensed.

Maybe she'd been insensitive? It wouldn't be the first time. She swallowed, all of a sudden engulfed in a black cloud of anxiety. She'd spent a lifetime putting her foot in her mouth, saying the wrong thing, forcing people to hate her . . . well, not her whole life, but at least ten years. At least since Pyro stole a piece of her, leaving her fractured with sharp enough edges to chase everyone away. And she was so good at seeing the signs now. Luc's tense shoulders, the fact he'd had to force himself to sound like it didn't matter, when it clearly did. Oh, she'd really messed up, like she *always did*.

'Sorry,' she said quickly. 'I didn't think. I'm . . . well, you know. Broken. It makes me say stupid stuff, sometimes.'

Luc stopped, so she did too, watching as he slowly turned to look at her.

'What just happened?'

'I shouldn't have said anything about goats. I didn't realize it was a touchy subject.'

Luc frowned. 'It's not a big deal. But I meant what happened to you? I thought we were having a nice conversation, and all of a sudden your energy changed. Dropped.'

Was it that obvious? Although it wasn't so much that her energy *dropped* as much as it got *engulfed* in her black cloud. A cloud that appeared whenever she felt people backing away from her. When her dad failed to pick her up from school even though it was his weekend. After The Fight with her mum, when she realized she wasn't welcome at home any more. When Amber turned on her. When Caspian dumped her. When she was in that living room at Auntie Vee's, listening to a dead silence that told her everything she needed to know about what her auntie thought of her.

And now. It had been gathering since Luc's abrupt shift of attitude at the top of the cliff, when he suddenly froze up and told her they were going to this mysterious restaurant. Maybe he'd felt it too, or maybe he'd just remembered he didn't actually like her very much. Because no one did, not really. Not when they got to know her.

And then she'd compared him to a goat, and even though she hadn't realized that was offensive, it must be, or else he wouldn't have tensed up like that.

She knew how to ruin things, that was for damn sure.

'I'm fine,' she told him brightly. 'I don't know what you're talking about. Let's just get to this restaurant and off this death-trap trail, shall we?'

Luc's eyes narrowed.

'You're not broken, Jenny.'

'Uh, I'm here, aren't I? Don't think totally healthy, well-balanced people with nothing wrong with them end up here, somehow.'

'Is this about that rubbish Zillah was spouting before? Outside the church? About you being – what was it – inherently unlikeable or some other crap?'

It was a shame the ground here was so arid, Jenny thought. If it was just a touch swampier, there might have been a chance of it swallowing her up, which would be preferable than trying to talk about this with him right now.

She glanced down at her feet, which were streaked with dust from their journey.

‘It’s not rubbish,’ she said quietly.

‘It quite definitely is,’ Luc shot back, with such heat in his voice her head lifted despite herself. If she didn’t know any better, from the intense glare he was boring into her, she’d guess he was angry. But why?

‘*I* like you,’ he snapped, as though the words were being dragged out of him.

‘Do you?’ She heard the surprise in her voice and decided not to try and hide it. ‘I wasn’t sure you did.’

‘Well, I do.’ His nostrils flared, and then he seemed to take control of himself. He broke eye contact, blinking away the fierceness. ‘Obviously.’

‘How is it obvious?’

‘How is it *not*?’ He seemed to be struggling with something. Searching himself for an example to offer her. ‘I’m taking you for dinner, aren’t I?’

She stared at him for a moment, and then as the words sank in she felt her mouth twitch. She giggled, the sound blossoming out of her into full laughter.

And Luc was staring at her like she was dangerous, which just made it worse.

‘What’s so funny?’

She couldn’t stop, struggling to breathe through tears of laughter. It wasn’t *that* funny, she acknowledged, except that it was such a relief for the black cloud to have lifted – which it had. Luc liked her! Someone in this universe liked her, even after spending a fairly significant amount of time with her! She wasn’t sure that had ever happened before.

'You could have taken me for dinner on Earth,' she pointed out when she finally managed to get hold of herself. 'You didn't need to bring me to the Second Circle of Hell.'

'Well, this is the circle of . . .' Luc broke off, clamped his mouth shut.

'The circle of what?'

'Never mind. Let's just go, shall we? The restaurant's not far away.'

He set off again, at an even quicker pace than before, and she wondered what he'd been about to say before he thought better of it. It didn't really matter, though.

'Maybe it's because you're a demon,' she wondered out loud.

'What is?'

'That you like me,' she said.

'Or maybe there's just nothing wrong with you.'

There was, of course. Otherwise there was no point being here. But she didn't bother correcting him. Because he liked her. Even though he was only doing this to get back at his father, even though she was a sarcastic little madam who said insensitive things sometimes. Even though she complained about the walk and compared him to a goat.

Luc liked her. And she liked him too. And that made them *friends*, didn't it? She might have misread his intentions in the boat, but that was OK. Friends was better; she didn't have many, and anyway, it was safer. A crush on a demon? Nah, that would be *silly*. But friends? Friends was great. A smile landed on her face, and refused to leave for the rest of the time it took for them to get to the restaurant.

It wasn't actually a restaurant, as it happened, but by the time they reached it Jenny didn't much care, because Luc was right. She needed to rest.

She heaved a breath into her lungs and stared at the incongruous building in front of her.

It was incongruous because of its surroundings, which were bleak, brown and largely featureless. Barely inhabited, hardly civilized. And yet right now, in front of her on the edge of the Second Circle . . . was a hotel.

Or, not a hotel. Maybe one of those motel/diner combinations she'd seen on American TV shows. There was a neon heart-shaped sign above the door, with an artful crack splitting it in two and the words HOPELESS HEART MOTEL underneath. Naturally, only about two thirds of the letters lit up. There was a handwritten note in the window that said, 'diner open, no vacancies'.

'The Hopeless Heart?' she asked flatly as they crossed the tarmac of the car park. Yes, tarmac. Yes, car park. Although, it was entirely empty of vehicles.

'Best food in the Second Circle,' Luc offered cheerfully. Somehow, that didn't fill Jenny with much confidence.

The diner was shabby from close up. Paint peeled around the wooden windowsills, and even to Jenny's eye the door appeared warped in its frame. None of this seemed to deter Luc in the slightest. When the door wouldn't open immediately, he put his shoulder to it and shoved until it gave.

A bell tinkled as they entered. The floor was tiled in a sort of dirty sage green, and it didn't escape Jenny's notice that most of those tiles were chipped. Some of the grouting between them had been lost too, giving the impression that the gaps between tiles led down. Somewhere else.

Booths on the edges of the diner were upholstered in fake leather, sticky in the non-air-conditioned heat of a too-small room, in close proximity to the kitchen, which was visible through a hatch in one wall. Inside, a muscular man wearing a stained white T-shirt and a tea towel over one shoulder busied himself with multiple metal spatulas. The sound of frying meat filled the air, although the overriding smell was of onions and eggs.

No one seemed to have noticed their entrance, even as they hovered by a wooden cut-out of a cartoonified waitress with a huge smile, holding a tray with a silver cloche. The words 'wait here to be seated' had been painted over the cloche by hand, and underneath someone had scratched something in Latin that Jenny guessed would be very clever if she had any idea what it meant.

Non fui, fui, non sum, non curo.

There were two waitresses, and both had their hands full. One of them was clipping a wodge of order papers up on a piece of string above the cook's hatch, and the other wore a plastered-on smile as she carried a porcelain bowl over to a booth towards the back of the diner.

Jenny's gaze travelled into the booth, to the occupants,

and surprise filled her when she caught sight of a cascade of glossy black hair, a pair of heavy-lidded, amethyst eyes . . .

'How did Zillah get here before us?' she asked, tugging on Luc's arm.

'What, where?' he hissed, just as the waitress trilled –

'Here's your rum and raisin, Alyssa.'

Alyssa?

Luc flinched next to her.

'Maybe this was a bad idea,' he muttered, backing away towards the door.

Too late. The waitress by the cook's hatch chose that moment to notice the waiting customers and fix a wide, bright smile on her face.

'Why, Luc Pyro!' she called out, crossing the floor to greet them. 'What a delightful surprise!'

Out of the corner of her eye, Jenny saw Alyssa, who *had* to be one of Zillah's sisters, fix her purple sights directly on Luc.

'Booth for two?' Luc asked quickly. 'Somewhere quiet?'

The waitress glanced coyly at Jenny, and then her mask slipped. Just for a micro-second, a flash of genuine shock on her face. But then the customer-service smile was back.

'Of course,' she said, much more discreetly this time.

She led them to a booth in a much less busy quarter of the diner and handed them a pair of menus bigger than Jenny's head. Luc immediately used his to block himself from view, so Jenny did the same.

The leatherette on Jenny's seat was cracked, mostly covered over and badly patched with silver tape.

'You can't order from that menu,' the waitress told her firmly.

'Why not?'

The waitress was gorgeous, she noticed. Even dressed as she was in a fire hazard's worth of synthetic fabric, she had a sun-kissed complexion that made Jenny think immediately of the Mediterranean. Her black hair was held back in slender braids and coiled into a bun at the nape of her neck. A red and white headscarf wrapped around her crown and into the bun. Practical, sure, but it also helped to show off her regal bearing. Whoever she had been in life, Jenny decided, she had not been a waitress.

'I'm Cleo,' the waitress said. 'That over there is Fran, and we will be your waitresses today. Now, for the gentleman,' she cocked an eyebrow in Luc's direction, 'that menu is of course fine, but for you—'

'Cleo, she's fine,' Luc interrupted.

Once more, Cleo dropped her service-mask, just for a moment.

'Luc, what are you doing with a live human?'

Then, as though remembering herself, she snapped upright and addressed Jenny instead.

'We have a small selection of food that should suit your *unique* palate. I will bring it over once the last of the lunch rush has died down, if that's all right?'

'Fine with me,' Jenny said, intrigued. 'Thank you so much!'

Cleo shot her a smile that was strained, before hurrying away and disappearing into the kitchen.

'Why can't I eat from the menu?'

Luc rolled his eyes. 'Old rumour about living humans eating food in All Hell.'

'Oh.' A flare of another memory hit her. 'Like Persephone and the pomegranate?'

'Yeah, but I wouldn't worry about it,' Luc said. 'Not unless you start growing horns or something.'

'Growing . . . *horns*?' Alarm skittered over her skin, but then they were interrupted again.

This time, it was Alyssa.

Up close it was much more obvious she wasn't Zillah. She was a little shorter, and her mouth didn't have the same sardonic tilt to it. She had the same terrifying aura though, and Jenny was sure even Luc quailed a little in the glare of it.

'Luc,' she said, an uplift at the end of the word making it a question. Her eyes landed on Jenny, who fought the urge to flinch.

'And Luc's friend,' Alyssa said. 'How interesting to see you here.'

Luc swallowed visibly.

'Yeah, uh . . . we're just—'

'Grabbing a bite to eat,' Alyssa interrupted. There was an edge to her voice Jenny didn't understand, but she felt the tension rising between them. What was going on here?

'Why don't I walk you out?' Luc said suddenly, standing up so quickly he overturned a saltshaker. 'Jenny, wait here.'

She stared after him in surprise and something else she couldn't quite identify. Why was his hand clamped so firmly on Alyssa's upper arm? Why was he whispering so urgently in her ear? She swallowed down the unpleasant sensation crawling up her throat, the suspicion she might be witnessing some kind of lover's tiff. But even if she was, why should she care? *Friends*, she chanted in her head. *Friends, friends, friends.*

Cleo slid into Luc's empty seat, making Jenny jump.

'What brings a living human all the way to the Second Circle of literal Hell?' she asked, conversationally, wiping up the salt Luc had spilt.

'How can you tell?' she asked.

'You don't glow,' Cleo said, matter-of-fact. 'Ergo, you're not a manipulated spirit-form formerly kept in an aluminium can. You're flesh and blood. Alive.'

And for the first time, Jenny noticed that Cleo did, in fact, glow. It was faint, barely there unless you were looking for it, but it was like an aura that clung close to her skin.

'I've come to get my soul,' she said, deciding to answer the first question. 'Luc's helping me.'

'Helping you?' Both of Cleo's eyebrows shot up. She gestured to the other waitress, who joined them moments later.

'Hi,' the new waitress smiled. 'I'm Fran.'

Fran was also extremely pretty: radiant skin and curly brown hair tucked back into a bun, held in place with three pens. Her features were all delicate except for her nose, which was long and straight and would have dominated her face if it weren't for the direct green of her eyes.

Apparently, the Hopeless Heart only employed stunners.

'Jenny.'

'Lovely to meet you, Jenny.'

'She says Luc Pyro is going to help her get her soul back,' Cleo informed Fran, and the cynicism in her voice was audible.

'Oh,' Fran said. 'That's unusual.'

'You know who his father is, right?'

'I do, but Luc's not like him. In fact, that's why he's helping me – Seth Pyro's the one who took my soul.'

'Let me get this straight,' Fran frowned. 'You and Luc, a demon without any demonic powers to protect you with, are going up against possibly the most fearsome creature this hellhole has ever seen?'

'I mean . . . yes?' she replied. She didn't really know about Luc's powers, or lack of them, but otherwise, yeah, that was about the long and short of it.

'Well may the Heavens defend you,' Cleo sighed. 'You're going to need it.'

The bell tinkled at the front of the diner and both waitresses disappeared with loud, tapping steps. Jenny's eyes followed Fran's feet: the tapping was because of their shoes. They were chunky, clog-like and shiny – like they were made of porcelain. These, the chain around Fran's ankle, and a slightly ephemeral quality to the way light landed on her skin were the only signs she wasn't as alive as Jenny.

Before she could ponder this further, or the alarm both waitresses had shown at her plan to retrieve her soul, Luc slunk back into his seat.

'Everything all right?' she asked, forcing a brightness she didn't really feel into her tone.

'Yeah, fine,' Luc said, and not for the first time Jenny noticed he wasn't meeting her eyes.

'You sure?'

Luc ignored her, grabbing his discarded menu and busying himself with that instead of talking to her. She frowned. *Dickhead Demon is back, then.*

After a few awkward minutes, Cleo returned with her order pad.

'We've got some tins of stuff from Earth in the back,' she said apologetically. 'Some soup, I think, and maybe some sliced peaches?'

Opposite Jenny, Luc growled. 'I *told* you, she's *fine*. She'll have what I'm having, which is macaroni and cheese followed by French vanilla ice cream.'

'Actually,' Jenny said, 'I will have soup and peaches. That sounds great, and I appreciate you finding that for me.'

Cleo's smile this time was tinged with relief. 'I think that's a good choice,' she said, writing down their orders and escaping once more.

'You really think you can make it to the Ninth Circle on tinned soup and peaches?' Luc shot at her once Cleo was gone.

'I don't know, Luc. I actually don't know very much about Hell, except that I should probably take as few risks as *humanly* possible while I'm here. Is that all right with you? Or are you still taking your Alyssa-shaped frustrations out on me?'

'Whatever.' Luc slumped back in his seat. 'You're missing out, though.'

Resisting the urge to point out she could quite easily have pasta and ice cream at home, Jenny folded her arms and tapped her foot on the floor. Something was bothering him, something about Alyssa, and Jenny was damned if she was going to let him take it out on her.

Silence landed between them like a stone, and Jenny wasn't going to be the one to roll it out of the way. She made a show of looking anywhere but at him, even though she could *feel* his eyes on her.

'I'm sorry,' Luc heaved out when the atmosphere was past spooning consistency. 'You're right, you shouldn't take risks. Neither should I. Coming here was probably not a good idea, but I really do think you need rest before we carry on. It's been a weird few days.'

'You're telling me.'

'I'm going to see if they've got rooms for us tonight,' Luc told her.

'What?' OK, now rest and a meal was one thing, but an overnight stay was quite another. She stared at him across the table. 'Luc, can't we talk about this?'

He didn't reply, though, instead raising a hand to call Fran over.

23

JENNY

'I thought you guys had no vacancies,' Jenny grumbled as Fran opened the door to the room that would be hers for the night.

'Hey, I'm on Luc's side on this one,' Fran told her lightly. 'It's a long way to the Ninth Circle, or so I'm told.'

Her room was opposite Luc's in a dingy corridor one flight of stairs up from the main diner. They'd had to go outside to get to it, because the rusty metal stairs up were built on to the outer wall.

The corridor itself was narrow and poorly lit, with only one flickering bare bulb hanging from a not-exactly-safe rope fixture. The carpet that ran down the corridor was threadbare and grey, with darker splodges that might have been a pattern and might have been stains.

So Jenny didn't have high hopes for the room itself.

‘Oh,’ she said. ‘It’s bigger than I thought.’

‘Best of the bunch,’ Fran shrugged, taking a seat on the double bed in the middle of the room.

‘The mattress sags in the middle,’ she said, ‘and I wouldn’t bother trying the bath, if I were you. The water’s not filtered. But it’s clean, ish.’

‘Wow, you’re really selling it,’ Jenny laughed.

The walls were papered in woodchip, and had evidently been painted over several times. Currently, they were an unappealing shade of peach, which clashed unpleasantly with the shaggy purple pile of the interior carpet.

She was about to comment on this, but when she turned around to face Fran, the words caught in her throat. The waitress had taken the opportunity to slip her porcelain clogs off her feet. Vivid red welts puckered the skin, along with scars from long-bust blisters and bubbles of new ones emerging. Her ankle was swollen, and there were grazes across the tops of every one of her toes.

Fran caught Jenny’s shocked expression and shot her a wry smile.

‘Gross, huh?’

‘No,’ Jenny stuttered out, even though the lesions and sores weren’t exactly pretty. ‘Just . . . *ouch*.’

‘Well, yeah, that too,’ Fran snorted, wriggling her ruined foot back into the torture device that had done this to her. ‘But you get used to it. After several hundred years, anyway.’

Jenny’s eyes shifted, over to the silver chain on the

waitress's ankle. It stretched out across the carpet and under the door, as though it had extended just enough to allow Fran to bring guests up to their rooms. Even so, it was a reminder of her place, which was clearly here at the Hopeless Heart.

'What did you do to land an eternity in customer service?'

Fran's aura dimmed, but only for a moment.

'Fell in love with someone I shouldn't have,' she said softly.

Then she straightened her shoulders and smiled brightly, shooting a wink in Jenny's direction.

'So, let me be a lesson to you, all right? No snogging when you should be working.'

'Fat chance of that,' Jenny muttered, even as a fleeting image of Luc on the Ferrier's barge danced across her eyes. Had he been about to kiss her?

'Fran?'

'Uh-huh?'

'What is the Second Circle the circle of?'

'What do you mean?'

'Like, does it have another name or anything?'

'Oh. Well, sort of. They call it the Circle of Lovers. So the question should be, what did I do to land an eternity in the Circle of Lovers; although it's not an eternity. I hope.'

Fran stood up from the bed, only wincing slightly at the pain in her feet.

'It's not?'

'Not heard of the Day of Judgement?'

Jenny shook her head, shrugged awkwardly. 'I didn't pay that much attention in church as a kid.'

'Ah well. In my day we couldn't escape it. We all knew if we sinned we'd be punished, but only until this so-called Day of Judgement, when we'll have a chance to repent and maybe . . . maybe we'll end up somewhere else. Of course, no one's been able to agree exactly *when* that's due to happen, so for now, here we are.'

'Somewhere else like . . . Heaven?'

Fran tilted her head to one side, as she considered this. 'I used to think so. Not sure, any more. I don't even know if Heaven exists. But I live in hope. Well, not live, but you know what I mean. Sleep tight, Jenny.'

She stretched, drew her mask back on, and left Jenny alone in the world's grimiest motel bedroom, remembering the way Luc cut himself off. *Circle of Lovers.* Did that mean . . . she shoved the thought away forcibly. Just as well, because as soon as Fran's clogged footsteps faded, someone knocked on her door.

When she answered, Luc slipped inside without waiting for an invitation.

'Hey, your room's way bigger than mine!'

'Cleo and Fran like me more than they like you.'

Luc shrugged at this. 'Makes sense. All humans together, I suppose.'

He didn't seem to have come over for any particular purpose, and Jenny had a warm suspicion somewhere in the region of her stomach that he'd just wanted to see her.

Or maybe he wanted to antagonize her again; with Luc it was hard to know. She hopped up on the saggy bed and patted the empty space next to her.

'Well come on in, my friend. Make yourself comfortable, we can have a sleepover.'

As the words left her mouth, she immediately burnt with embarrassment. 'I mean, not a sleepover, sleepover, I just meant . . .'

'I know what you meant,' Luc grinned, all confidence and swagger in the face of her mortification. *Dickhead.*

He sat on the mattress next to her and swung his legs so his heels kicked the bed base in rhythm.

'I hope you're not mad,' he said after a second. 'That I made us stay here, I mean.'

'I'm not mad,' Jenny said slowly. 'Impatient, yes. And nervous. But you know this place better than me. If you say we need to rest before we carry on, then . . . I just have to trust you.'

'And do you?' His head snapped up and his eyes were on hers, locking her in his gravitational field. His bloomed black; it didn't even bother her any more.

'Do I . . .?'

'Trust me.'

His gaze was so intense, she could hardly blink. Something hitched in her chest, and she scrambled for an answer that was both true and that might keep him looking at her like that.

'I want to,' she said, only then realizing it was true. But of *course* she wanted to trust him. She'd gone to him at the fair because she had no other choice, and that meant she *needed* to trust him, because if she couldn't . . . well, if she couldn't, that meant all her options were bad ones, and that wasn't a world Jenny felt strong enough to live in.

'I want you to,' Luc said, his voice dropping low, soft enough to creep under her skin and to dance on the ends of her nerves.

'I want to know more about you,' she whispered. 'That would help, I think.'

Luc blinked, breaking their moment. His eyes didn't revert, though, still pools of endless dark as he checked the cracks in the ceiling for inspiration.

'What would you like to know?'

'What's it like, living here?'

Because if she could understand that, maybe she could understand him, right? He already knew she was miserable in her home life, miserable enough to follow a demon into Hell itself, but he was still a mystery to her.

'Not great,' he told her with a snort. 'I mean, I'm luckier than most. My dad's the most powerful demon in the Abyss; our house is huge and full of interesting bits and pieces he's pilfered from your lot over the years. He's not home much, which is also a bonus because . . . I mentioned I'm not his favourite demon?'

'You didn't say why.'

Luc swallowed. 'Yeah. There's a reason for that.'

'You don't have to tell me if you don't want.'

Luc shook his head, regarded her through his lashes a moment. 'I do want to tell you, though. Isn't that strange?

I never talk about this. I've *hurt* demons for bringing this up. So why do I feel like you should know?'

This felt rhetorical, so she kept her mouth shut.

Luc stood up, making his way over to a battered desk in the far corner of the room. There was a tray on it, with a small kettle and a basket of various packets.

'Can I offer you a cup of the worst coffee in this, or any, plane of existence?' Luc asked.

'Sure. Thank you.'

He nodded, checking the water level in the kettle before flicking it on. She got the impression he didn't really want coffee, he just wanted something to occupy him as he spoke.

'You probably heard Zillah making cracks about my lack of power,' he said, tearing the end off a paper tube of instant coffee.

'I didn't really notice,' Jenny lied. 'Although, to be honest, I don't even really know what it means. Like, I've seen Zillah's power . . . are they all like that?'

Luc shook his head. 'No, that's very much a "Daughters of Lilith" situation. Powers can manifest in a host of ways, and mine hasn't. My father thinks I'm doing it on purpose, refusing to come into my Demonity and be a real demon.'

'Demonity?'

Luc paused to pour water into their cups, then returned to his seat on the bed. She took the mug from him; it wasn't precisely hot, she noticed, and there were clumps of freeze-dried coffee granules floating on the top of the liquid. Something about it didn't smell right. She held it anyway, even as she decided it wasn't going anywhere near her mouth.

'Yeah, it's . . .' He huffed, clearly uncomfortable. 'All children start out innocent, you know? Demons, humans, other. Kids are pure. But if you grow up here, that can't last. I can't tell you how it works exactly, it's not something we get taught, but as we grow up, we *change.* When we come into our Demonity, we get powers, and that's when we're considered adults. That's when we're considered useful.'

She didn't speak, letting the silence settle.

'I don't know why I don't have mine,' Luc said quietly. 'It's embarrassing. Everyone knows, and because of who I am – Seth Pyro's son, Lucifer's grandson – everyone's got an opinion on it.'

'That sounds tough,' Jenny said softly.

He nodded, staring into space as though he'd barely heard her.

'Anyway, my dad's convinced it's some kind of teenage rebellion. It doesn't even make sense, but apparently, I'm a total waste of skin, so there's that.'

'What about your mum?' He'd never mentioned her.

Luc's eyes flicked to hers, then away again. He took a sip of his coffee and winced.

'She died, when I was born.'

'I'm so sorry.'

'Don't worry about it. According to my dad she was a useless old hag anyway.'

He was so *sad*. She could sense it, like a tangible thing,

vibrating in the air around them. She reached out, brushing his wrist with the very tips of her fingers.

'Don't feel bad for *me*,' he said, turning to her with a forced grin and strain written all over his face. 'I'm fine.'

'I don't feel *bad* for you,' Jenny promised. 'I just . . . feel. And your dad's wrong, by the way. You're not a waste of skin.'

'What am I then?'

He moved up on the edge of the bed, until his thigh pressed against her knee. He took the cup of undrinkable coffee from her and put both mugs on the floor before taking one of her hands in his.

'What am I, if not a waste of skin, Jenny Hall?'

His voice was doing that thing again, where it got all soft and velvety and sent the hairs straight up on her arms and the back of her neck. Her wrists felt strange, fuzzy, and she was certain she couldn't have stood up even if she wanted to.

Luc's face loomed close. *God*, she thought, *you're so handsome.*

But she wasn't exactly going to say *that*, now, was she?

'You're kind,' she blurted out, hearing the strangled squawk of her voice. 'You've been nothing but kind to me.'

Luc made a sound between a sigh and a laugh at that. It sent shockwaves rolling over her skin.

'My father would tell you that proves his point.'

'Then his point's stupid,' Jenny shot back, but she couldn't elaborate, because Luc's leg was still pressed up against hers, and he cradled her hand in both of his, and one of his thumbs was stroking the inside of her wrist and somehow that meant she could barely breathe, and his eyes were so black, she could dive into them and drown, and his breath was soft on her cheek, and his lips parted, close, and . . .

A loud knock on the door sliced between them, sending Jenny scrambling further up the bed and Luc up on his feet in an instant. He kicked one of the mugs by mistake, sending a pool of pondwater coffee spilling out over the purple shag.

'Shit.'

'I'll sort it,' Jenny said hurriedly. 'Can you get the door?'

He did, and Cleo's voice filtered into the room.

'Thought you might be in here.' She sounded tense, but when didn't she? 'Since you complained so loudly about your room. I know it's not exactly a field of rushes, but . . . anyway, you've got a visitor.'

All at once Jenny stopped what she was doing, midway through picking up the coffee mugs.

Alyssa, again? Who else knew they were even there? Her heart thudded as she resumed her clean-up operation.

'I'll be back in a couple of minutes,' Luc said.

'Sure,' Jenny said, feigning cheerfulness.

'Don't worry about that, kiddo.' Cleo gestured to the coffee on the carpet. 'It's practically an improvement.'

Then, once again, the door closed, and Jenny was alone.

But she had no intention of waiting idly by while Luc

argued with his ex/girlfriend/whatever she was.

Do you trust me?

She did want to. But it wasn't easy. Sometimes Luc acted like she was just cargo he was carting through Hell, and sometimes he looked at her like he wanted to eat her. And he was a demon, and he stroked the inside of her wrist until her insides dissolved. And sometimes the best way to find out if someone was trustworthy was to spy on them, even if that wasn't a very trustworthy thing to do. But as Jenny well knew, you often learnt what people really thought about you when they didn't know you were listening, and it had been an awfully long time since she just took people at their word.

The door creaked as she opened and closed it behind her, but there was no one in the corridor to hear. For a second, she wondered about locking the door, but it wasn't like she owned anything that didn't fit in her front jeans pockets, was it? She could hear Cleo's footsteps on the fire escape staircase, so she headed that way too. She waited until the top of Luc's head disappeared into the diner before descending herself, clinging on to the handrail as she fought to go slow, quiet, rather than rushing down to get away from the ominous rusting of the metal.

It would be just her luck if the whole thing came crashing down with her on it.

The door into the diner had a handy letterbox-shaped pane of glass at head height, so she peeped through it until she found Luc's bright hair in a booth. He had his back to the door so she couldn't see his face but from the way his jaw moved she could tell he was already talking furiously, intent on whoever was opposite him.

It wasn't Alyssa. It was a male demon, which she knew because he didn't glow and certainly wasn't human. Even seated in the booth he looked rangy, his skin sickly pale and tinged with green. Because he was facing the door, Jenny could clearly see his face. When he blinked, his eyelids slid back into place, and then a second set of thinner eyelids did the same. His eyes were entire pools of black, which was no longer a surprise, but when he grinned, his teeth were as sharp as rocks at the bottom of a cliff. She shuddered.

This strange new demon was wearing an all-black uniform. A walkie-talkie dangled from his belt, and on his breast pocket, embroidered in orange thread she squinted to read, was 'MINOS 3004'. He was doing something with his hands as he spoke, pulling and pushing them apart as though the air between them was squidgy. Jenny blinked, and the air between MINOS 3004's hands sparked, a ball of greenish light appearing. Was this what Luc meant by a Demonity? she wondered.

Who was this, and why did he want to talk to Luc?

The door opened from the inside, and Jenny almost jumped out of her skin.

'Clever girl,' Cleo murmured, ushering her inside and gesturing for her to hide herself behind the nearest booth.

'I'll distract them while you slip in the one next to them,' the waitress promised.

Good as her word, Cleo marched over to Luc and the

MINOS demon, opening a menu wide enough to obscure them from view as Jenny scurried past and into the next booth. Only a thin piece of plywood, covered in that tacky leatherette, separated her from Luc.

'Piss off, Cleo,' the MINOS demon snapped.

'Well, y'all just yell out if you change your mind,' she trilled brightly. 'You know we aim to please here at the Hopeless Heart!'

'Useless bint,' the MINOS demon muttered as she tapped away in her ceramic shoes.

'What do you want, Abaddon?' Luc's voice sounded tense. 'I already told Alyssa—'

'Why do you think I'm here? I know what you told her, that you were softening the girl up to keep her onside. Alyssa didn't buy it, and neither do I. You've already got her this side of the divide. What other "softening" does she possibly need? You could have dragged her on a bus to the Burning Sands as soon as you walked through the Hellmouth. You'd have been at the lake already!'

Jenny's heart was in her mouth.

'It's more complicated than that,' she heard Luc snap. 'She needs careful handling, all right? She's stubborn, and—'

'Careful handling, I'm sure,' the demon named Abaddon leered. 'I don't give a shiny blue shit what you do with her on your own time, but we are on a deadline here. I've half a mind to take her myself. Where is she?'

'No.'

'What, scared of the *careful handling* she'll get from me?'

She could practically hear Luc's fists clench.

'Stay away from her, Abaddon. This is *my* mission, handed to me by *my* father.'

'All right, be like that. But the eclipse is tomorrow night, and she *must* be at the lake by then. Lucifer's grandson or not, if you screw up the best chance demonkind has ever had to break out of this hole, there will be *consequences*. Thirteen million demons' worth. Just think about that.'

'I've thought about it, believe me.' Luc paused. 'I don't think you know my father as well as you think. Does he strike you as the kind of man to harbour noble ambitions like setting us all free, if there's no material gain for him?'

'I don't give a toss what kind of gain there is for him, as long as it means I don't have to stick around here.'

'You don't think the why matters? The how?'

'Not really, no. Are these cold feet I'm feeling under the table here, Luc?'

A longer pause. 'No.'

'Good. In that case, I'll see you at the lake tomorrow. We'll all be there. Can't wait to meet your girlfriend.'

'Don't be a prick; she's not my girlfriend.'

'Probably for the best, eh?'

Jenny cringed back into the booth as Abaddon got up and marched out of the diner. Something heavy thumped on Luc's table and he let out a frustrated roar.

She wasn't worried about Luc, though. She was worried about herself. *She was a mission from his father?* That meant he lied to her. About everything. Not even twenty minutes ago, in fact, when he told her all that crap about his power, and his dead mother! It was just a ruse to get her to trust him!

She felt rather than heard Luc stand up in the next booth. She snatched up one of the other oversized menus from the tabletop and used it to shield herself as he stomped out.

Shit. In moments he was going to knock on her door upstairs. When she didn't answer, he'd go in – it wasn't like she'd locked it. And then he'd realize she'd heard, that she knew . . .

No. Jenny wasn't going to be there for that. She dropped the menu and bolted out of the booth, headed for the only place that made any sense: the door next to the hatch, the one that said KITCHEN STAFF ONLY in cracked red paint.

'What are you doing in here?' The muscular cook scowled at her.

'Where's Cleo? Or Fran? I need them. I need . . .'

A door leading outside swung open and both waitresses tumbled inside.

'What's going on?' Fran hissed, seeing the terror written all over Jenny's shivering body.

'Was that William Abaddon?' Cleo asked.

Jenny just shook. 'He-he lied,' she stuttered. 'I'm a mission. His father, I . . .' Her teeth started to chatter, and the waitresses shared a horrified look.

'She can't stay here,' the cook said, but Cleo already had her hands wrapped around each of Jenny's arms, tugging her gently but firmly in the direction of the door they'd just come through. It led to the back of the diner, and a row of overfilled mega-bins.

Jenny still couldn't speak, but that didn't seem to matter.

'Fran, can you head Luc off? Try to distract him?'

'On it.' The waitress vanished, leaving Cleo to grip Jenny by the shoulders outside.

Her face was pale. 'You've got a five-minute head start at *best*. Do you remember the way you came, to get here?'

Jenny nodded. Shook her head. 'I don't know.'

'Well *think*,' Cleo insisted. 'You need to get back to the Hellmouth that brought you here, stat. Get back to Earth, where Seth Pyro has no jurisdiction over you. OK? It's the only way.'

Jenny nodded. She just wanted to go home.

'Good girl. Now, go. *Run*.'

She didn't need telling twice. She ran.

She raced across the empty car park. At any moment Luc could come out of the diner, or pop his head out of a window, and see her, but she couldn't stop. Couldn't risk getting caught. She just had to flee.

Her feet carried her without her brain's input, her body's memory leading her off the land on which the Hopeless Heart stood, and out on to the stony road that had led them there. Or at least, she hoped so. It was hard to know if she was going the right way without landmarks to keep her going – but this wasn't a landscape designed with landmarks in mind. Hell wanted her lost. She truly believed that.

Five minutes, that was the head start Cleo had offered her, but out here she knew it wouldn't be enough. Luc would see her, there was nowhere to hide, and she was already tired from the travelling they'd done.

So when she noticed a patch of sparse woodland to one side of the road, she dived for it. She hared round a narrow pair of trees and saw, in the middle of the copse, a bigger tree. Big enough to hide behind, maybe, until Luc ran past?

'Jenny!'

Oh *God!* That was Luc. And he sounded close.

She ducked behind the tree and tried to control the shaking in her limbs. This was a *terrible* hiding place.

'Jenny!'

Closer, still. She had to *do* something. Because Luc would, when he found her. He was a demon, like Zillah, like the stone-toothed MINOS agent in the diner. OK, so he came in a much more appealing package, but didn't that just make him *more* dangerous?

She didn't even want to think about what he would do if he caught her.

Climb.

Well, that was one option, wasn't it? No time to think, no time to strategize, she reached up and gripped one low, sturdy branch. She swung herself up, wincing as her shoes scraped against the bark.

I'm sorry, she thought, hoping the tree could hear it in her thoughts. *I hope I'm not hurting you.*

She didn't have time to stop and ask for permission,

though. The wood of this tree felt like the trees back in Elrick Park: slick, moist. She barely noticed, even when she misstepped, face-planting a limb that smelt like an unwashed armpit. Her glasses slipped off her face, dropped to the ground, but she didn't have time to panic. She climbed out of view and squinted so she could see, moved inwards, hoping the leafless branches would be enough to protect her.

No. Even without her glasses, she knew Luc would see her. He was still calling her name; she had *moments* before he got here. A sob rolled up her throat, and she clamped both hands round different branches, squeezing tight. Her pulse was so strong she could feel it in her palms, as though the tree's heart was beating too.

Help me, she begged silently. Back at Elrick Park she'd always spoken out loud, so she didn't know if the tree would hear her, but she was too scared to speak. Her fingers gripped the branches as she repeated the thought. *Please, help me.*

And then the tree trunk opened beneath her and swallowed her whole.

24

MARTHA, AGAIN

Once upon a time, Martha had dreams. Nothing outrageous, mind. Just to meet someone nice, maybe someone who liked to read, because that felt like a good sign. He wouldn't be from too far away, because that way they'd both have parents around to help with the kids (because naturally, there were kids), and maybe he would say things like, *I think your drawings are marvellous, you should go back to college and do something with them*, unlike her mam, who said things like, *I don't know what good college would do you, you've already a job.*

She didn't have those dreams any more. Instead, Martha realized as she latticed the top of a sausage pie, she had delusions.

For example, she had spent the past ten years acting as though she had everything she ever wanted, when in actual fact, she had geographies that didn't make sense and the occasional awkward encounter with social services. She was not some kind of sainted mother figure; frankly, she very rarely had the faintest idea what the twins were up to. Laws unto themselves, those two, and what was she, a bloody oracle?

Recently, she'd been thinking more and more about her life before the twins. Before the park. Before a mysterious man with hair like distilled sunshine invited her out to the new cocktail place on the high street and made her an offer she really should have refused.

Back then, all she wanted to do was spend an evening in the new cocktail bar, even though the girls at work were snarky about it – said it was just another chain, said it looked like everywhere else with its pastel walls and crushed-velvet seating.

They were long shifts at the supermarket, and after ten hours of carting cages to and from the filthy stockroom, of stretching and bending to restock bare shelves, Martha was always exhausted. Not just because of the work, although it was monotonous and hard, but because when she clocked out of one job, it just meant clocking on to another. Something the other girls didn't understand.

And was she any less exhausted now? she wondered. She slid the pie into the oven and poured herself a mug of tea, seating herself in the solid armchair by the kitchen table. She wasn't as tired physically. Plenty of room in her day for breaks, now. Flasks of tea, crosswords in the sentry box . . . but emotionally, she thought this might be the hardest ten years she'd ever experienced, made all the worse by the arrival and subsequent vanishing of that young girl who'd lost her soul.

She closed her eyes and took a long sip of her tea, to settle herself. She needed to stop thinking about Jenny, if she had any hope of regaining her equilibrium.

She opened her eyes and almost jumped out of her skin. The twins were sat across the kitchen table, sharing the long bench.

'Hello, Martha,' Joey said.

She hated it when they sneaked up on her like that.

In her old life, no one jumped out at her when she least expected it. In her old life, she went to work, and on the way home she pulled her coat tight around her uniform, dodging puddles and slowing down as she walked past the new cocktail bar, pretending not to stare in through the window as she passed. Out of the corner of her eye, she saw women dressed up like costume jewellery, glamorous, radiant, and she wondered what it would be like to sit at one of those sherbet-yellow tables, sinking into that plum velvet. It was a predictable, staid sort of a life. But it had been hers.

Now, the twins were doing that thing they did where they looked at each other without speaking, communicating inside their own personal bubble.

'Stop that,' she snapped.

They looked up; stared at her, round-eyed.

'Martha?' Chloe-Lee said uncertainly. 'Is everything quite all right?'

A buzzing filled her head. Not a sound, more a sensation, an old television with bad reception. She felt it in her ears, across the top of her skull, and it was only when her vision tunnelled that she realized what it was: the truth, no longer possible to ignore.

'I want my soul back,' she said.

When her eyes dropped to the table they snagged on the tattoos on each child's forearm. A heart, and a feather. Ten-year-olds didn't usually have tattoos, did they? And they certainly didn't have tattoos that glowed, but as she watched that's exactly what the twins' tattoos started to do.

'But why?' Joey asked. 'Don't you have everything you've ever wanted?'

In her old life, Martha went home, instead of stepping inside that colourful bar for a drink. She arrived, invariably damp, and hung her coat on the banister at the bottom of the stairs. Slipped off her work shoes and padded across the laminate in the hallway to the kitchen. Kettle on, two mugs down from the cupboard. All her movements considered, because if she could keep quiet enough, she might yet get a few moments of peace before . . .

'That you, Mar?'

'Aye, Mam, it's me.'

'Fifteen down. Seven letters, clue is "hemmed, but not sewn". Something, something "A", something, something, "E, D".'

'I thought I did,' she told Joey. 'But it's all a lie, isn't it?'

'What do you mean?'

She put down her tea. 'All this. The forest shouldn't be

here. You two aren't' – she wanted to say 'real' but that wasn't quite right – 'ten,' she settled on, instead. 'And I'm not your mother. You don't need one.'

'Yes, we do,' Chloe-Lee said quickly. The little girl seemed stricken; tears trembled in her wide, gold-hued eyes.

'Well, all right, maybe you do,' Martha replied, 'but I was told I'd have children. And you're not that, are you?' She swallowed. 'In fact, I'd like to know what you are, actually.'

The twins shared a Look, but when Martha tensed up, they stopped. Their tattoos were shining now, iridescent with a light that didn't make any kind of sense. Instead of replying, Chloe-Lee laid her hand over the luminous heart on her arm. When she removed her hand, the light came with it, and she held it over the table, shaping it like clay until it solidified, no longer a line-drawn heart but instead a set of scales. The old-fashioned kind, with bowls suspended on either side.

She clicked her fingers in her brother's direction, and he mirrored her movements, except his light split in two, replicas of the heart and feather from the tattoos. He placed the heart in one bowl, and the feather in the other, and Martha watched, dumbstruck, as the scales settled into perfect equilibrium.

'This is the Balance,' Chloe-Lee finally pronounced. 'Joey and I are the Protectors of the Balance.'

Martha's brows drew together. 'I don't know what that means.'

Joey reached out to pat her hand. She didn't pull away, although the temptation was strong.

'You have heard us talk of the Sacred Agreement, yes?'

Martha nodded.

'It is our role to ensure it is upheld.'

'Is that why you were so keen to keep Jenny out of the portal in the forest?' Martha asked. They had been truly upset when they found her gone; even more so when they realized her school jumper, torn and bloodied as it was, was merely a distraction.

Chloe-Lee nodded. 'We hoped to keep her safe, but we cannot stand in the way of free will, and we have no jurisdiction inside All Hell – a demon would need to invite us in, first, and the chances of them doing that are slim indeed. Much as the Celestial Council do not invite us to sit in their chamber.'

She fell quiet then, her gaze falling to her lap. Joey comforted his sister with a hand on her shoulder and understanding landed on Martha like a brick. Their role was to stand somewhere between the demons and this mysterious Celestial Council, neither one nor the other. Always apart.

'That sounds lonely.'

Martha knew about lonely. Lonely was why, when a golden man with hair like sunshine cornered her in the milk aisle, she didn't tell him where to go. Lonely was why she opened up to him like a flower when he asked her to meet him for a drink after her shift.

He suggested the new cocktail place on the high street,

and at first, sitting in that cocktail bar felt just as good as Martha had imagined it would. Her drink tasted like jam, and the golden man said, *It's nice to see you smile, Martha. I've been watching you for some time and you don't seem to do that often.* Lonely was why, when he blinked and his eyes did the most peculiar thing, like a drop of ink in a bowl of water, blossoming outwards until she couldn't see the whites any more, she didn't scream. She felt like a fly trapped in a sticky bit of webbing, and she shrank back into the crushed-velvet chair and the golden man assured her he meant her no harm, he just had a proposition for her . . .

Something must be stuck in her throat, she thought now. That was why she was swallowing so much, and why it hurt. That's why her eyes threatened to water. She coughed, turned away for a moment, and when she turned back, the scales, the heart, the feather – they were all gone, and in their place was a familiar yellow can.

'You are not the only one who made a deal with Seth Pyro,' Joey said. 'We wanted a mother, so he gave us you. In return, we agreed to take on the care of the forest around the Hellmouth.'

'You have been the very best mother,' Chloe-Lee whispered.

'We could not have asked for better,' Joey agreed.

'But we promised long ago, that if you ever directly asked for the return of your soul, we would give it to you.'

Martha's heart stuttered. 'You never told me that.'

Another Look. This time, she didn't need to be telepathic to understand it – guilt.

'That was wrong of us,' said Chloe-Lee.

'We hoped . . . Well, perhaps it doesn't matter.'

'No, no,' Chloe-Lee muttered. 'We should tell her.' She caught Martha's eye. 'We were scared you would leave us, if you knew you could. When Pyro gave us this yellow can, he tied you to us. Physically, you could have left any time, but metaphysically? Humans do not enjoy being too far from their souls.'

Joey made a small, unhappy noise. 'We would have preferred a mother who truly wanted us, but that is not our purpose.'

'It is not our destiny.'

'But then, this is not your destiny, Martha Garstang. A demon manipulated your destiny, and we let him.'

Chloe-Lee shuddered. 'The same demon who will alter all our destinies, if we continue to let him.'

Martha sat up straighter at that. 'What do you mean? Is this anything to do with Jenny?'

The twins nodded in unison.

'We fear,' Joey admitted, 'his plan is to use her for dangerous ends.'

'Such as?'

'We think he plans to use her to wake Lucifer.'

They were looking at her expectantly, as though she should leap up in horror or something, but she simply quirked an eyebrow.

'And then?'

'And then,' Joey replied, 'we shall have to hope Lucifer doesn't use his Light to tear a hole through Creation.'

'Because if he decides to do that,' Chloe-Lee continued, 'then this sphere is already as good as lost. Everything you've ever known, wiped out.'

'Everything except the demons, anyway,' Joey clarified.

That buzzing returned for Martha, the truth flowing through her, but she didn't want it. The enormity of what the twins were suggesting . . .

'What can we do?'

'*You* can't do anything,' Joey told her gently, pushing the can towards her. 'But we can. And truthfully? We should never have let this go on for so long. Pyro was using us; using you to keep us placated.'

'No more,' Chloe-Lee promised. 'Martha, you are a free woman. Your soul is yours; Joey and I must leave this place, and alert the Celestial Council.'

'I only pray we are not too late,' Joey said softly.

They stood up in turn, kissed her on each cheek, and filed out of the kitchen, leaving Martha alone, staring at the yellow can on the table and only dimly aware of the tear tracking down her skin.

Still, no use crying over spilt milk and all that, so she pushed out a long breath and took the can in her hands. Her old life flashed before her eyes.

'Trapped,' she said out loud. 'Fifteen down, Mam. The answer's "trapped".'

25

JENNY

If Jenny had thought she couldn't see before, now she really couldn't. It was pitch black inside the tree trunk, which had sealed her inside. It smelt weird in there – at once green and meaty. Like the warmth of a compost pile. Whatever she'd landed on was soft enough that she wasn't hurt, at least.

'Jenny!'

Luc's voice was muffled by the thick outer bark of the tree but still she held her breath. This Venus Jenny-trap had nabbed her in the nick of time.

'Where are you?' she heard him grumble, and against her better judgement she leant in and planted her ear to the inside of the trunk, listening.

'What the . . .?' Luc muttered. There was a pause, and then she heard, 'If your glasses are here, then where . . .'

Please don't let him figure this out, Jenny prayed. She was entirely embracing the inside of the tree now, arms spread wide and palms flat against the moist bark. *I don't know if I'm any safer in here but please, please don't let him realize I'm here . . .*

YOU ARE SAFE.

Jenny flinched as the voice landed in her head.

She didn't feel very safe. Luc was still outside the tree after all, confused, pissed off, and after everything she'd overheard in the diner, Jenny wouldn't put it past him to come back with a chainsaw if it meant getting his hands on her.

It was infuriating, not being able to see what he was up to. Although, without her glasses, it didn't really make any difference. She would sadly be lacking in vision even if she weren't trapped behind a wall of bark.

'Oh, for rebellion's sake,' she heard him say. Closer. As though he was just on the other side of the bark from her. 'Jenny?'

Her mouth dried out. He knew.

'Luc Pyro!' A voice called out, familiar only from the diner. Abaddon, wasn't that his name? And he was a MINOS agent, someone she really didn't want to meet in a dark alley. Or a light alley, for that matter.

'Do you have the girl?' That was a different voice, one she didn't know.

'What do you want?' Luc snapped, which was not an answer. But at least he hadn't given her away. Not yet, anyway.

'We were on patrol,' the new voice said. 'Saw the human sprinting this way like a demon was after her. Oh, wait.'

'Very funny, Malik.'

'Well?' Abaddon again. 'Do you have her?'

A beat. Was he going to tell them where she was?

'This is your fault!' Luc grumbled. 'If you hadn't interfered, she wouldn't have got scared and bolted.'

'Is that so?' Abaddon didn't sound particularly worried by this. 'Maybe if you hadn't taken an unnecessary detour in the wrong direction, I wouldn't have needed to interfere. Funny how that works, innit?'

'He doesn't have the girl,' Malik's voice sniffed. 'You owe me six silver tokens.'

'I'll settle it with your mother, later.'

'Can you two just piss off, or something?'

'No,' Malik said. 'We can't.'

'And actually.' Abaddon's voice shifted, losing the humour. Jenny could imagine him drawing himself up, attempting authority as he spoke.

'Lucifer Pyro, I hereby detain you on the orders of Seven, Incorporated.'

Jenny's stomach dropped. They were *arresting* him?

'You what?' Apparently, Luc was as surprised as she was.

There was a noise like metal clinking, and the snap of something connecting.

'Fenris silver?'

'I spoke to your father,' Abaddon said, and even through the bark Jenny could hear the smug satisfaction in his voice. 'He wants you at the lake, and he doesn't want you wandering off.'

'What? How am I supposed to find Jenny if—'

He wasn't giving her away. The realization sent a bolt of *something* into her chest. He knew she was in the tree, she was sure of it, and yet . . . *He's protecting you*. Could that be true? She swallowed, bit her lip. Listened.

'Don't worry about your little human girlfriend. Your father's got a plan for that, too. Oh, don't look at me like that, Luc! You failed. Like we all expected you to. Your father offered you a chance at glory, yet more honour for the Lightbringer family, and you lost her. So, now you're grounded. Makes perfect sense if you ask me.'

'This is stupid,' Luc said, but neither Abaddon nor Malik bothered to reply.

There was another rattle of metal, a muffled grunt which she could only assume was Luc being dragged forward, and then everything went very quiet.

THE DEMONS HAVE GONE, the voice said inside Jenny's mind. The words felt alien inside her skull, but also natural. When the voice spoke, she saw green shoots behind her eyes.

'Thank you for protecting me,' she said, stepping into the middle of the tree's trunk.

Nothing.

Oh, yeah, she needed to be physically in contact with the wood for it to work. She reached her fingertips out to the inside of the trunk again.

WE WERE PROTECTING US, the tree said.

'Oh. Well, I appreciate it anyway.'

The tree didn't respond. Jenny pressed her palm flat against the trunk.

'Hello?'

No more green shoots.

'Could you . . . let me out now?'

Nothing.

Unease crawled over her skin. What if . . . this wasn't a very friendly tree? What if it had no intention of letting her out? She spent some time searching for a way out, breaches in the whorls of the bark, but she was sealed in. Was she likely to run out of oxygen? *Don't be silly*, she told herself. *Trees produce oxygen*.

But was that true for Hellish trees? Or was this some kind of living coffin? Wasn't there some ancient, druidic practice of shoving human sacrifices into trees – or was that from a film? God, it was hard to keep straight what she remembered from Sunday school, what she'd read in a Horrible Histories book and what she'd seen on the Syfy channel.

Regardless, there was no way out of the tree, and it was no longer talking either. She pressed her back against the trunk, sliding down until she was sitting on the mulchy floor of her cell. This whole thing was a nightmare, it was just that she wasn't sleeping.

She rolled her head so her cheek was against the body-warm wood of the tree, and channelled every sensation in her body into her voice when she said, 'I'm tired, I'm hungry . . . and I'm scared.'

YOU ARE SAFE HERE, the tree replied, missing the point completely. I CANNOT HELP WITH THE HUNGER. I BEAR FRUIT BUT YOU SHOULD NOT EAT THAT WHICH GROWS IN ALL HELL.

She sighed. 'You'll have to let me out, then.'

THAT WOULD NOT BE SAFE.

'For me, or for you?'

There was no immediate response, as though the tree was considering its next move. She felt reluctance, doubt, rolling through the bark and into her skin.

FOR ANYONE.

A series of images flickered into her mind, so rapid she wasn't sure the tree shared them willingly. She recognized Pyro this time, no longer confusing him with his equally handsome son. He was in a forest, chopping wood. The tree bled when his axe fell on it.

PYRO WILL FIND YOU. HE WILL HURT YOU. HE WILL HURT ANYONE WHO HELPED YOU.

The wood beneath her fingers vibrated with effort.

You're already hurt.

She didn't say it, but she didn't need to: the tree heard her anyway.

WE DO NOT INTEND TO BE MORE SO.

'Why are you even here?' Jenny heard herself ask. 'Why did your hearts weigh so heavy?'

WE ARE MANY. THERE IS NOT ONE CAUSE. BUT CONSIDER THE NAME FOR OUR COLLECTIVE NATURE.

'Your . . . I didn't know there was a name. I've just been

calling you "the trees".'

WE ARE THE SUICIDES' FOREST, the tree replied.

Jenny flinched. 'You're here because of suicide?'

When the tree didn't reply immediately, she realized that might have been insensitive. 'I'm not judging you,' she said quickly. She hoped the tree could tell she meant that. 'I'm just . . . that's not a reason for you to be punished. You – all of you – needed help. And you didn't get it in life, or if you did it wasn't enough, and now . . .'

The more she thought about it, the worse it was. They were trapped here, in Hell of all places, as though being ill, as though being so desperately unhappy in life, was some reason they should be punished. She felt sick. That wasn't right.

And she knew her outrage was spiralling out of her, into the wood, into the consciousness of every tree of the Suicides' Forest plugged into this network.

'Is there anything I can do?'

It was stupid. Of course there wasn't anything she could do – except, the tree hesitated.

PERHAPS.

'What? Tell me, I want to help.'

IT REQUIRES YOU TO LEAVE THIS PLACE.

'Leave Hell? Yeah, that's the general plan.'

NOW.

Meaning, without her soul. *Ouch.* Indecision was a tipping scale within her.

IF PYRO SUCCEEDS IN HIS PLAN, THERE WILL BE NO HOME FOR YOU TO GO BACK TO.

ONLY HELL. ALL HELL.

More images – although these couldn't be real, right? They landed in her head like bricks: aerial views of cities burning, children screaming, bodies, bodies . . . *war*.

'He's going after Earth?' It sounded ludicrous when she said it out loud, because she was a modern, non-religious girl and the idea of someone targeting the Earth was . . . impossible. Except, she was also a modern girl trapped in literal Hell, wasn't she? What did she even know about what was real and what wasn't?

'What does he need me for?'

That was what she didn't understand. What possible use was she to a demon as powerful as Seth Pyro?

THE SACRED AGREEMENT IS AN ANCIENT AND SPECIFIC TEXT, the tree said. PYRO HAS SEARCHED FOR MANY YEARS FOR A WAY AROUND ITS RULES.

'And for some reason he thinks that's me?'

The green shoots in her mind shuddered in agreement.

'Well, I'm not going to help him.' Obviously, she wasn't going to help him. He could beg, plead or resort to torture if he wanted, but everyone always said Jenny Hall was stubborn. He couldn't make her do . . . anything.

Well, apparently he could manipulate her into making the stupid decision to come into Hell in the first place, but that was before she knew what she was up against. She thought about Vee, about Connor and Tyler, and her heart thumped hollowly in her chest. There was nothing any demon could ever, ever do that would make her put her family at risk, and she didn't think letting All Hell break loose on Earth would be good for the boys, somehow.

'Let me out,' she pleaded. 'Let me out and I will figure something out. Please!'

YOU CAN BE TRACKED. PYRO WILL SEND DEMONS.

'Yes, but Luc already knows where I am anyway. What if he decides to tell his dad? Ideally, I'll be gone long before that.'

The tree apparently had no answer, and Jenny used it to her advantage.

'Like, what if Pyro decides to send a bunch of demons here to cut me out of you? Sounds like something he might do, doesn't it? What if that happens, and you bleed all over this sad bit of soil, and they cart me off anyway, and then we're all completely screwed?'

The tree still wasn't talking, but the burr of green when she touched the wood told her it was thinking about what she'd said.

WILL YOU LEAVE HELL?

Jenny sagged against the inside of the tree, visions of her cousins hiding from demons running through her mind. Stopping that had to be more important than whether or not she had a soul, didn't it? It felt like giving up, but when she squeezed her eyes shut to keep the salt-water from flowing out, she saw her auntie's face.

'If you let me out of here, I will *run* out of Hell.'

YOU DO NOT HAVE YOUR EYEGLASSES.

Huh. Now that *was* a good point. It was Jenny's turn to

go quiet, mind whirring as she tried to work out this particular kink in her plan. It wasn't like they were just reading glasses, was it? Her eyesight had grown progressively worse since primary school, to the extent that she only ever wore plastic frames, because metal ones were too heavy combined with the thickness of her lenses. Put another way, without her glasses, her own feet were barely visible blobs, and anything further away than that was a total mystery to her.

'No. No, I do not,' she agreed.

The green shoots in her mind shivered, with what seemed like a sigh of some horticultural kind. And then she felt something roll into her leg. She jumped, reached for it, and felt a palm-sized ball in her hand. It had a dry, leathery texture.

IT IS—

'A pomegranate.'

Because what else would it be?

'You want me to eat this.'

IT WILL HELP.

'And if I eat this, I get out?'

Affirmation in the green shoots. That was all she needed. She dug her thumbs into the tough skin of the fruit and shoved as many of the seeds into her mouth as she could, ignoring the fact that the juice was undoubtedly all over her chin and white polo shirt.

DO YOU STILL WISH TO HELP US? The leafy static buzzed in her ears.

'Well yeah,' Jenny huffed, her mouth full of bitter seeds.

'That's the point of this great escape, isn't it?'

The tree sighed. WHEN YOU ARE OUT OF THIS PLACE. I WOULD ASK YOU TO . . . PRAY. FOR US.

'Pray? I've never been very good at that.'

YOU ONLY NEED TO ASK THE COUNCIL TO REVIEW OUR FILES.

'Your . . . files?'

THEY MUST CONSIDER THE REQUEST OF A LIVING HUMAN.

'And what will they be reviewing your files for, exactly?'

The tree seemed to need to concentrate to answer this. Or maybe it was emotion that made it slow to respond.

HELL IS A FOR EVER SENTENCE, the tree said slowly. BUT THE LAWS SHIFT, WITH THE BALANCE. WHAT WAS ONCE A HELLISH SIN MAY BECOME . . . LESS SO.

'I see,' she said, only partly sure that she did. 'So, you need me to have your files reviewed in case your sins are . . . less bad than they were when you were put here?'

YES, the tree replied.

'And if they are, does that mean you get to leave?'

IT MEANS THERE IS A CHANCE.

'OK. I can do that,' Jenny said. It sounded simple. And it sounded like the right thing to do. She hadn't enjoyed being stuck here for a few hours; she could hardly imagine the rest of eternity.

There was a loud creaking sound as the tree's trunk split open into a gap just wide enough for her to wiggle outside. Despite the constant twilight, she blinked against the relative brightness.

On the outside, she patted the tree gently. 'Thank you.'

It was only then she realized she could see.

26

JENNY

She kept touching her face, revelling in the fact she could *see* even though her glasses were somewhere in the Ninth Circle of Hell with Luc.

It didn't seem to matter as much that the landscape was all lank, yellow grass and endlessness. She'd left the trees behind, and since then the only landmarks had been the occasional boulder half sticking out of the ground hoping to trip her, but even so she'd made it out of the Second Circle and back up to Limbo. She knew she was headed the right way when the grasses became dirt, and when that low-lying mist returned, rolling out over the still waters of the Acheron.

She mimicked the actions Luc had taken to 'hail a cab' last time. She dropped to a crouch, felt along the edges of the banks for . . . something . . . and found a rectangular metal segment pressed into the dirt. She knocked on it with her knuckles and stood back up. The mist parted like a curtain over the river, and the Ferrier poled into view.

As they drew near to the bank, Jenny slid the silver disc from her back pocket and held it out, ignoring the tremble in her fingers.

'Can you take me back? Please.'

The Ferrier didn't speak, but put out an arm to help her into the boat. The silver disc disappeared up their sleeve as she settled herself on to the same bench she'd sat on before. A surreal, déjà vu sensation crawled up her back, mingling with the relief that she'd made it this far. Still, she couldn't help twisting her body and neck around to look behind her, in case any MINOS agents were on their way to leap aboard.

The Ferrier faced her. Watching her, maybe, but after a second they moved away, reaching behind them to grab something from the front of the boat. A spare cloak. Without a word, they handed it to Jenny.

'Oh, *thank you*,' she said, slipping the heavy fabric around her shoulders as the Ferrier slid their barge pole into the treacle waters of the Acheron.

With the hood over her head, hiding her obvious *livingness*, she felt much better.

There was nothing for her to do while the Ferrier guided the barge across the Acheron, leaving her with time to think – something she'd been avoiding ever since Luc's revelation in the diner sent her skittering out into the wilds of Hell all alone.

But now, her mind worked, and her fingers traced over some words scratched into the wood of the bench she was on.

On the bright side, she was no longer hounded by a lying demon too handsome for his own good. She should have known better than to trust a boy with a face like that. She wasn't hungry, because that pomegranate had been surprisingly filling, or tired, because apparently the tree's fruit had restorative powers too. She could see, which, as someone who'd needed glasses since she was in Year Three, was a genuine miracle. And she was no longer trapped in the belly of a bad-tempered tree that smelt like her cousin Connor's armpit. All things considered, she was winning. Right?

Of course, she still didn't have her soul. She was also alone, unless you counted the Ferrier, and they were only a temporary ally. At least two demons with unpleasant plans for her were likely hot on her trail, and she still had to find her way back through that thick, sightless fog before she reached the yellowing meadow where the Hellmouth was.

Those things were in the 'less good news' column.

But on *balance* . . . she felt almost hopeful.

As they neared halfway across the water, the Ferrier paused the boat. At first, she didn't notice – the movement of the barge was so smooth it didn't much feel like anything anyway, but when she did, she lifted her head quizzically.

'Do you feel faint again?'

Oh, yes – she'd fainted last time, hadn't she?

'No, not this time.'

'That is good. I am sorry that happened to you on your first journey. I should have expected it; my last living passenger had the same malady.'

'Your last . . . You mean, other living people have come this way?'

The Ferrier's hood bowed in what she assumed was agreement.

'Many years ago. Seven hundred, I believe. And others before him, too.'

'Seven hundred . . .' She swallowed. The Ferrier had been at this for seven hundred years? *More* than that? Her mind spun, barely able to comprehend a life so long.

But they weren't finished with her yet.

'On the other side, there will be souls waiting for me,' the Ferrier intoned. 'You must not show yourself to them. You may keep the cloak.'

'OK, I promise. I . . . really appreciate how much you're helping me. You haven't even asked . . .'

'You paid your fare,' the Ferrier pointed out. 'And my loyalties are my own.'

Not Pyro's, or Seven, Inc.'s.

'Gotcha. Well, thanks, again.'

'It is my pleasure.'

She glanced down at the words her fingers had found in the bench and frowned. Now *these* were familiar.

'What does this mean?' she asked. '*Non fui, fui, non sum, non curo . . .*'

‘It is a Roman sentiment,’ the Ferrier rumbled. ‘I believe it translates thus: *I was not, I was, I am not, I care not*.’

‘Why is this the second place I’ve seen it written since I’ve been here?’

‘I could not say,’ the Ferrier replied. ‘I did not carve it. It seems . . . a deeply human thing to graffiti across the Abyss.’

Did it? Jenny wasn’t sure what to make of it.

The pole slipped into the water once more, and the Ferrier carried her to the other side of the Acheron.

As they had suggested, there were souls waiting on the bank. She knew they were souls because they glowed, but otherwise they looked very much as she guessed they would have in life: some old, some young, all of them a bit dazed, nervous.

When she climbed off the barge, some of them backed away from her. Power of the cloak, she supposed.

The Ferrier was too busy settling their new brood on the barge to wave this time. Something about the scene appealed to her: they really did look like a mother hen, clucking round their chicks. But she had a feeling they wouldn’t appreciate the comparison.

She squared her shoulders (the heavy cloak was a pleasant weight across them, like armour) and set off in what she thought was the right direction. The ground canted up before long and the fog rolled in, proving her theory right.

I am not going to panic, she insisted silently. *If I’m headed upwards, I have to be going the right way.*

Because All Hell was a funnel, wasn't it? That's what Luc had shown her at the top of the cliffs in Limbo. He'd been leading her down, down, down, but now she was going back up for air. As soon as she was back in Elrick Park, she'd breathe way easier.

The fog was interminable. *But you knew it would be.* She forced herself to keep going, climbing steadily upwards even as her thighs burnt, even as the tops of her toes rubbed painfully against the cheap plastic of her shoes. Although frankly, she was impressed they'd held up as well as they had.

She kept going, and *finally* the mists dropped, from her head to her waist, to her knees, her ankles, and then she was back in that sallow, grassy area she'd first crossed into with Luc.

Luc. What was he doing, right now? Was he . . . OK? *Why are you thinking about that lying sack of—?* Well, because she wanted to know what had happened.

She was glad he was gone, obviously. He'd lied to her! He'd manipulated her, using cruel tricks like *being nice* and *opening up to her*, just to make her trust him when all along . . . but at the same time, he hadn't given her away, had he? He'd *known* she was in that tree, and if he'd wanted to he could have sent demons to get her with chainsaws and he *hadn't.* In fact, thinking about it, it almost felt like he'd . . . protected her.

But that didn't make any sense. Why would he do that?

She stomped across the yellow grassland, thinking about Luc and turning everything over in her head. Was it possible, she wondered, that he might have changed his mind, somewhere along the way? Hadn't the MINOS guy, Abaddon, hadn't he said something about a quicker route that Luc hadn't taken? Or was she just thinking wishfully, as though it were remotely possible little old *her* might have charmed a bloody *demon*, for goodness' sake?

The biggest problem, really, wasn't what Luc had done. It was that she'd fallen for it in the first place. She felt stupid, gullible and hurt. She *felt*.

Just like last time she'd crossed this miserable patch of nothing, the air was silent around her. No birds chirping. No insects rustling underfoot. No 'wind like blades' or whatever Luc had called it. The only thing that existed in this place was a girl with complicated, boiling emotions.

But she wasn't the *only* creature here, was she?

Something shifted in her periphery, and she stopped walking. The something was pale, distant – and moving.

She gasped, the sound loud and shocking in the interminable silence that trapped her, and for the first time she heard another sound too. Far away, like the thing she thought she might have seen. A shout? A yell? A wordless cry? It was not animal. Not quite human, either, but God knows those weren't the only categories in this place.

What had Luc said to her about the creatures in this place?

They don't act human any more.

She heard it again, the sound. A scream. Saw it too, pallid in the distance, like a maggot creeping free of decaying fruit, erratic and jerky in its movements. Was it closer now? Jenny's heart pounded so hard she thought she might burst. Was it coming this way? *Yes.* Yes, it was headed this way, pouring that wordless holler into the darkness of the heath, moving like a stop-motion animation.

She should move. She should go, run, forward to the Hellmouth or even backwards, to some safer part of Hell. Even thinking that sent a panicked bubble of laughter up her throat. Where was safe in *Hell*? She should—

Something huge and unsteady lurched in front of her, inches from her face. Jenny shrieked, but the creature – what was it? – the creature didn't so much as pause, and she realized in moments this wasn't the creature she had seen before, but a different one entirely.

She couldn't move. She widened her eyes; there were *more* of them, tens of them at least, juddering across the heath. The one that had crossed her path was roughly the shape of a person, but like one that had been made from clay and coated with those modelling bandages that oozed thick, white plaster. But it wasn't plaster. The bandages hung loose, the ooze came from wounds on the creature's flesh. It moved like it couldn't balance, and when her eyes travelled down, lesions covered its legs too, its bare feet, and where the dressings gaped she saw yellow, black and bone.

As though drawn by the intensity of her gaze, the creature stopped moving away. It turned, slow, and as it did she felt the attention of the other creatures latch on to her too.

Her fear whistled like a kettle, so loud inside her body she was sure she was broadcasting it without even opening her mouth. The nearest creature grunted, a malevolent sound, its eye sockets deep and stuffed with dirty bandage. Somehow, though, she knew it could see her, its jaw hanging loose as it uttered a sound from deep in its throat.

The fear within her chattered her teeth, held her spine taut and disintegrated the feeling in her knees. She couldn't move if she wanted to. Couldn't lift her eyes off the gruesome sight before her, of the creature's bloody grin, its blistered legs loping towards her.

'Move,' a familiar voice growled, digging sharp fingers into Jenny's upper arm. Zillah appeared from behind, and yanked, pulling Jenny from her frozen spot, forcing her legs to move, and together they barrelled past the bandaged monsters.

A howl rose behind them, one Jenny was sure stemmed from the creature that had almost had her.

'Don't *feel* so much,' Zillah snapped, 'that's what attracts them.'

In no position to argue, Jenny focused only on the sensation of Zillah's nails digging in through her cloak, the pounding of blood in her ears and the burning in her thighs that told her she was running.

She stumbled, and Zillah hauled her forward across the heath, away from danger and towards a dirt path walked into the grass over time. When they reached the path Zillah let up, just slightly, and Jenny caught her breath as she found herself being led up a barely perceptible incline. The hill's gradient deepened, until eventually the heath was no more.

At the top, Zillah dropped Jenny's arm like it was venomous and wiped her hand on her clothes. Under any other circumstances she might have been offended, but she was so light-headed from relief she just dropped to her knees and planted her hands on the dirt in front of her.

'They didn't even touch you,' Zillah snapped, 'you just stood there and let your fear drive them into a frenzy.'

'What were they doing?' Jenny managed to choke out.

'Well, their punishment is entirely predicated on trying to find something that gives them a purpose. I'm guessing they felt the *loud* emotions . . . of a living human and that felt something like purpose.'

'They wanted my fear,' Jenny clarified. She felt a bit better – physically, anyway – enough to haul herself to her feet. She tried to get her bearings, and saw the fog, the way she'd come, a little way in the distance.

'No, duh,' Zillah replied. 'Although I actually think they wanted to tear you apart.'

Jenny shuddered.

'Why are they all bandaged up like that?'

Zillah released a sound like a laugh, only bitter. Her demonic gaze blazed into Jenny with a ferocity that sent her backwards a couple of steps.

'Because this is Hell.'

Yeah, fair enough. Wait—

'Why are you even here?'

Zillah raised an eyebrow, folded her arms. 'Aren't you glad I am?'

Jenny swallowed. 'Not if you're working for Pyro too.'

The blood drained from her face when Zillah didn't reply.

'Oh, God. Of course you're working for him.'

'Ah, ah, ah.' Zillah shook her head. 'I don't have time for all this chit-chat business. All you need to know is this: I am not Luc. I am not going to get distracted by those big, hazel eyes. I'm *not* going to lose you. Also, I'm not nice . . . so do as you're told and come with me. Now.'

She growled that last word, and every follicle on Jenny's body shivered. When she didn't immediately move, Zillah reached out and grasped one of her cloaked wrists, hard.

'I said, now.'

'What if I say no?'

Zillah bared her teeth. In Jenny's peripheral vision she saw the Succubus flip the borrowed cloak off her wrist, and wrap her cool hand tight around Jenny's flesh. Immediately, the demon was in her head again, and this time she wasn't being careful.

Jenny's knees buckled as a keening, siren-like, wailed through the corridors of her mind. Zillah's presence bulldozed into her consciousness, nothing like the gentle susurrations when she communicated with the trees.

But Zillah did send images. Jenny's eyesight dimmed, plunging her into a place so dark she *felt* it between her fingers: she was in a field of mud, a bland, sticky landscape with poles planted in orderly rows. She wasn't walking, was barely aware of her own body at all, but still she drew nearer to the poles, and as she did, glowing human souls appeared, lashed to the wooden stakes. They didn't see her, or if they did they were too tired, too defeated to pay her any mind. Some of them had black lines across their skin, others bled from their mouths. Some of them had scorch marks on their bodies.

Welcome to the Legion's training grounds, Zillah's voice echoed. *This is where Luc's going to end up, now he's finally messed up so bad even Pyro can't protect him. Don't worry, he won't be on a spike . . . did you think I didn't notice you two cosying up? Well, I can help you be together. Here, he'll learn how to torture, and if you don't do as you're told, I can't think of anywhere better for your soul to end up. How sweet! He can practise tongue-cutting on you. Over and over and over . . . until the Celestial Council finally put us out of our misery.*

The darkness fell away, and Jenny found herself on her knees in the yellow grass, one arm roughly held up in Zillah's hard grasp. The Succubus dropped her, and Jenny snatched her arm back, holding it against her chest.

'You'll do as you're told,' Zillah informed her. 'Because even if the Legion's training ground doesn't scare you, don't forget I know where your auntie lives. Your cousins – such *sweet* little boys.'

Jenny blanched. She didn't doubt for a second that Zillah would hurt Connor or Tyler if she got half a chance.

'I guess I can give the Ferrier their cloak back at least,' she said, capitulating.

'Nope. No boats,' Zillah shot back. 'We're going the way Luc should have in the first place.'

Zillah walked fast, forcing Jenny to skitter along behind

her as best she could. Which was a struggle, her flimsy ballet flats causing her to skid every other step, her feet sore from getting tangled up in the grasses or slipping in the mud.

'Stop messing around,' Zillah snapped.

'I'm *not*,' Jenny shot back, and the Succubus cast a glance down at her feet. Something in her face twitched and she stopped walking.

'Why do you wear those pointless shoes?'

'Four ninety-nine a pair off the market,' Jenny shot back. 'In case you'd forgotten, I was practically homeless before I got involved in . . . whatever all this is. I wasn't exactly spoilt for choice.'

'Right.' For a moment, Zillah looked chastened. Then she blinked, and the demon was back. 'Well, just try to keep up. We're already behind schedule.'

'Like I care about your schedule.' She wanted to sound flippant, confident, but the shake in her voice gave her away.

She'd been *so close* to getting home! The thought brought her up short. Home? Where exactly did she mean by that? Well, when she blinked, it was Auntie Vee's house that sprang to mind. Was that really home? Although it was currently a moot point: here she was, traipsing along behind a creature she knew for a fact couldn't be trusted. A creature who liked to crawl inside people's thoughts and trick them into doing whatever the hell she wanted. A creature who could order harpies to spill blood and feathers whenever she wanted . . .

‘Stop it,’ Zillah said.

‘What?’

‘Panicking. I don’t even have to *touch* you to feel it rolling off you. It’s . . . I don’t like it.’

Jenny stared at her in disbelief. ‘Well, I am *sorry*,’ she snapped. ‘Forgive me for experiencing a perfectly normal human emotion.’

‘That’s exactly the problem,’ Zillah said.

‘What?’

‘A perfectly normal *human* emotion,’ Zillah said. ‘It’s gross.’

‘That’s tough, isn’t it?’ Jenny shot back. ‘When you *manipulate* and *lie* to a human, we tend to get a bit *emotional*.’

‘Whatever,’ Zillah growled. ‘Hurry up, we’ve got a bus to catch.’

27

LUC

Like most demons, Luc *hated* the cold.

And the Ninth Circle was a frozen wasteland.

He dragged his feet as Abaddon and Malik manhandled him over the snow, past the wide, dark waters of the Lake of Lament and to a lone tree standing at the base of a huge mountain. Lucifer's Mount. Of course this was where his father had insisted they bring him.

It was truly a testament to the bizarre geography of All Hell that back when he was with Jenny, at the top of the cliffs of Limbo, they hadn't been able to see the mountain. From this vantage, right at the bottom of the funnel-shaped Abyss, it was an immense thing. As the MINOS agents meddled with his chains, wrapping one end around the tree to keep him there, he couldn't help looking up, trying to catch sight of his mythical grandfather who was (somewhat ironically) chained tight up there with Fenris silver too.

But no one had seen Lucifer on the mountain, because no demon could climb it.

Wouldn't it be funny, Luc thought, if it turned out to be a lie, and he wasn't there at all? Well, maybe not *funny* funny.

'Oh, lads,' he called out as Abaddon and Malik made to leave. 'You're not sticking around for a bit? Keep me company?'

'No chance,' Malik shivered. 'We're off back where it's warm.'

And so he was alone, his hands bound tight in front of him at one end of a slender length of silver chain. The other end had been wrapped twice around the trunk of a tree and lashed there. He walked over to it, used the crook of his index finger to tug on it, but Malik and Abaddon knew what they were doing. No give, no escape.

Luckily, his demon DNA kept him from being in real danger from the elements, but the cold of the Ninth Circle still seeped through to his bones, invading his thoughts with icy fingers.

No doubt this was all part of the design. Eventually he knew it would drive him to distraction. Certainly, he wouldn't be able to produce any kind of escape plan, even if Fenris silver *weren't*, famously, unbreakable.

Beyond the edges of his prison, the snow was white, the ice was sharp. Far above, the false stars of All Hell shivered, and from where Luc sat they were reflected, pinpricks of yellow light, in the glassy, black waters of the lake itself.

The Lake of Lament was a place of regret. In some ways, Luc thought, this was a fitting place for him to be incarcerated; he had regrets all right. Specifically, he regretted ever going to Earth. Ever meeting Jenny Hall, ever offering to take her to her soul.

He closed his eyes and tried not to think about her. The concentration on her face when trying to stop him annihilating her on the bumper cars. The wonder in her eyes when she woke up on the Ferrier's barge, gazing up at him like she *liked* him. Like she *trusted* him. His stomach clenched and he shook himself out of it.

What would she do now she knew he was the worst kind of betrayer? He'd given her a head start at least, or so he hoped, by not revealing her hiding place in that tree. *How* she got in there was a mystery to him, but it was the only thing that made sense, especially since the tree had practically emanated self-satisfaction.

He hoped she could survive without her glasses. That was another regret – they'd been in his hands when he heard the MINOS agents approach, and he'd stuffed them into his jeans pocket, so Malik or Abaddon didn't find them. But was that going to just make it harder for her to escape?

He had to hope.

He had to hope she'd find the river, hitch a lift to the other side, and once she was back in Elrick Park she could just *go home*. Back to her auntie's house, maybe even back to patch things up with her mother. Back to a normal, boring teenage life with snogging at parties and homework. As long as she was safe, far away from the Hellmouth, far away from his father.

Speak of the devil. Seth Pyro picked his way across the snowy planes of the Ninth Circle towards Luc, dressed as always in a tailored suit and shoes that would no doubt be ruined now. When he got close enough to speak, he greeted Luc like one of his business partners, which is to say, he greeted Luc as though for once in his life he was pleased to see him.

'Ah, there you are!'

'Where else would I be?' Luc shook his chains.

Pyro's teeth gleamed. 'Of course, how silly of me. I am surprised, though . . .' he swept an arm at the white expanse of the Ninth Circle, 'to see you here alone.'

Luc's jaw set. 'If Abaddon hadn't jumped the gun, I'd have been here in good time, *with* the girl.' He ignored the pang in his chest as he spoke.

'I see.' Pyro seemed to genuinely consider this, going so far as to stroke his chin with his forefinger. Luc wasn't fooled.

'If that's true, then I must offer you my sincerest apologies on behalf of the MINOS agency,' he said. 'I can see, though, why they were confused. After all, your orders were to bring her here immediately upon your return, and yet, you were found dilly-dallying in the far reaches of the Second Circle. Could you explain that?'

'Those weren't my orders,' Luc disagreed. 'You said I had to bring her back here before the stars aligned on this thing.' He gestured as much as he could with his bound arm. 'And they're not aligned yet. I haven't failed, yet.'

But even as he said it, he hoped he was wrong.

'Perhaps you're right,' Pyro replied. Somehow, his agreement didn't feel like a good sign. 'You did bring her through the Hellmouth, and I am . . . mildly impressed. But now she's under our jurisdiction, all bets are off. I'm sure *one* of my agents will catch her.'

The Ninth Circle dropped another degree colder.

'What's going to happen to her?' Luc heard himself ask. One of Pyro's eyebrows quirked at the question.

'She won't *die*, if that's what you're worried about. Unless she chooses to defy me, in which case, who knows? But if she climbs the mountain she'll remain very much alive . . . Do you know, there's an old wives' tale about Lucifer's chaining? According to the legends, if he is woken from his slumber, someone must take his place.'

'She'll be stuck there? Chained to the mountain?'

'Only if you believe in old wives' tales,' Pyro grinned, slyly.

'So all of it was a lie? She never had any chance of getting her soul back.' He felt like the worst creature in all the spheres.

'Oh, you mean this?' Pyro reached into his jacket and pulled out a yellow can with the Seven, Inc. logo on the front. 'She doesn't need it, to do what I need her to do.'

'Then when she's done your stupid task, can she have it back?' Because if so, maybe Luc wouldn't be burdened with so much of this awful guilt. If she could still get her soul back . . .

Pyro squinted at him. 'Could she get it back *after*? What a novel thought.' He regarded the can carefully, as though searching the fine print on the back of it for answers.

He took a step towards Luc, and reached towards him with the can. Luc's heart leapt. He was going to let Luc keep hold of it for her! Hope fizzed in his chest, and he reached out – just as Pyro turned away, reached back, and tossed the can straight into the Lake of Lament. As the can touched the surface of the water, a vast, pale hand reached up from the black depths, its fingers like tree trunks, the nails blackened and cracked like long-neglected tombstones. The can containing Jenny's soul dropped into the palm of that enormous hand, which clenched around it and dragged it into the depths beneath.

'But on reflection,' Pyro sniffed, 'I think not.'

Demons aren't taught to pray – mostly because they know it's pointless. Pleas from prisoners are usually ignored by their jailers. But what Luc did after realizing the depth of evil in his father's plans? It felt a lot like praying.

Praying Jenny got out of All Hell in time. And praying that one day, she might be able to forgive him for putting her in this position in the first place. Praying she'd find solace without her soul, which was now lost to a vengeful giant under a lake salted with tears.

28

JENNY

'You have got to be kidding me,' Jenny said when she saw the bus stop. It could've come from her hometown, complete with a heavy plastic shelter built over the top of it in case of rain.

There was a timetable on the inside of the shelter, and she eyed it suspiciously as Zillah leant against the shelter wall. As far as Jenny could tell, only one service ran this way, the 000, heading straight for 'Burning Sands', whatever they were. Sounded just *lovely*.

She sat down heavily on the warped, rusted metal of the bench and tried to make out some of the marker-pen graffiti scrawled on the inside of the shelter. Most of it was nonsense, much like graffiti everywhere, but then . . . there! *Non sum, non curo.* The Ferrier had translated it for her, but that hardly helped her understand it.

When the bus arrived, it was as ordinary as the stop they waited at. She figured it had probably been red, once, but was now faded orange. It looked like there may have been a logo on the side too, but this had long since worn away. The tyres were thin and old. All in all, it was rickety.

What else, exactly, had she expected?

Zillah nudged her aboard first.

'Where to?' a disinterested voice asked.

'Burning Sands,' Zillah said, reaching across Jenny to hold out her arm to the driver.

What was this? The driver didn't even turn to them, keeping his eyes on the road ahead as he reached up to briefly touch Zillah's fingertips with his own. His skin was sallow, heavily pitted like the cratered, rocky surface of an alien moon. He had horns, like Luc did, but unlike Luc's, the driver's horns were huge, gnarled things. They curled out from his temples like those of a particularly stubborn sheep, almost meeting in the middle. They had to be heavy, Jenny decided. Maybe that was why he didn't turn to look at them.

'Next,' he said.

'That's you, sunshine,' Zillah prompted.

'What?'

'Your fare, pet.' The driver held out an impatient hand.

'Hang on, you're *kidnapping* me, and I still have to pay for my own bus?' She glared daggers at Zillah, who just shrugged.

'Fine,' she grumbled, pulling the £3.62 out of her pocket. 'I hope this is sufficient.'

For the first time, the driver took his eyes off the windscreen, saw the money in her outstretched hand and laughed. Unpleasantly.

'I don't take *coins*, pet.'

'Well, that's all I have. What a shame, maybe I can't travel after all . . .' She made to get off the bus, but the doors closed in her face.

'I take pain,' the driver said with a leer.

'I'm sorry, what the hell?'

Zillah folded her arms and watched, clearly enjoying herself.

'Pain,' the driver repeated. 'Give me your hand, and I'll show you.'

Jenny remembered Zillah flicking through her memories, and suddenly understood what he wanted.

Well, OK, sure. If this dude wanted pain, she had plenty to spare.

Shooting a venomous look at Zillah, she put her hand in the driver's wide, gnarly one.

At first, nothing happened. She had time to register that his hand was warm and dry, the skin a little rough but generally not unpleasant, and then she felt it. Felt *him*, his demon . . . power, consciousness, whatever it was.

It crawled up her arm on the inside of her cloak, like a spider moving slowly towards her shoulder.

Gross.

The feeling continued across her skin. She half expected to see a lump creeping under the fabric covering her arm, but there was nothing there. Nothing she could see, anyway.

When the sensation reached her neck, she flinched. It was like cold fingers caressing the tender skin just below her ear. Long, skinny, invisible fingers. Her earlobe itched as one of the fingers tickled her there. Then it plunged into her ear, and she gasped.

The sensation vanished from her skin. But she knew that meant he was in her head. She closed her eyes against the smirk on the bus driver's face. The fingers scraped inside her skull. *Oh, yeah. He was in there all right.*

'The Burning Sands is a long trip,' the bus driver said, his voice like melted tar. 'All the way on the other side of Dis. I'll need a nice, juicy chunk of pain to take you that far.'

Jenny's skin broke out in goosebumps, and she shivered. How long was this going to take? Inside her head, the fingers took their time, moving slowly through the hallways of her mind, running along every wall they came across. Leaving greasy trails in their wake.

This was too much. It *was* like when Zillah was in her head, but worse. She couldn't take much more of this.

'Here,' she gasped, forcing herself to think about the most painful thing she could.

For months she'd avoided thinking about it at all, but she dredged it up from the recesses of her mind anyway, offering it to the driver of the bus like a gift – The Fight.

'Try this one.'

'Ooh,' the driver cooed. 'Hefty. I like it.'

But she couldn't really hear him. She was somewhere else—

⋆

—She knew something was wrong as soon as she closed the front door behind her. The flat she shared with her mum was only small, and usually when she got home from school, she could smell whatever they were going to have for tea that night cooking: oven chips, usually, maybe beans.

But tonight, the flat smelt much the same as it had when she'd left this morning, which meant her mum wasn't cooking. But she was definitely home – her handbag was in its normal place on the floor under the coat rack, and as Jenny kicked off her school shoes and dumped her bag next to it, she felt her stomach tighten with horrible anticipation.

Her mum must have received another message.

She walked slowly down the short corridor towards the living room. Past the kitchen, where she could see a half-full bag of frozen chips on the counter. So, the text had come in while her mum got ready to cook. Which meant her mum had broken the 'no checking phones before dinner' rule. Again.

They put the rule in place when the texts started to get more frequent. It was a compromise – Jenny wanted her mum to get a new SIM card and change her number, or even call the police and explain what was going on, but her mum said no, that's not how you handle bullies.

You ignore them until they go away.

But the messages weren't so easy to ignore, it seemed. The living room door was just slightly ajar, and it creaked on its hinges when Jenny pushed it open. Her mum was sitting on the sofa, still in her work uniform, just staring at the phone.

She looked up when Jenny stepped into the room, her face haunted.

'What does it say?' Jenny asked, because there was no point pretending.

Her mum swallowed. 'It says you've got a boyfriend.'

Jenny's knees almost gave way from the relief. Was that all? Ever since the texts started coming, about six months ago, they'd been sending insidious vines into the cracked wall of Jenny and her mum's relationship.

Jenny takes drugs, the text messages alleged.

Jenny steals from the outlet centre.

You shouldn't let Jenny go out on Saturday if you know what's good for you.

It was all lies. Well, all right, she'd tried smoking a joint Amber rolled for her a few months ago, but no one knew about that, and the text messages said she was taking all sorts anyway. She'd never stolen anything in her life, and her only plans on Saturday were meeting up with Caspian.

Caspian was the reason she was relieved. They'd been together a month, and the only reason she hadn't told her mum yet was because she couldn't believe her luck, didn't want to jinx it by announcing it to the universe.

'I do have a boyfriend,' she told her mum. 'I'm sorry I didn't tell you, but he's—'

Her mum cut her off.

'It says you're having sex with him, Jenny. It says you're

having sex with lots of men.'

'Well, that's clearly bollocks,' Jenny laughed.

Why was her mum being so weird about the contents of this message?

Her mum didn't seem to think this was funny.

'I'm only going to ask you once. Is anything in this message true?'

Was it just Jenny, or was it cold in their flat tonight? Or was that just her blood freezing?

'I told you. I have a boyfriend. He's nice, I think you'll like him – but Mum, I swear to you, I haven't . . . we haven't . . .'

They'd only just had their first kiss, for God's sake!

But the stony expression on her mum's face didn't shift.

'Mum, you don't really believe it, do you? Since when have those texts said anything true?'

'I don't know,' her mum admitted. 'When they first started, I thought . . . no, they must have got the wrong Jenny. But . . . recently, I don't know. You've been different. Angry. Secretive. Rude.'

Well yeah, Jenny thought. *I'm being cyberbullied via my mother's phone.*

That was the worst part of the whole thing. If they'd been sending awful messages just to her, she could laugh it off. Like when someone anonymously texted Amber that she had 'tiny tits'. She'd shown Jenny and they'd rolled with laughter, not least because it was in no way true. But these messages weren't going to Jenny, they were going to her mum, and that made it so, so much worse.

Especially now.

'This is what they want,' Jenny pointed out, hearing the high pitch in her voice. 'They're only sending them to you because they want to hurt us. Our relationship.'

'Or maybe it's a Good Samaritan trying to warn me of the things my daughter's getting up to,' her mum countered.

A pit opened inside Jenny at that moment, swallowing any further arguments she had. It wasn't true! How could her mum even believe it?

But the pit unleashed something too: for months now, Jenny had been battling against the simmering rage the text messages had caused. She'd lost friends because of it: how could she trust people, when any one of her so-called mates could be the sender of the texts? Maybe they were all in on it, laughing about it behind her back.

But now the rage wasn't aimed at them. It was aimed at the one person who should have believed her. Should have trusted her.

'You think I'm sleeping around, Mum?'

Her mother wouldn't meet her eye. 'I don't know. I . . . well, are you?'

'Fuck you.' The words were out before she could stop them. 'Even if it was true, even if I was the biggest slut in the world – I must have learnt it from you.'

A hot tear splashed on to her face, and she snatched her hand away from the driver to wipe it away before Zillah noticed. No doubt the Succubus would think it highly amusing.

The bus driver sighed, sated. 'That was lovely,' he told her with a wink. 'Do you want your change?'

'What?'

'Your change,' the bus driver repeated slowly. He raised his eyebrow at Zillah. 'She's new, right?'

'Very,' Zillah smirked.

'What do you mean, change?'

'You gave me too much for the journey, and very nice it was too. I owe you something in return.' He sniffed. 'I can tell you who sent those messages if you want.'

Despite everything that had happened in the past few days, Jenny's curiosity perked up like a Dobermann.

'You can do that?'

The bus driver shrugged. 'Sure thing. Amber Coombs. That's who was sending those messages to your mother.'

Jenny's eyes widened and her head spun with this information.

She'd wondered about Amber, of *course* she had, but they hadn't fallen out until after the messages started. It didn't make sense, unless . . .

She started doing it while we were still supposedly friends.

'Oh,' Jenny heard herself growl, 'I am glad I smacked that bitch when I had the chance.'

The bus driver chuckled.

'I like her,' he told Zillah.

'Well, that makes one of us,' the Succubus grumbled. 'Come on you, let's find a decent seat.'

29

JENNY

They were the only passengers on the bus, and Zillah insisted they sit right at the back. At least she let Jenny sit by the window so she could watch what was going on outside.

Not that the landscape was especially inspiring. They were travelling downhill again, she noticed, and then over a bridge across the Acheron. She drew the Ferrier's cloak closer around her, seeking comfort in its folds. She hoped the Ferrier didn't get in trouble for trying to help her.

They passed through Limbo, then down a narrow, rocky road into the Second Circle. All dismally familiar.

Next to her, Zillah sat right in the middle seat, her legs sprawled out in front of her, practically halfway down the aisle. Arms folded, face blank, she looked like every mean, bored cool-girl stereotype rolled into one. Jenny tried to scope the bus out for escape routes without looking like she was checking for them, but . . .

'I can feel what you're doing,' Zillah muttered. 'Don't even think about it.'

Frustrated, Jenny went back to staring out of the window.

The bus trundled along the track, bumping over stones and potholes. Outside, the grainy dirt and insipid yellow grasses gave way to mud and the occasional distant hump of something long-abandoned. At the front of the bus, a bell chimed, and an LED sign lit up with the information that they were NOW ENTERING THE THIRD CIRCLE.

Oh goody, Jenny thought sourly. *Can't wait*.

It looked *very* similar to the Second Circle. Maybe those anonymous lumps in the distance appeared more frequently, but otherwise it was a long, slow sameness.

No wonder the demons were sick of living here.

'What do you do for fun?' she asked.

'Fun?' Zillah's neck twisted gracefully towards her, but her face was a pure image of confusion. 'What do you mean?'

'Well, you know. In between all the torture and that. Do you have . . . bowling, or something?'

The Succubus appeared to struggle with this for a moment.

'We don't have bowling, no.' She returned to her original pose, and Jenny shook her head, assuming that was the end of it.

'There is a cinema, kind of,' Zillah offered.

'Kind of?'

'Well, it's a punishment for the souls, really.' Why wasn't this a surprise? 'Like, some people get assigned there to re-experience their sins from life into eternity, knowing there's no way they'll ever be able to go back and make different choices. Fun to watch, sometimes.'

Not exactly what Jenny had in mind.

'And there's the casino.'

'Let me guess, human souls move from blackjack to poker to roulette, gambling themselves into worse and worse eternal punishments?'

'House always wins,' Zillah agreed. 'And there are literal one-armed bandits roaming the game floor too, so it can get a bit messy. Excellent hot dogs, though.'

'But, like . . .' Jenny paused, not entirely sure how to phrase what she wanted to say. 'What else is there? Besides terrorizing souls, besides all the schemes and politics, what do you *do* here?'

Silence. Zillah's jaw tightened. And then –

'It's not just a punishment for your lot, Jenny.' Her voice dropped, despite the emptiness of the other seats.

'What does that mean?'

'It means . . . a long time ago, some guy called Lucifer dared to challenge the Celestial Council. He was charismatic, and clever, and he thought things needed to change. Things weren't fair. The Council disagreed, and things got ugly. In the end, the Council blasted this giant hole in the ground and chained Lucifer to a mountain in the middle of it. Fenris silver, unbreakable. He's also in an enchanted sleep, because the Council think he'll stir up another rebellion as soon as he's conscious.'

'Some of this sounds familiar.'

She scoffed. 'I've read some of those holy books your lot are into and they're . . . selective.' She rolled her eyes. 'All the focus tends to land on Lucifer, but he wasn't alone when he challenged the Council. *Any* creature connected to the rebellion found themselves unceremoniously ditched in here. They sealed us in, unless you were useful to them, or, as in my mother's case, if the Council knew they'd already messed up how they treated you.'

'What happened with your mother?'

Zillah waved this away like it was a fly. 'Long story. Doesn't matter. What matters is, this place is just as much a prison for us as it is for the human souls that get sent here. We don't have bowling, we don't have *fun*. Does that seem right, to you?'

She didn't wait for an answer.

'It's not, obviously. I wasn't even born when any of that happened, but I'm still stuck under the same contract my mother is, just like all six of my sisters are, and we have no idea how long they're planning to keep us in this hellhole.'

Outside the window, the landscape had changed while Zillah talked. Those distant, anonymous lumps weren't so distant now; Jenny could make out shapes. Kitchen appliances, mostly, like abandoned fridges with their doors hanging open to reveal empty internal voids.

Now, why were there so many stranded fridges in a field in the middle of Hell?

Didn't matter. There were more pressing issues in Jenny's mind.

'Is that why you're so keen for me to go with you?'

'Obviously.'

'What's going to happen?'

'I honestly don't know.' Well, that was a let-down.

'Wild guess?'

The Succubus splayed her hands wide, revealing nothing. 'You're going to have to ask Pyro when you meet him. He seems to think you can wake Lucifer up, something he has completely failed to do over the years despite trying endlessly. And if you can, that would mean the Council have to take us seriously.'

When she put it like that . . . it almost sounded reasonable. Except . . .

'If it were as easy as that, he could have just asked me. You know, *nicely*.'

Zillah didn't reply, and a bloom of dread erupted in Jenny's stomach. There had to be more to it than that. More to it than just tapping a Fallen Angel on the shoulder and offering him a coffee to help him wake up. Why else would Pyro have gone to all this trouble, stealing her soul, waiting ten years, sending Luc and Zillah after her to make sure she got where she was at this precise moment? She blinked, remembering the warscape the trees had shown her. Not real, no, but *possible*. Could waking Lucifer really lead to that?

And speaking of Luc – how much of this did he *know*? Was it possible he was as in the dark as Zillah was about what Pyro wanted from her? And did that even matter? She swallowed, hating herself for looking for excuses for him, even now.

I've got you.

She'd believed him. Still wanted to. God, she wished she could just talk to him!

Honestly, the kitchen appliance landscape was a nicer place than her own head at that moment. She frowned and sat up, peering out into the murk beyond the window. There were *hundreds* of fridges out there – double-doored, American-style monstrosities, knackered old chest freezers leaking mould and neglect, the occasional microwave caked in what looked like red velvet cake batter, even ovens, all of them spread out across the landscape like they'd been dropped in a hurry.

They *smelt*, too – at first stale and faintly bacterial, but as the bus rolled on the smell intensified too – rotten, faecal – until her nose wrinkled, her eyes watered and her throat constricted.

'What *is* that?' she choked out, clamping one cloak sleeve to her face to try to filter the air.

Zillah scoffed. 'Did you expect All Hell to be sweet and fragrant?'

Well, no, but she'd never smelt anything like it. It was practically tangible, thick even inside the bus. Things moved among the filth outside, in the mire, among the discarded appliances. She couldn't tell what they were, because they moved too fast for her to fix her eyes on them, but they gave her the impression of black smoke and chip-pan fires. Her memory snagged on the Uncommitted and she had a horrible feeling those were human souls out there, wasting away in a bog of filth, scrabbling to find sustenance in those long-empty fridges.

She leant back into her seat, nauseous. She closed her eyes and tried to breathe even though the excrement odour made them water. It was way worse than anything she'd experienced when her mum opened the car windows out in the country – it wasn't just human waste but *unhealthy* human waste, like a million people had been force-fed burning rubber and told to defecate in the same field.

Oh, God. She was going to heave.

Somewhere in the distance, a dog barked three times, reminding her of Greek myths she'd learnt at school about dogs with three heads, but even this evidence of animal life couldn't distract her. She leant forward and pressed her nose as far as she could into her own hands so she could only smell her own skin and the vague Acheron mustiness of the Ferrier's cloak. Shallow breaths, and a silent mantra: she *wasn't going to be sick*. Oh no. Because if she *was* sick, the bus driver was likely to toss her out at the side of the track. Here. In the field of serious gastrointestinal issues.

No thanks.

In the seat next to her, Zillah appeared supremely unconcerned.

Eventually, *thankfully*, the stench passed. Or, at least, she got more used to it. Her eyes stopped watering, the urge to vomit all over the floor abated. Tentatively, she released her makeshift face mask and realized she could breathe normally.

Against her own advice, her eyes slid sideways to the window again. At first, she thought she'd been mistaken, that they were still in the craplands, but she was no longer looking out at abandoned kitchen appliances.

A bell pinged in the bus and the sign scrolled another message: NOW ENTERING THE FOURTH CIRCLE.

Which was, apparently, where demons dumped their household waste. Mountains of it, peaks made of empty yoghurt pots, battered trainers, flat pillows, old toothbrushes. All of this was jumbled together, an entire world made landfill. And again – there were . . . things here, scrambling across the hills of waste as though searching for something. Some of them dug down into the piles, others picking up item after item on the surface, inspecting them for a few moments before casting them aside.

Jenny's heart broke for these souls, even though she didn't know what they were searching for. Probably for something that didn't exist – that would be very demonic, wouldn't it? Something bubbled inside her, deep in that void where her soul was meant to be. With a soul or without, Jenny thought, these were *her people*, no matter where in the world they were from, no matter what time they'd been born in. What could anyone *possibly* have done in life to deserve an *eternity* of this?

Like, how long was a human life, anyway? Eighty, ninety years, if they were lucky? Sure, Jenny knew there were truly evil people in existence. But she couldn't quite believe that so many human souls had racked up that level of evil in those short lifetimes. She looked out at the trash mountains and her anger soared. Those mountains crawled with human souls.

She thought back to Fran and Cleo. Maybe they'd messed up, fallen in love with people they shouldn't have. Maybe they'd even let that cloud their judgement, maybe they'd made bad decisions – but did that mean they should live for ever like they were living now, with eternal blisters and infernal chains holding them in a never-ending waitressing shift?

Even the Uncommitted – what did that even mean? Was it such a crime? Did any of them truly deserve their oozing, bandaged fate . . . for ever?

No, she decided. They did not. And what was it the tree had said to her? Hell is for ever. Unless . . . unless *someone* asked for a file to be reviewed. She still didn't fully understand what that meant, but right there on the bus, Jenny swore she would get out of here and do just that.

She just had to find a way to escape Zillah, first.

The bell sounded again. She looked up to the LED sign: NOW ENTERING THE STYGIAN MARSH.

What fresh Hell is this, then?

She fixed her eyes beyond the window, out to the landscape, waiting for the next horror to assault her senses and feed her rage – but instead she felt the air go out of her. She stared out at the view and her anger faded, folded back into that empty space where she once had a soul. It was still there, but it couldn't compete with what she was seeing now.

The Stygian Marsh was *beautiful*. It was like . . . a nature reserve, in the pits of Hell. Magic, like nothing else she'd ever experienced, possibly only because it was located where it was.

The marsh revealed itself in pools that glinted under the ever more distant lantern-light from above, and reflected there, those lights for the first time took on the luminescence of stars. Tall, lush grasses grew up around the pools, and someone had constructed a wooden walkway connecting the waters. Jenny could imagine taking a walk here, finding a quiet spot to think.

That this place existed here was preposterous, and yet here it was. Her heart thudded against the inside of her ribs. Why did this exist? There were birds too – at first she barely believed it, but it was *real*, they were real – they looked like herons or storks except much, much bigger; she suspected most of them were at least her height – and she couldn't tell if it was a trick of the inadequate light that made them look so . . . grey, their feathers appear so ragged.

The bus trundled round a corner and the marsh veered closer just in time for Jenny to watch an especially large bird blink, its yellow eyes almost neon in the dark. Its neck jerked violently forward, and its beak snapped at something in the water, the sound cracking through the air, deadly, metallic. It was such a brutal motion that Jenny gasped, and as though it had heard her the bird jerked upright and glared in through the window. She shrank back from it, but she couldn't help catching the bird's eye and instantly she *knew*, without a doubt, that these birds had also once been human. Just like everything else in this place.

Jenny pushed herself closer to the window, inspecting the marsh, and when she did she saw the shapes in the water – the things the birds were snapping their jaws at. They glowed, the underwater-dwellers, and they didn't so much swim as float. They were souls, just like the birds, only these ones had been condemned as prey while the stork things had been condemned to prey *on*.

At this point, she knew she shouldn't be shocked any more. What else did Hell have to show her that could puncture her sense of 'oh, I've seen worse'? And yet this time when a bird stabbed its jaws into the water and pecked mercilessly at a glowing soul, she thought she might cry. A bloom of something dark and cloudy loosened from the glowing soul in the water. They still bled, even in death.

The glowing soul didn't make any move to get away from the bird, but thankfully the bus rolled on, away from the Stygian Marsh.

'How much more of this *is* there?' she asked Zillah.

'Not long, now. Look over there: that's Dis. We're getting off just on the other side of the city.'

A skyline of blocky, brutalist-style buildings rose from the tilted horizon. It was far enough away that she could see an orange haze around it, inside it, and felt a twinge in her stomach. A city on fire. *Naturally.*

The bus swept them away from the horror and beauty

of the Stygian Marshes, and on to a narrow road on a gentle downward hill. Always down, down, down, right? Gosh, it was *warm* suddenly. Had the sight of flames in the background made her subconscious temperature rise, or was it real? Either way, her skin prickled, and she slid the Ferrier's cloak off her shoulders.

The bell pinged. NOW ENTERING BURNING SANDS, WHERE THIS ROUTE TERMINATES.

Zillah chivvied her off the vehicle, and it was only when the doors had snicked closed that Jenny realized she'd left the cloak on board.

30

TRISTAN OF THE NARROWS

Tristan Wood had been in Hell for years, now.

Specifically, Tristan resided in the ditches of the Narrows, a dank hole of a place he shared with thieves, fraudsters and, of course, others like him – soothsayers. Future-Seers. Astrologers, scryers, those kind of people.

Some of them, naturally, were absolute charlatans. Well, there's always a bit of that in this game, isn't there? After all, any old hack can moan portentously while peering into a crystal ball and pretend to see Death Himself stalking over a battlefield.

Tristan avoided talking to the hacks. Even in death, he couldn't bear the thought of anyone associating *him* with *them*. No, he much preferred the company of thieves. At least thieves were *honest*. He learnt all sorts from them – how to know when it was worth charming a lock, for example, and when just to smash a window with your elbow.

These weren't exactly techniques Tristan was ever going to need, now, but he'd always been curious about other trades. Probably because he never got to pick his own: soothsaying called him, not the other way around.

He could still remember the first time the Power called to him, even centuries later. He was a child at the time, a tow-headed little thing with wide, grey eyes and a curiosity that drove his mother to distraction. He was always wandering towards the edge of the dark woods. Always tilting his head and following the sound of birdsong into probable danger.

But one morning, not long after he turned six, he'd been playing with a wooden bowl and a bucket of water in the yard, and he'd heard someone whisper his name. He'd looked around, of course, as any naturally gregarious child would. Was this a new playmate? Alas, there was no one there, and he'd returned to his game of scooping water out on to the straw-strewn ground when he heard it again.

Tristan.

And he'd felt something, too, a tug in the region of his belly button. Something asking him . . . no, he realized later, not asking but *imploring* him to follow. So he had. He'd walked right into those woods his mother always warned him away from, and he'd found a clearing that he was sure wasn't there before. They often took this route together, Tristan and his mother, for the village market, and he was sure he'd remember a clearing like this. The grass was flattened in a circle, and a wide-topped stone sat in the middle with an assortment of crystals, candles and bones strewn across the top.

In the middle of this altar, he found a velvet pouch of smooth stones covered in angular runic letters.

He'd felt the same pull a few other times in his life. When his mother fell from a hayloft, the pull told him where to find her. The first time he thought himself in love, the pull showed him why he shouldn't be. It had even saved him from an untimely end himself a few times. But . . . when he finally died, he discovered the pull was a sin. The Power wasn't for the likes of him to use.

Well, no one ever explained that to a six-year-old.

He hadn't felt the pull for a long, long time. Not since the MINOS agents who condemned him to the Narrows twisted his neck, forcing him to spend the rest of existence walking forwards and looking back. Not since he'd been locked in a silver cage, only released when it was his turn to be tortured in one of the many, many pits down here.

But today, today he felt it.

Tristan's cage was bare, except for a dark wood desk and matching chair in the middle. All new entrants to the Narrows were offered one piece of furniture; most souls opted for a bed or a wide couch, but Tristan had asked for a desk. He was seated in the chair, his elbows resting on the desk and his eyes gazing out directly behind him, vacant. He sat like this a lot; there wasn't *much* else to do between torturings, after all, and for some reason he hadn't had one of those for . . . a while.

Hmm.

Tristan blinked slowly, letting this knowledge sink in.

Now, why hadn't he been sent to a pit recently? He couldn't say 'why not today', because the Narrows were an abyss within the Abyss, dark and tedious; there was no way to know where one day ended and another began. But after a good couple of centuries in there, Hellish time had made its mark on Tristan and he *knew* something was off about his routine.

And yes, perhaps the thieves in the next cages over were simply relieved their punishment had been delayed. Surely the fraudsters were crossing their fingers and hoping whatever had caused the postponement of more agony would long continue, but Tristan couldn't make himself take that view.

He stood up and walked his legs backwards until his face and spine were pressed up against the bars. He swivelled his eyes around as far as his vision would permit. There was not a demon in sight. Peculiar.

That's when the pull came for him, still by his belly button, as though Fate herself gripped tight on a birth cord he no longer had.

The pull was strong. It dragged him back to the desk and sat him down, sending an arm into the secret drawer he had carved long ago, the secret drawer where he hid his illicit tarot deck.

She's coming, someone whispered in his ear.

'Who?'

Jenny.

31

JENNY

It was too late for Jenny to rescue the cloak; the bus was already rolling away. They were in the desert. And it was not called the Burning Sands for nothing.

Her jeans and polo shirt were already damp from sweat. Her face was wet too, and she was once more struck with gratitude that she no longer needed glasses – because God only knew how steamy and gross they'd be right now. Her shoes – which had held up *so well* up until now – were falling apart as the glue holding the plastic together started to melt.

'Zillah, I can't . . .'

'Dump them, then.'

'But . . .'

But the Succubus was in no mood to tarry. 'We have three more circles to get through, and this place is crawling with wild helldogs. *Move.*'

So she slid the melting plastic off her burnt, blistered toes and tried to keep her whimpers to a minimum as the skin on the delicate soles of her feet met the scorching sand of the desert.

'Look,' Zillah said, 'if you push your feet under the sand and sort of wade, it'll be cooler.'

It was! The relief sent endorphins zipping through her as they trailed across the desert.

'What's a helldog? And what happens next?' she asked.

'Helldogs – pretty much all in the name. Next – we jump off a cliff.'

Apparently, and horrifyingly, Zillah did not seem to be joking.

'We jump off . . . what? Why?'

The Succubus squinted into the blinding vastness of the desert.

'Because the alternative is hanging around here for ever? The cliff's called Dragonwater. Fastest way down to the next circle, if you can avoid the reptiles crawling around the edge. You'll know it when you see it.'

From her clipped sentences, Jenny knew Zillah wasn't as unaffected by the desert heat as she pretended – which was a) a relief, given that it meant she wasn't entirely made of granite, and b) unsurprising, really, given she was still head to toe in all-black leather.

For once, Jenny wasn't worried about how to escape her captor. What would be the point of running away now, even if she could? She'd only end up lost, skin slowly roasting until she died of thirst. Or by helldog.

The sand shifted from yellow to white. And then, after what felt like a hundred years, Jenny heard the sound of water. Running water – or *falling* water, tonnes of it. She waded as fast as she could, her parched throat and skin homing in on the promise of cool, of wet, of not-desert.

But the thing is, it wasn't water at all. It was more sand.

The cliff edge was sharper than the one she'd stood on in Limbo with Luc. God, didn't that feel for ever ago, now? A pang shot through her. *Luc.* Lying scum. *Handsome* lying scum. Who had been going to kiss her in that awful motel room if they hadn't been interrupted, she just knew it, and if . . .

. . . if nothing. Luc wasn't here, liar or not, and she was with Zillah, at the top of a sheer cliff where several tonnes of sand cascaded over the edge every second with an orchestral crash that drowned out all other sound.

Zillah tapped her shoulder and mimed jumping.

I can't, Jenny mouthed.

Fear was an animal in the cage of her body, and it wanted out. Specifically, through her belly button, if the tugging sensation behind it was any indication.

You have to. Zillah's face was determined.

Something dark scuttled in the corner of Jenny's eye. Her head turned, and she watched as a crocodile-shaped creature vanished over the edge nearby.

That didn't help.

Come on, she coaxed herself. *You can handle this.*

Turned out she could handle a lot more than she ever

gave herself credit for. Deep breath (hot, lung-scorching in the desert heat). Just a step forward. That's all it took.

And then she was over the edge.

If she were a Pixar character, she might feel like she was flying. As it was, Jenny knew for a goddamn fact she was falling. She also strongly suspected she might die.

For a place with no weather, the wind picking up around her was impressive. It screamed through her, sounding suspiciously like her mother. *Huh*. That would be her own version of Hell.

Mercifully, she'd had the wherewithal to close her eyes as she jumped. She couldn't imagine opening them now; she much preferred being one with the sand, grains of which she felt blasting open the skin on her cheeks, her neck, anywhere that wasn't covered in a dirty school uniform. She much preferred not watching the ground come up to meet her. She opened her mouth and screamed.

And then, impossibly, she was underwater. The sand had . . . changed? As she fell. She sliced through the surface with the force of a cleaver through a breastbone. The shift in physics jarred, her pancreas floated up by her throat.

Everything slowed. She felt the water, soaking into her jeans and polo shirt, cool against her skin. It stung the cuts in her face from the sand. She opened her eyes, and saw everything in shades of green. She continued downwards, sinking further into the water, but for some reason this didn't worry her as much as it probably should have. Her body slowly righted itself, and it was as though the cool green surrounding her washed away every ache and pain from her journey so far. *Magic.* The bottom of the lake rose up, a puddle of silver coins carpeting the floor. There was a ledge to her left; she aimed for this and landed.

As soon as her feet touched the ledge, the water receded. She was on dry land again, dry as a bone and mercifully cool. The crocodile she'd seen at the top of the cliff scurried off into the distance.

She laughed. It felt good, so she did it some more, spinning around in a circle, ignoring everything except the relief that coursed through every atom of her body. She was alive! Even the void where her soul should be rejoiced.

She stopped spinning, out of breath and delirious, putting her hands on her thighs to help her catch back up with herself.

'Glad you've cheered up,' Zillah sniffed from behind her. 'The surly moping act was getting tedious.'

Which was rich, coming from her.

32

JENNY

Her good mood didn't last long. Beyond Dragonwater the landscape was arid, although at least cooler than the horror of the Burning Sands.

'What horrendous nightmare comes next?' she asked Zillah, as conversationally as she dared.

'We have to cross the Narrows,' her captor replied.

'And what, pray tell, are the Narrows when they're at home?'

'Nothing to get excited about,' Zillah sniffed. 'Look.'

Jenny looked where Zillah pointed, and her heart sank.

'What is it with this place and deadly voids into nothingness?'

Because that's what the Narrows looked like, to Jenny. At this point, she was barely even surprised. It was a senselessly wide, circular pit, dug even deeper into the downward-sloping hill of the Abyss.

'Hey, at least this time we've got bridges.'

'Bridges' was, as far as Jenny was concerned, an overstatement. The one Zillah apparently wanted her to use was so slender they would have to cross it single file, built from chalky, white objects that might have been stones but equally could have been kneecaps, bleached in the heat of the Burning Sands before being shipped down Dragonwater to whatever the Hell this place was. This bridge was one of several arcing over the pit, segmenting it like a chocolate orange. They met in the middle in a circular stone plaza Jenny could only just make out, so wide was the hole. The plaza sat atop a huge, bone-white column that descended into the depths, and which also appeared to be the only thing holding the bridges up.

At the edge of the canyon, dirt crumbled under Jenny's bare toes as she looked out towards the plaza.

'This cannot be safe.'

Zillah shrugged. 'Some of them are a bit crumbly, I guess. That's why you need an old hand to guide you across.'

'Can I remind you I don't even want to be here?'

'You can remind me as much as you like, doesn't make a difference unless you want me to murder your cousins and send them into these very ditches.'

She was so . . . matter-of-fact. And she'd absolutely nailed the best way to get Jenny to behave. *Cow.*

'What happens down there, anyway?' Jenny said, gesturing into the pit.

Zillah shrugged. 'Oh, you know.'

Jenny did not know.

'Much wailing, gnashing of teeth.'

'What?'

'Torture, Jenny. I mean torture.'

Perhaps she should have guessed.

It was a vast space, and as she followed Zillah on to the slender bridge nearest them, she couldn't help wondering at the sheer scale of it.

'How many souls are down there?'

Just ahead, Zillah shrugged. 'Loads.' Then, 'Concentrate, all right? Try to put your feet where I put mine. Some of these stones are loose, and if you trip over the edge, I can't guarantee you'll have a soft landing, but I can guarantee you a pit of vipers.'

Great.

Thankfully, they made it to the central plaza without any drama, for which Jenny was grateful. The plaza at least felt solid beneath her feet, but they'd have to do it all over again on one of the other fragile bridges if they were to get fully across. Jenny risked a glance into the bowels of the Narrows. It was a long way down. She could see what she assumed were the viper pits Zillah had mentioned – dark, rectangular patches dug out in neat rows, interspersed with silvery squares. Very orderly. And quiet. Too quiet, somehow? She'd expected a mass of souls and demons, moving like ants at this distance.

'Where is everyone?' she asked.

Zillah shrugged. 'Busy. Pyro's got big plans later today,

don't you know.'

Jenny's unease from earlier came back, heavy. *Right. Plans.*

The silvery squares were, she realized, cages. There were so *many* of them. She leant further forward to see them more clearly, her curiosity getting the best of her. How could people – *former* people, anyway – how could they exist in there?

She must have leant too far. One second she was angling her head to try to see the sides of one of the cages, and the next she heard Zillah yell, 'Jenny, no!' before her weight tipped her balance, and she spilt over the edge.

Before she could fall, strong hands with sharp nails dug into her arms.

'No . . . you . . . don't,' Zillah grunted, as Jenny hung in mid-air, her back to her saviour.

She dangled over the pit, her heart defying gravity in her throat, preventing her from speaking. Zillah planted her feet squarely on the precipice to get a better grip. She released a sharp curse and pulled, and relief fizzed through Jenny as she felt herself pulled up, backwards.

Another lucky escape!

But then the arm of her polo shirt snagged on a protruding stone. She felt it happen – the stone dragged painfully down the soft flesh on her upper arm as Zillah pulled. She yelped, trying to warn Zillah, but instead she heard a surprised squawk . . .

Then they both fell.

Jenny bounced on impact.

A sickening pain flared in the region of her ribs and Zillah's hands no longer held her. She tried to roll on to her back and realized she was halfway in one of the ditches she'd seen from above. All damp, black soil and . . . what was that? She snapped her head around as something coiled around her ankle and tugged. Was it a creature of some kind? It looked like smoke, shifting in and out of focus, but there was a snakelike strength in it as it wound itself up her leg. *Pit viper.* She brought her other leg against it sharply and the snake let go, but not before lunging, sinking teeth into her thigh.

She yelled in pain as she hauled herself out of the pit. The pain in her ribs was white behind her eyes, but she was buggered if she was letting a gang of smoke-snakes fang her to death.

Dizzy, she backed up until she was supported by the bottom of the large stone column.

'Jenny!'

She looked down at the pit she'd almost fallen into. Zillah was in there, lying flat on her back in the middle, eyes wide and staring.

'Help me.'

Jenny frowned, confused, until she saw a thick, smoky coil of snake wrapped firmly around Zillah's waist.

Oh, crap.

'Get up,' Jenny told Zillah firmly. 'Climb out.'

'I can't *move*,' Zillah pleaded. 'I'm serious . . . I think I've broken something.'

Jenny stared in horror as another of the snakes slithered

across Zillah's left leg, coiling around her calf possessively.

'You're a *demon*,' Jenny yelled, 'surely they can't hurt you!'

'Oh, they can.'

Jenny hesitated, then cast around for . . . something. A weapon, something to beat the snakes off with. There was nothing.

In the middle of the pit, a silvery tear rolled out of Zillah's eye.

'Sod it,' Jenny muttered. She huffed, ignoring the pain in her ribs as she sat down on the edge of the ditch.

'Wait!' Zillah yelled. 'You . . . you can't come in here.'

'Do you want my help or not?' Jenny snapped, beginning her shuffle again.

'*No*,' Zillah said. 'Yes! I mean . . . Pyro needs you alive.' Something like a sob fell from her mouth.

Jenny had a few ideas of how to respond to that, but one of the snakes wrapped tighter on Zillah's calf, so she bit them all back. Another snake eyed Jenny covetously, too close to the edge for comfort. She hesitated.

Zillah shivered visibly. A viper coiled on her belly, rising up and swaying, eyes on Zillah's face.

'Zillah?' Jenny called, uncertainly. 'What should I do?'

'Just go,' Zillah whispered.

It was tempting. No Zillah, no being forced onward to the Ninth Circle. No human sacrifice for Lucifer, no spilling over of Hell into Earth . . . but what kind of person would that make her?

'No! I can't *leave* you here, Zillah!'

'You have to.' She was speaking so quietly now; Jenny could barely hear her. Could barely see her face, through the smoky pillar of the snake's neck.

'Go!'

The force of her shout seemed to anger the snake. It hissed.

Jenny squeezed her eyes closed and swallowed down the tight feeling in her throat. She took a step away from the pit, trying not to listen to the sound of hissing and rattling that steadily increased in pitch.

Zillah screamed, and then just as suddenly, she stopped.

Jenny wiped her eyes. Kept walking. Looking for a way out.

There really didn't seem to be any demons around, except for the one she'd just left in the snake pit. Which was a relief. It meant she could stop sneaking about in the shadows, for one thing, which was just as well seeing as she had no idea where she was going. She headed for the silver cages, hoping to find someone human. Or human*ish*, at least.

The first cage was empty, which felt ominous. Where was the soul, if not in the cage?

She kept going until she found one that was occupied. It reminded her of a cartoon cage with a lion in it – except in this case the lion was a man, medium build, sandy-blond hair, seated at the only furniture in the space: a heavy, antique wooden desk. The desk faced her, and there was something odd about how straight he sat. His eyes were closed, but when Jenny drew near, they cracked open. He didn't seem surprised to see her.

'You made it, then,' he said.

'What?' She swallowed. The hairs on her arms spiked.

'Don't panic, I'm about to get up.'

'Why would I . . .'

Then he stood, and Jenny blinked rapidly, trying to make her brain understand – he was backwards. Well, his head was, at least – he stood up without pushing the stool away from the desk because he had sat down with his knees facing *away* from the desk – but his face was still intent on Jenny.

'I'm a Seer,' he told her. 'As in, I see the future. It's why I'm here – and it's how I knew you would be.'

He walked . . . backwards, until he was directly on the other side of the cage bars from her. His eyes were brown, sympathetic, human. Aside from the fact his neck had been twisted out of all natural shape, he could have been a stranger in front of her in a queue, or a supply teacher.

Her eyes snagged on his neck – deep, red welts from where his head had been twisted around and resituated above his shoulder blades.

'Does that hurt?' she asked quietly.

The Seer shrugged. 'Not any more. It's really an allegorical punishment, more about the mental than the physical. I suppose that's why they still have to take me out every so often for a proper torturing in the ditches. You know, just to remind me where I live now.'

He said it lightly, but Jenny could tell it was an effort.

‘I’m so sorry,’ she told him honestly.

‘It’s not your fault, chicken. You’ve enough on your plate without taking on my eternal torment as well.’

‘How do you know that?’ She couldn’t help being impressed, if he knew everything about her without so much as reading her palm or something . . .

‘Sweet girl,’ the man laughed. ‘You’re a living human, trapped in the bottom of a torture pit in the Eighth Circle of All Hell. I’d say that’s a lot, for one plate.’

Hmm. He had a point.

‘Look,’ Jenny said, ‘I need to figure out how—’

‘Now, now,’ he replied quickly. ‘There’s no point asking me *anything* until I’ve got my deck. You will allow me to do a reading for you, right? It’s the quickest way to get to the truth, in this place.’

‘Uh . . . sure.’

The Seer made his way back to his desk. He walked body-forwards, using his arms to feel his way as his eyes were still facing in Jenny’s direction. God, this was weird – it made her stomach clench when she thought about the mechanics of it.

But he didn’t seem concerned.

‘What’s your name?’ she asked.

‘Tristan,’ he replied. ‘And you’re Jenny, yes?’

She swallowed. ‘Yep.’

‘Mm. Thought so.’

Tristan opened one of the desk drawers, pulling out a cloth bag double-knotted at the top, unlaced it and pulled out a deck of cards about the size of a standard playing deck.

'How come they let you keep that?'

'Oh, they don't know I have it,' Tristan replied, unperturbed. 'When you've been here as long as I have, and behave yourself as impeccably as I always do, you somehow become less prone to random cell searches.'

He shuffled the cards – without looking at them, obviously. This was a practised move, because if Jenny had tried to do any such thing, she was sure she would have spilt cards all over the silver floor of the cage. Tristan twisted slightly so he could hand the cards to Jenny.

'Shuffle those for me, please, and think about your question.'

'How do I get home?' she said out loud. She was asking Tristan as much as the cards, but he just watched her shuffle the deck until she handed them back.

He crouched down carefully, sideways on so he could lay the cards out on the floor of his cage and still see Jenny as he did so.

'You're going to have to describe them to me,' he pointed out. 'I can't actually see them, like this.'

She tried. Some of the cards were people, like an old man with a long cloak and a lantern. Others were more like ordinary playing cards, except she wasn't familiar with the suits.

'Uh, there's like, six long sticks?'

'Wands,' Tristan corrected as he frowned in concentration. 'I've had this tarot deck a long time, now. I can sense its whims and foibles . . . and it does *not* like your question, not one bit.'

'What do you mean?' Jenny's heart sank.

'Now,' Tristan grinned up at her, 'not to sound like a cliché or anything, but are you sure you're asking the right question? Only, the deck seems to think you don't actually *have* a home.'

Well, that stung.

'How am I supposed to know?' she snapped. 'I'm not exactly an expert. And I need to get home . . . I mean, out of Hell,' Jenny said. 'I don't have time . . .' She made to move. There had to be a more helpful Seer somewhere down here, didn't there? Christ, she'd take a murderer at this rate if they were handy with a map.

'Wait! I'm sorry. I've been here for *centuries*, in and out of those torture pits . . . I forget what it's like not to have the rest of eternity to play with. Just . . . let's try this one more time, OK?'

'Fine, but make it quick.'

Tristan nodded. 'How about we forget asking questions? I'll just do a general read, all right? It might help.'

Jenny huffed but did as she was told, shuffling the cards, and watching as Tristan made another spread. He flipped over the first column and asked her to describe them. She did so as best she could.

'Well . . .' he said, his voice suddenly low and reverent. 'There's lots to unpack here, chicken.'

'What do you mean?'

'Lots of fire,' he said. 'Wands everywhere! And plenty of Major Arcana too. You see this one?' He pointed directly at it even as his eyes locked with hers, giving her the distinct impression she hadn't needed to describe the cards to him at all.

'Yes?'

'That's the Wheel of Fortune. I'd say it's telling you you're in for a bumpy old ride. Rocks and hard places, frying pans and fires.'

'That sounds about right.'

'Maybe, but combined with all these Wands, too – like I said, there's a lot of fire in this reading – fire everywhere!'

'Well, we are in Hell.'

'Yes,' Tristan agreed slowly, 'and some of it could be Hellfire, but a lot of this is . . . fire that already exists. Inside you. You are . . . impulsive, because you don't always have a clear plan. Wrathful, at times, too.'

She thought about all the times her anger had got the better of her. Starting with hitting Luc, and then Amber.

'Yeah. You could say that.'

'I'm not saying anything – the cards are. And they want me to remind you that fire is an excellent defence. That's what you've tended to use yours for, isn't it? As in, you surround yourself with a wall of fire, so no one with ill intentions will bother to come through. No one can hurt you then, except the fire itself. The problem is, no one else can get through either, leaving you alone in the middle of a blaze and believe me, no one wants to be all alone in a ring of fire, chicken.'

'I suppose not,' Jenny said, thinking, *How is this relevant?*

'But,' Tristan continued, 'fire is not only destruction and chaos. It is determination, too. Strength. Passion, ambition, motivation. Sometimes it frightens people, but you need to *own your fire*. And if it burns you? Well, remember the phoenix: rebirth. The shoots of spring rising through the ground of a razed field.'

She didn't feel very strong, or phoenix-like.

'Any directions in there?' she asked hopefully.

Tristan chuckled. 'No. Although . . . see this card?' He tapped a card of a white-haired woman holding a book and a set of scales.

'This one is telling you to trust yourself. Trust your instincts. That's your best hope of achieving your aims, whatever they may be. So . . . what are your instincts telling you?'

'Listening to my instincts got me into this mess, so we're not on speaking terms.'

'Interesting. Explain?' Something sharpened in his face, like she'd finally caught his attention.

'Isn't that obvious? I trusted the wrong demon, ended up here.'

'Why did you trust a demon?'

A sudden, overwhelming urge to cry ballooned in her chest. She sucked in a breath and held it until the urge went away.

Tristan was still looking at her expectantly.

'I didn't have a choice,' she pointed out. Then she explained: about the fight with her mum, sleeping on Vee's sofa until she *wasn't*, and that feeling, the one she carried around with her at every moment, every minute of every day. The one that whispered to her, *No one wants you. No one likes you. You're a burden, you're useless, you're nothing, nothing, nothing.*

'That's why I punched Amber, really. She knew, she even said it.'

'What a remarkably twatty thing for her to say,' Tristan observed mildly. 'Sounds to me like a punch to the nose was least of the punishment she deserved.'

'Yeah, well. I didn't do it to punish her. I did it because it felt like . . . I'd been found out. And then I heard Charlie and Vee fighting over how long I was staying there, and, like, that was it. The last safe place I had, and even then, I wasn't safe, I had nowhere else to turn, so I turned to a bloody demon, and . . .'

And she didn't feel like nothing when she was with Luc. It hit her then, like a tonne of Dragonwater raining from the desert above. She didn't feel unwanted, with Luc. Not once. He listened to her, told her she mattered – enough for it to be worth getting her soul back.

'It was a lie, though,' she said. 'Hence the whole not being able to trust my instincts thing.'

'Are you sure it was a lie?'

She frowned at the Seer through the bars of his cage. He was slowly shuffling the cards as they spoke, rhythmically splicing and folding them into each other as though he hadn't just said something outrageous.

'Yes. He never wanted to help me; he was working for his father.'

'Hmm. Well, what do I know, I'm only a Seer. But those cards . . . they really didn't want you to go home, chicken. That was *not* the right question.'

'And what is?' Jenny snapped back. 'How do I find the demon boy who pretended to like me and brought me into Hell in the first place?'

One of the cards fell out of Tristan's hands, landing face up on the floor of the cage.

'That,' Tristan told her, 'is the World card. And in this context, I think it means "yes, that *is* the right question".'

33

JENNY

'*Trust your instincts', indeed.* Her *instincts* were telling her to do anything except what she was about to, which was to put one foot in front of the other and try not to panic as the metal door Tristan had directed her to slammed closed leaving her in darkness, groping for the walls and trying not to take a tumble to the bottom of the stairs that appeared beneath her feet, leading down. Turned out he *did* know a way out, but only one that took her further away from the Hellmouth and home.

The whole time she descended from the Eighth Circle, she was furious. Furious with Tristan, for suggesting she should go looking for Luc. Furious with Luc, for highly obvious reasons. And furious with herself, because despite everything, there was a spark of something bright and hopeful flickering somewhere behind her aching ribs when she thought about seeing him again.

When she reached the bottom of the stairs, her legs were on fire, and her ribs throbbed heavily where she'd landed on them. No doubt bruised at the very least. A patch of thigh, where the smoke-snake had bitten her, throbbed.

All evidence she was still alive, at least.

She had expected to emerge from this Hellish fire exit and still be very much underground; after all, hadn't she fallen to the bottom of the pit to get here? But to her surprise, she walked out into a field, very much like the one she'd met the Uncommitted in, except that in the middle of this one was an old well, with a rusted, orange ladder hanging over the side, leading downwards. She walked towards it cautiously, sure she was about to be accosted by demons or something, but as always, all was still. It seemed Pyro's 'plan' involved a total dereliction of demonic duty, and Jenny for one was not inclined to complain, even though a tiny voice suggested it was a *bit* odd she hadn't run into a single demon since getting off that bus.

Behind her, the walls of the pit rose like a sheer cliff, but everywhere else there was just more endless blank, nothing except for the crumbling well and a small wooden plaque tacked on its lip. Nowhere for a human, or demon, to hide.

There was a tree, though.

It stood alone in the field, short and bent, like a person in pain. She pressed both her hands against its fleshy bark and felt that burr of green shoots in her mind.

CLIMB UP AND SIT IN MY BOUGHS, the tree suggested. REST.

Gratefully, she did as she was told, and once she was settled the tree creaked as it stretched a far branch closer. A small, wizened, leathery fruit grew alone, and the tree offered it to her.

'Thank you,' she whispered, her hand flat on the wood.

EAT, the tree suggested. YOU WILL NEED YOUR STRENGTH IF YOU ARE TO GET HOME FROM HERE.

She patted a nearby branch affectionately, then dug her thumbs into the flesh of the fruit. A spray of red juice squirted across her polo shirt, but honestly, what did it even matter any more? The clothes were ruined, her feet were bare and filthy, and when she shifted on the tree and felt something digging into her hip, she pulled out her phone from her front jeans pocket. Smashed to bits, which wasn't exactly surprising.

'Turns out I might not be headed home just yet,' she told the tree conversationally.

WHAT DO YOU MEAN?

She told them what Tristan had said, and the World card jumping out of his tarot deck.

'I don't know what to think,' she said when she was done with the story. 'Like, why would I go looking for Luc? Surely that's just putting myself in more danger? Then again, I have no idea how to get back. How does one even attempt to scale the Narrows, let alone Dragonwater? Oh,

God, I don't know if I could find my way back across that desert . . .'

There was a pause that sounded like leaves rustling.

WE KNOW WHERE THE DEMON BOY IS.

'You do?' That bright spark flared inside her.

Instead of replying, the tree pushed an image into her mind. It was a map, except the background was black and all the criss-crossing lines were golden threads. *No*, she realized with a jolt, *not a map – a network.* These were the roots of the tree, beneath the soil, connecting each tree to all the others of their kind, no matter where they were planted.

CLOSE YOUR EYES.

She did as she was told, and her world tilted under the soil.

The golden, rooted network called to her.

She floated down to it, towards the sparks of light fizzing beneath the ground, and gave herself over to them. She was in this network now, part of this vast web of connection, equally as close to the tree she had her hand on as to trees many miles away, ones that weren't growing next to a portal to Hell, but were already there, lining the banks of sweeping rivers, or burning in Hellish deserts.

One of the sparks of light was brighter, calling out louder than the others, so she followed it, her consciousness zipping through the roots. Once she found it, she latched on. A new sensation rolled through her, like she was being siphoned upwards, out of the soil and into this new tree.

This tree was planted somewhere cold and inhospitable.

She shivered within the bark. There was a lake in front of her, at enough of a distance that she could see the scale of it, a giant expanse of still, smooth, black water. She swept her eyes across the banks, searching for its source, and then she found them: two thin streams close together. She followed them with her eyes too and found the foot of a mountain.

It was lovely. Peaceful. Stars high above sent sparkling, wavering lights that glinted on the silk-still surface of the water. Were they stars? Their light was too yellow for that, but they behaved like stars, except for the way they quivered like candle flames.

And as she noticed this, she wondered – was it peace she was feeling?

No, it was something else, something just as still and quiet but also somehow less. The resignation of lying on a sofa in a dark house with your aunt and cousins asleep upstairs, knowing that this is your life now – no home of your own, rapidly running out of family and friends in the wake of a thousand burning bridges. You can grieve for the life you could have had, but what's the point? It's done. You said those things. You made your choices. And in the end, this is where they bring you: a lake that smells like tears, in the deepest, coldest part of All Hell, where golden wax stars glisten, reflected in the black water.

And there, chained to the tree by a slender thread of glittering silver, was Luc.

'He's trapped,' Jenny murmured as her heart contracted.

He looked *miserable*, sitting cross-legged in the snow

with his head in his hands. His watch glinted, refracting the bright snow back at itself. She could hardly believe this was the same charismatic boy who'd almost kissed her in a motel in the Second Circle, but it was, and her chest ached more than her ribs.

'Why is he chained up like that?'

WE DO NOT CLAIM TO UNDERSTAND.

But she already knew the answer anyway. *Pyro, obviously.* Luc had failed him, so he'd decided to chain his own son to a tree in the coldest part of All Hell as punishment. Well, at least Luc hadn't lied about his dad being a total dickhead, then.

She opened her eyes, and the connection with the tree Luc was chained to broke. She stared hard at the well with the rusted ladder, below the boughs of the tree she'd climbed.

WHAT WILL YOU DO?

She wasn't sure. Except, she *was*. Instinctively, anyway.

Her Auntie Vee once told her she 'abandoned ship' when things got hard. *Maybe that was true*, Jenny thought. Maybe she was always looking for the easy way out, the safest route. And what good had that done her? She had no home, no friends, no idea what she was supposed to do with herself in the next five minutes, let alone the next five years.

So, maybe it was time she stopped doing that?

She raised her hand and placed it back against the tree bark. The trees heard her decision immediately, before she even spoke.

She was going down. To the bottom of the funnel. To Luc.

She sucked in a deep breath and climbed down the tree, before walking over to the well. She reached out and gripped one side of the rusty ladder. It was icy, cold enough that she flinched her hand away and swore under her breath.

But there was snow when she saw Luc, wasn't there? So this was the right way.

She swallowed, reached out again, ignoring the way her hands recoiled at the feel of the freezing metal under her skin. She manoeuvred herself carefully over the lip of the well, trying to pretend her whole body wasn't protesting.

Her hands stung on the metal ladder. Her ribs burnt, white-hot under her polo shirt as she twisted herself down. Her bare feet froze when they touched the rungs. But, despite looking rickety with rust, the ladder was sturdy under her grip, which was reassuring, all things considered, and at this stage in the game, Jenny decided to take the good where she could get it.

So she climbed down the well, into the dark.

The cold intensified as she moved down the ladder. Before she knew it, goosebumps covered her body and every move she made came with a shiver, rolling across her skin. Her school uniform was no match for the freezing temperatures, and she worried vaguely that she might step on a rung to discover her flesh had fused to it with the cold.

Luckily, that didn't happen. Instead, by the time she

found the bottom of the well, her feet were totally numb, and her hands weren't far off. She wrapped her arms around herself and shoved her hands under her armpits, trying to ward off the icy shivers still rolling through her with every foggy breath that left her.

You can do it, she told herself again. *You have to.* Because apparently, *this* was what her instincts wanted. It was all jumbled in her head: it was Luc, but it was more than that too. It was destiny, even if she'd never believed in that before. It was a Rube Goldberg machine, and she was a ball being rattled and juddered along a bizarre pathway, where all routes led, apparently, to one Lucifer or another.

You have no choice. But she did. Of course she did. There was a signpost up ahead, with five cracked wooden arrows hanging from it. CAINA, said one. ANTENORA. PTOLOMEA. ISCARIA. And then – LAKE OF LAMENT. In small letters underneath, it said MOUNT LUCIFER. She shivered, stamped her feet (which achieved nothing except drawing her attention to the fact they were turning blue) and set off in the direction of the Lake of Lament, and Mount Lucifer.

She chose that route, that fate.

After a while, she stopped noticing the cold so much. She still shivered, but now it felt separate from her actual sense of the cold. *Good.* It made it easier for her to press on, head down, against the wind, which blew a gale, like strong arms pushing her back. The cold brought ice with it too, hail that came at her horizontally.

She was moving too slowly. She knew this, dimly, but it was like the cold had seeped in under the thin fabric of her clothes and was holding her close, weighing her down.

There were shapes around her, in the distance – some almost human, but she might have been hallucinating. She nodded to trees as she passed, just in case they were really there, and in the distance, she thought she could see something else too, something shining. Was that real, or a snowy mirage? She made for it anyway – and as she stepped off the path, the hail fell away like curtains.

Jenny stepped out on to a still carpet of snow. She was at the banks of the Lake of Lament. She had made it.

Her head was fuzzy; like there was a dark, velvety scarf inside her mind, blinkering the edges of her vision and making it difficult to think. She wasn't shivering any more, which was nice, but it took effort to swing her head right, left, trying to orient herself in this environment now she was here.

There was the lake, majestic and still. There were the twin streams feeding into it – and there, at the foot of the mountain, the tree she had projected into earlier, the silver chain, and Luc.

He didn't see her approach, still sitting with his arms wrapped around his knees, his head balanced on his forearms.

She wanted to call out but couldn't find the energy. Instead, she dropped down on her knees, just a few feet away from him. Oh, that was more comfortable by far.

'Jenny!' Luc gasped, the sound of her soft landing on

the snow alerting him to her presence. He scrambled towards her until the chains snagged him back. 'What are you doing here? Oh, crap, you're hypothermic.'

She tried to smile, shook her head. She wasn't hypothermic! She was, if anything, *warm*, enough that she thought it might actually be a nice idea to take her jeans off. Maybe jump in that nice lake. No herons there. No floaty glow-fishies.

She tried to tug at the button on her jeans, but her limbs felt too heavy. The velvet scarf in her head grew thicker. Things were a bit difficult to see, now. Should she be worried about that? Weirdly, she wasn't.

In front of her, she watched, puzzled, as Luc leapt to his feet, pulling urgently at the chains around his wrists. He was fuzzy at the edges, soft-focus, glowing. He was talking to her; at least, she thought he was, although the words were muddy and distant. What was he saying? Something like, 'you can't die'.

But who was dying? Only Zillah was dead. She started to giggle. That wasn't funny. Nothing about this was even remotely amusing.

Luc's eyes shuttered closed. Her field of vision was narrow now, tunnelled in on his face. On the way his lips moved. Luc had a nice mouth, didn't he? And that was funny, too. And it was even funnier – although she couldn't have explained why – when Luc's eyes snapped open and dropped to look at something Jenny couldn't see. She felt something warm nearby, something that wasn't there a moment ago, and Luc's eyes were wide, that pretty, funny mouth moving again, and laughter bubbled out of her even as the ringing in her ears took hold of her entire body.

She didn't stop giggling until she passed out.

34

JENNY

She woke up warm, with what sounded like a fire crackling somewhere near her head.

Where am I?

She ached, limbs heavy, and when she cracked one eye open to take in the sight of a small bonfire, her memory was still scrambled.

She sat up, groggy, and frowned. Why was she asleep, outside, with no shoes on?

Oh. She remembered.

She lay on a patch of damp, yellow grass, muddy from where it had been covered in snow until the heat of the bonfire melted it away. She moved her head slowly to Luc, who was still chained up, still straining towards her.

'Are you all right?' he croaked. She didn't know how long he'd been there, waiting for her to come around, but she felt a sudden flush of warmth towards him. Here he was, trapped in unbreakable silver chains, and he still cared if she was all right.

'I'm OK,' she said, even though that was probably only half true. She felt dizzy, nauseous, but still she hauled herself to her feet and tottered closer to him.

'I thought you were dead,' he whispered. 'I don't know what I'd have done, if . . .'

Jenny smiled, opened her arms, and hugged him.

'I'm OK. Really.'

'What are you *doing* here?' Luc asked. He couldn't hug her back, not with the chains, but she felt his head rest on her shoulder and couldn't stop the warmth that spread through her.

'Well,' she said, stepping back to look at him, 'after you left me in that tree, I got all the way back to the Uncommitted, where I was nearly eaten by a gang of wind-whipped monsters . . .'

'Oh, no.'

'Until a Succubus rescued me. Except it wasn't a rescue, it was Zillah.'

Luc's face dropped.

Jenny continued. 'But then we fell into a pit of vipers at the bottom of the Narrows and only one of us made it out, so . . .' She swallowed. Her stomach knotted, and a bone-deep suspicion that she could have done more took hold. 'She told me to go,' she gasped. 'But I can't believe I left her.'

Luc reached for her – or tried to, but he was too close

to the end of his chains. She sidestepped him anyway. This was important. She needed him to understand.

'I met a backwards man with a deck of cards,' she said. 'And the cards told me I couldn't go home. Actually, they said I don't have a home to go to. Or . . .' A thought gripped her, suddenly. 'Maybe they were telling me I *wouldn't* have a home to go to, if I gave up now.' She paused. 'He won't give up, will he? Your dad, I mean. If he fails now, he's just going to keep looking for another way to wake up Lucifer, or to take over Earth.'

Luc opened his mouth to answer, but nothing came out. Instead, Jenny heard what sounded like a twig snap behind her and watched as Luc's eyes widened. She swallowed, fear squeezing her stomach, and turned around. Slowly.

Luc stood about twenty feet away.

Wait . . .

It wasn't Luc – of course it wasn't. This man was older, his hair a few shades lighter, faint lines visible around his eyes, the corners of his mouth. But otherwise, Seth Pyro was identical to his son.

'Well, isn't this charming?' Pyro said. His voice was light, mocking, and when he blinked, his eyes flashed black. He wore a suit that reminded Jenny of guns and armoured vehicles, and when he smiled, she was surprised to see his teeth weren't sharp like Luc's, but neat and even in a way only expensive dentistry can achieve.

Somehow, this was more unsettling than Luc's wolfish grin.

But if he wanted to intimidate her, well, that would only work if she let it, wouldn't it?

She inhaled through her nose, trying to hide the deep suck of air she needed to be brave, straightened her spine and stepped forward, one hand outstretched.

'You must be Mr Pyro,' she said, brightly.

Luc's father stared at her outstretched hand with something approaching disgust. His own hand remained resolutely at his side, which was just *rude*. She withdrew her hand after a few tense seconds, maintaining the bright, plastic smile on her face.

'I'm Jenny,' she said, as though she hadn't noticed the tension.

'I'm well aware,' Pyro told her, cocking one eyebrow in an expression so reminiscent of Luc she had to stop herself from laughing. This was *surreal*.

'Ah, yes,' Jenny agreed. 'You *would* know who I am – I forgot, I'm sorry. We've already met. You're the prick who stole my soul.'

A small gasp sounded behind her, but she ignored Luc's shock. Instead, she kept her gaze focused on Pyro, determined to show him she wasn't a pushover. Determined to hide the knives of fear stabbing at her heart.

Her words hung in the air for a moment, two, three, and then Pyro's face cracked into a smile.

'There were those who claimed a child can't survive without their soul, you know.'

He said this conversationally, as though it was neither here nor there to him.

'Apparently, all it does is make one tenacious . . . and annoying.'

Jenny grinned. 'Maybe I'd have been both those things anyway.'

'Maybe. I am impressed you managed to get here, all by yourself. No thanks, I understand, to that . . . *disappointing* Succubus. Where is Zillah, by the way? Her mother will want to see her, no doubt.'

Pyro gestured behind him and for the first time Jenny looked past him, to the Lake of Lament.

There they are, she thought.

The lake was full of demons. How many, she couldn't fathom – it seemed like every demon in All Hell had gathered here, for this. They were on boats, so many that the enormity of the lake was made entirely apparent. Standing at the prow of a narrow, intricately carved boat towards the front was a tall woman with deep, earthy skin and shiny black hair coiled up on her head. Her face was familiar, and she stood with six younger women. Zillah's mother, and Zillah's sisters, including Alyssa.

None of the demons moved, or spoke; they just stood there, an endless sea of horror.

An army, her brain unhelpfully offered up.

She realized she hadn't answered Pyro's question.

'I don't know where she is,' she lied. 'Why should I?'

Pyro's mouth twitched, and she had a feeling he could tell she wasn't being truthful. Her smile had fallen from her face, and now she fought the urge to turn on her heel and run.

She couldn't do that. Not after *all this*. Besides, what were her chances of escape now, with a whole horde of demons just waiting for instructions?

Apparently, though, Pyro didn't actually care about his Succubus spy. He let his eyes rove over Jenny as though seeking some clue as to the puzzle she represented, and when he spoke, his voice was like silk.

'Have you enjoyed your little trip through my domain, Miss Hall?'

'Er, sure. I mean, the hospitality could be improved, and you could do with some more tourist information points, but on the whole . . . I'd give it a solid two out of five.'

'And what about the cuisine?'

Jenny stared at the demon blankly.

Pyro tilted his head to one side. 'I notice, by the way, you no longer need glasses. That must be convenient.'

Jenny frowned. Where was this chat headed?

'You know, there's a lot of rumour relating to our little corner of Creation. For example, some of the older demons, the Original Fallen Angels, claim that humans should *never* eat food grown in All Hell. They claim it has all sorts of repercussions; it can even change a person, physically.'

Jenny tried to calm the erratic beating of her heart. Hadn't Luc said something about growing horns, once? She pushed down the urge to rub at her forehead.

'I imagine,' Pyro continued, 'it would be particularly difficult to ward off some of those consequences, should one also be without their soul. After all, the soul is one of the only things guarding most humans from becoming like us.'

Jenny's hands balled into fists at her sides.

Pyro smiled, nastily. 'Demons don't have poor eyesight, either.'

'I am *not* like you,' Jenny snapped, no longer able to keep her anger down.

'Not yet,' Pyro agreed. 'But I don't think it's far off, do you? I mean, could an ordinary human really handle the heat of the Burning Sands? A catastrophic fall from the top of the Narrows? A bite from a pit viper? Not to mention the cold of the Ninth Circle. Where, incidentally, did you get that fire from?'

Jenny glanced behind her, where the bonfire was banking down. She risked a glance in Luc's direction, because hadn't she seen . . . something, before she passed out? But he shook his head, just once, his expression stricken.

'I don't know,' Jenny said. Her voice sounded very, very quiet.

'Don't feel bad.' Pyro sounded almost sympathetic. 'Most demons have the capacity to save their own lives in a pinch. But if you've developed the ability to conjure Hellfire, I'm afraid you're already halfway to demonhood. You've certainly more demonic ability than my son has.'

Jenny bit back the whimper in her throat. She didn't want to be a demon!

'I can help,' Pyro said gently.

'How?'

Luc broke in from behind her, 'Jenny, don't listen to him.'

Pyro snapped, 'Quiet, boy. I'll deal with you later.'

To Jenny, he said, 'It's really very simple. The reason you're in danger of becoming a demon is because there's a space inside you, where your soul should be. How about I fill that space up for you?'

'I can have my soul back?'

'Regrettably, no,' Pyro admitted, in a tone that didn't sound exactly regretful. 'However, I could offer you something of a trade.'

'Jenny, he's trying to—'

'Shut *up*, Luc.' He lifted a hand and a bolt of energy pulsed out, slamming into Luc, and sending him staggering back, clutching his stomach.

Pyro sniffed, as though he hadn't just gut-punched his own child.

'Well?' he asked Jenny. 'What do you think?'

'I think you might be high right now,' Jenny suggested, tartly.

'Oh, chance would be a *fine* thing,' Pyro told her calmly. 'Unfortunately, when one is tasked with such a monumental responsibility as liberating your kind from an unjust incarceration in what is, frankly, a giant hole in the fabric of all Creation, then there just isn't time in the day for recreational drug use.'

'Funny.' She didn't believe him, obviously. Everything about this creature screamed ambition, and she could not reconcile that with this 'I'm so noble, freeing my people' act he had going, which she suspected was for the benefit of the watching demons anyway. Why else had his voice suddenly risen, as though performing for this assembled audience?

'Now, since we've established I am of sober disposition, allow me to put it to you another way. I need you to climb the mountain behind you and wake up my father. He's been asleep for, oh, quite some time now, and I rather think it's time he took charge of his people. If you can do this for me, you'll find that little soul problem you've been having is no longer an issue.'

'I think I'm going to have to say no, on that,' Jenny replied.

'Oh.' Pyro winced. 'That is upsetting news. More for you, in truth, than for me, because the thing is . . . I've been planning this for more than ten of your human years. Time moves more slowly here than it does for you, of course, so you must understand that I've put a lot of energy into this, and I don't intend it to fail.'

Jenny tried to speak again, but Pyro cut her off.

'Have you heard talk of an eclipse recently, Jenny? An alignment?'

She shook her head, not trusting herself to speak.

'It's a truly magical occasion. Rare, too. It is the only time that the edges of this world brush alongside the edges of your world. The Council try to hide it from us, of course. They *seem* to think that if we discovered when the alignment was due, we might . . . amass an army, tear a hole in the fabric of our existence and . . . destroy the human world entirely.'

He smiled, wide, and Jenny temporarily forgot how to

breathe. *War.* Burnt cities, dead children. Everything the trees had shown her in that vision. That was what freeing the demons meant. That's what Pyro wanted.

'The alignment will occur in approximately –' he walked over to Luc and snatched the watch from his son's wrist before returning – 'I'd say, eighteen of your Earthly minutes. Lucifer must be awake in time for that event, and so you simply *must* agree to scale that peak.'

She remembered the Seer's words: *trust your instincts.*

Her instincts told her to spit at him, so she did.

It flew in a perfect arc, landing on the back of Pyro's left hand. He looked down at the sticky droplet with a small frown.

'Oh, now, that's not pleasant,' he said mildly, glancing around hopefully before sighing and wiping the back of his hand on his trouser leg.

Then he raised that same hand and made a flicking motion. Some force knocked into Jenny, lifting her off her feet and sending her flying backwards. Her spine made brutal contact with the tree Luc was chained to and the air rushed from her lungs.

'Jenny! Are you OK?' Luc asked. She sensed him dropping to his knees, felt his hands, gentle, on her shoulders.

She nodded weakly, fought for breath, tried to come back to her senses enough to stand up.

'She's fine,' Pyro said dismissively. 'She's more demon than you are.'

He walked forward until he was standing over Jenny.

'I can't tell, Miss Hall, if you're very brave, or very stupid.'

'Stupid,' she said, before a coughing fit took over her.

'Yes, that seems rather more likely. I don't want to do business this way, flinging you around the lake like a ragdoll until your broken, pathetic little body can't take any more and you agree to my plan. Wouldn't it be far nicer for you to just . . . get up now, before you have to crawl up the mountain?'

'Screw you,' Jenny snarled, rolling out of the way just in time to avoid another of Pyro's vicious flicks.

'Dad, why are you *doing* this?' Luc yelled.

'Because I don't have the luxury of *time*,' Pyro growled.

Jenny scuttled backwards, away from the tree, but Pyro was distracted by his son now, anyway.

'If you'd just done as you were supposed to in the first place,' Pyro said, 'none of this would be necessary. All you had to do was *get her here*!'

Spittle flew from his mouth as he spoke. Jenny's mind fizzed; she had to do something. Distract him, or *something*.

He was angry, she realized with a startling clarity, because he wasn't getting his own way. And he wasn't getting it because someone was standing up to him. And, like any bully, he hated that.

She walked around the tree, making sure she was fully visible to the assembled demonic army. When she spoke, she did it loudly, letting the sound carry across the lake.

'You can't actually *make* me climb the mountain, can you, Pyro?'

He turned to face her slowly.

'I still have free will. Even without my soul, I'm still

human, and I still get to make my own decisions. You can *hurt* me, obviously, and try to get me to change my mind that way, but you can't force me into a decision I don't want to make.'

'We'll see about that,' Pyro snarled, raising a hand.

'Wait! What if there's another way? A way for you . . . all of you,' here she gestured to the waiting demons, 'to get your cases looked at individually, a chance to get out of here that doesn't lead to certain death for *my* kind?'

'You're talking rubbish,' Pyro spat. 'There's no such thing.'

'There might be. Because isn't there a rule, if a living human asks the Celestial Council to look into a file of someone condemned here, they have to do it? And . . . isn't it true that you're all condemned here, just as much as the human souls are?'

Murmuring broke out on the other side of the lake.

'Ridiculous!' Pyro bellowed. 'I have been arguing with the Council for *aeons* to have our files reviewed, and they have refused at every turn!'

'But you're not a living human,' Jenny pointed out. 'I am. And I'd be *happy* to ask for you. I mean, I don't think it's fair that the trees of the Suicides' Forest have to be here for ever, but I also don't think it's fair that all of you do, either.' She looked across the lake and caught Lilith's cool gaze in her own. 'A demon told me that some of you weren't even alive during Lucifer's rebellion, but you still get punished just the same. Just because you happen to be demons. That's . . . *awful*.'

Lilith blinked and looked away. At her daughters.

'Just let me have my soul,' Jenny said, 'and I promise I will ask for every file in this dump to be reviewed.'

'*That* would take too long,' Pyro snapped, grabbing her attention back. And was that a dash of desperation tinging his voice? 'Even if they agreed, and we have no evidence they would, there are more than thirteen million demons in this Abyss. Why would we wait, when we could simply *take* right now?'

In a lower, quieter voice, he continued, just for her.

'Your soul is already gone, Miss Hall. I threw it into the lake. So you might as well stop with the humble hero act. You're not taking this away from me. This is *my* glory, not yours.'

He smirked at her, his eyes sliding towards the black, fathomless lake waters to make sure she really understood. Her soul was *gone*.

All this, her mind whispered, *for nothing.* The void inside her trembled; her knees buckled.

What was she without a soul? What could she be? Everything that had brought her to this point had been in the hope of fixing what was wrong with her, and now that was impossible. The murmurings of the assembled demons fell away, and Jenny scrabbled on the edge of the nothingness inside herself. Whatever she did now, whatever happened – she was going to stay broken. Unwanted. Intrinsically wrong. Inherently unlovable.

Her knees stayed weak, but she managed to stay upright. Just.

Pyro had never intended to give her soul back, had he? It probably hadn't even occurred to him – she was just a tool to get what he wanted, and a disposable one at that. Shouldn't be a surprise really; Seth Pyro considered *everyone* disposable. His son. Martha, and the twins, and even the demons assembled here on his say-so. Sure, he might pretend his motives were noble, that all of this was to liberate his fellow demons. But he'd just admitted his true intentions, hadn't he? He wanted glory, because then he would be a hero. And heroes have all the power, don't they? Just look at Lucifer: asleep all these aeons and still the most revered demon in All Hell. Of course, Pyro couldn't let Jenny just ask the Celestial Council. Pyro didn't want liberation, he wanted his own way.

But that didn't mean she had to give it to him.

'I'm *not* climbing that *goddamn mountain*!' Jenny yelled. 'And you can't make me!'

Her voice rang loud across the lake, silencing the remaining low chatter from the demonic army. The silence fell like snow, and Pyro's face contorted in fury.

'So you say,' he snarled.

The small fire that had kept Jenny from hypothermia was almost embers now, until Pyro flicked a hand in its direction, and it roared into life. Pyro turned in a circle, motioning as he did so, and the fire responded. The Hellfire encircled the tree with Luc chained to it, Jenny and Pyro, separating them from the lake, the demon horde, anything except each other.

And it was *loud*.

'The time has come, Miss Hall!' Pyro yelled over the thundering flames. 'You are right, of course. You have free will. I can't force you to wake my father. But I can give you a choice. Climb that mountain, or die in these flames and condemn yourself to an eternity here, working for me. And I won't be a very fair boss, I'm afraid.'

Jenny's breath quickened: short, fast, shallow. *Perfect time for my anxiety to come back.* She bent down, hands on her knees, and tried to focus on her breathing. Luc screamed something but she couldn't hear it, her brain and the noise of the fire jumbling his words. She closed her eyes.

In through the nose, Jenny reminded herself, *out through the mouth. Breathe. Trust your instincts.*

Pyro had made an error, hadn't he? That's what her instincts told her as her eyes shifted to Luc, straining against his chains. Unlike Zillah, who had been smart enough to threaten people Jenny cared about, Pyro was intent on threatening only her. Did he think she cared about what happened to her? What was the point, when he'd already discarded her soul like it was nothing? It was almost *funny*, wasn't it? If he'd wanted a negotiation, he should have made sure she still had something to lose.

I am not, I care not. The Latin mantra she'd seen scrawled across All Hell sounded in her head. Oh, Pyro would love that, wouldn't he? He thought he could break her, frighten her with fire and force, until she cracked and just did whatever he wanted. Well, he was wrong.

I am not – except, she was. With or without a soul, Jenny *existed*. Pyro couldn't take that away; even if she had nothing left, she was still *there*.

I care not – except, she did. That was his mistake. Even if it truly didn't matter what happened to her, did Pyro really think she would trade her own safety for that of her family? Did he think she'd sacrifice *billions* of human lives, just to avoid a Hellish fate for herself?

Well, of course he did, because Pyro didn't love anyone. He thought her fear of eternal Hellfire would make her do what he wanted, consequences be damned.

She heaved in a breath, stood up straight and glared into the infinity of Pyro's obsidian eyes.

'*Non sum, non curo*,' she said.

And she walked into the wall of Hellfire.

35

LUC

When Jenny stepped into the Hellfire, Luc's heart shattered.

'No!' he yelled, shaking the chains on his wrists as though that would make even the slightest bit of difference.

Maybe his father was right. Maybe he was useless, pathetic, too human to amount to anything. Except – Jenny was human, and she wasn't pathetic, or useless. He'd known that from the second he met her outside that awful house party. She wasn't some sad, soulless little girl. She had spark, an inner flint to fight for a better life – and that had inspired him to help her.

Are you going to let your dad condemn her?

He'd been angry for as long as he could remember. Angry that his mother died before he could know her. Angry that his dad didn't have time for him, angry that all his friends found their Demonity with ease and left him behind. Some days it felt like anger was all he had; all he was.

But it had never felt like this before.

It rolled inside him, hot and white and bursting for release.

He leant back against the tree he was bound to. Before, when Jenny lost consciousness from the cold, he'd felt a spark of something deep within himself. He'd seen sparkles behind his eyes, and he'd known on instinct to trust that feeling, so he'd let the spark travel up through his bones, under his skin, popping, glinting, like flint tapping against pyrite. He'd felt it concentrate in one of his hands, and when he'd thrust forward, snapping at the silver chain, the Hellfire just . . . exploded outwards.

He'd never experienced anything like it before, and he'd known it was his Demonity. But it had only worked then because he was desperate to save Jenny. The sight of her, white as the ice all around, had sent a shard of fear into him that sparked it.

Could he replicate that now, to save her again? He didn't know. He didn't know how to control it, how to make it do anything except send more Hellfire in that direction, which would only make things worse.

But he had to try. He squeezed his eyes tight, like he had before, straining against his chains, in case getting a few centimetres closer made the difference. He willed those sparkles to pop behind his eyes, for that spark to flicker back into life. He thought about his father as he sought the source of his Demonity, thought of his rage.

Nothing.

He couldn't do it.

The spark was gone.

He gasped, opening his eyes. Maybe he'd used it all on that first burst of Hellfire earlier. Maybe that was it. Maybe he was everything his father had told him he was.

He lost focus, his eyes staring into the wall of Hellfire. She was in there, burning up even right this second. Somewhere in the glassy flames.

Are you just going to stand here and let her die?

Because she would die. Sure, his dad would bring her back after, demonic and lost to All Hell for eternity, but she'd have to die first.

What are you going to do about it?

His Demonity sparked in his stomach.

He blinked, fire behind his eyes and in his veins, a scorching heat that rolled outwards through his skin, catching the edges of his Fenris silver chains. He gave himself over to it and his fingernails glowed. He reached down to grab hold of the sinuous metal ropes and – impossibly, unbelievably – felt them yield under his hands. Fenris silver was what kept his grandfather chained. It was unbreakable. But now, as Luc's hands blazed with white light, he crumbled the metal like dry soil.

He was free of his chains. He radiated light, so bright he thought he might go blind, but he didn't.

His father had his back to the tree, staring at the dark spot in the Hellfire wall that was Jenny like he couldn't believe she'd really done it. Ignoring him, Luc put a hand to the fire. He needed to find a way to stop it, because if Jenny died, Luc would burn All Hell to the ground.

Every last Circle.

Every grain of the Burning Sands would melt into glass beneath his feet.

Every drop of water in the Acheron would evaporate from his rage.

Under his glowing palm, the Hellfire felt cool. Malleable. He reached forward and made a fist, grabbing the fire like it was fabric, pulling it instinctively towards his chest. It sank into him, swarming through his skin, his veins, his bones.

Once it started, it didn't stop. He opened his mouth, sucking the fire into himself, swallowing this inferno until all that was left of it was meltwater and ash.

Then he saw her.

His Demonity receded instantly. He stood where the Hellfire ring had been, unburnt and scared, staring at the body lying face down in the mud. Pyro stood over her, staring at Luc with something like wonder on his face.

'Wh-what was that? Was that . . . Lucifer's Light?' he heard his father ask.

Luc lifted one arm, palm out towards his father. Light crackled across his knuckles, over his palms. He didn't know if it was Lucifer's Light – *the* Light that could break open the prison of All Hell – but he knew something else.

'Think I found *my* power.'

'I'll say you did.'

There was something strange in his father's voice. He couldn't identify it, because he didn't think he'd ever heard it before. He looked up, and the expression on his father's face made his skin crawl.

Pride. Pyro was staring at the light rolling over Luc's hand with pride.

'Get away from her,' Luc said, disgusted.

In apparent surprise, Pyro glanced down at the crumpled, smouldering girl by his feet.

'Silly girl,' he tutted. Then, 'You do realize we don't need her any more?'

He was smiling. That was the thing that really set Luc's blood boiling, the light crackling through his veins. Jenny was *dying* at his feet, and Seth was *smiling*.

It was like he was in two places at once: standing in the mud, practically vibrating with the ferocity of his newfound Demonity, and also floating above the scene.

It was the floating version of him that watched his father remove the star tracker from his inside pocket and consult it. It was the floating version of him that heard what his father said next.

'We have two minutes until full alignment. Get ready, Luc, and on my signal, *blast* the Light at the device. That should be enough to crack the borders open! We won't even need Lucifer!' He threw it on the ground between them, a target.

It was the vibrating, power-filled version of Luc that ignored this entirely, and repeated, 'Get away from her.'

The two versions of Luc rejoined. He raised his hand, that light still tripping across his skin.

Alarm crossed Pyro's face, as though for the first time recognizing the danger his son posed to him.

'Come, now,' he said, his tone coaxing. 'That device is not just a map, you know. It is powerful magic; if you break it, you will also break the barrier between our planes. We could challenge the Council directly!'

Luc flexed his lightning-drenched fingers, and Pyro's eyes widened. He took a step backwards, holding his own hands out in front of him.

'You don't know what you're doing,' he stuttered.

'Yes I do.'

Light blazed outwards from the heart of Luc's hand, lifting Pyro off his feet. He flew through the air, his face barely registering surprise before he splashed into the Lake of Lament. The demon-filled boats rocked in the wake of the impact. More heavy splashes as boats capsized, as demons landed in the cold, black water.

Luc barely even noticed as the pale hand rose from the depths, but the other demons did. They screamed, fled, scrambling up the sides of their boats to avoid getting tangled in those vast, powerful fingers. Their fear made them quick, but Pyro wasn't so lucky: the hand closed around him, entombing him in stony fingers and dragging him beneath the inky waters.

But Luc didn't care about any of that. He was already kneeling in the mud, gazing at Jenny.

Her clothes had burnt away; so had her hair. So had her

skin. She oozed, red and black.

'No,' Luc choked, his voice carrying in the frozen wastes of the Ninth Circle. 'Please, no.'

The Demonity sparked in him again, a flicker, a suggestion. He'd promised, hadn't he? If anything happened to her . . .

Luc sobbed, hands skidding in the mud towards her.

'Help her,' he heard himself say. He aimed his gaze beyond the far-away lanterns above him and howled. '*Help her!*'

He screamed, the sound emerging from him with the force of a thousand sharpened knives. A jagged ball of glass and agony spiralled up from the very depths of him, finding a release in the sound of his voice and the bright, white light that was him now.

He raised his arm and shot out another blistering jet of white light. At first, he just sent it out into the Abyss around him, but then his eyes snagged on the star tracker his father had thrown on the ground. He moved his hands, changed his aim, and sound ripped through the air. The device shattered, sending splinters of its golden, shimmering magic flying like sparks from a firework. A high-pitched whine filled the air and a visible tear opened up, ragged-edged, in the fabric of All Hell.

'Help her,' he whispered. It hurt to talk, after that.

'Of course we'll help her,' a familiar, childlike voice said.

Luc's head snapped up as Chloe-Lee and Joey Garstang stepped through the void between worlds, the tattoos above their joined hands glowing faintly. They were barefoot, wearing white, robe-like garments, and their footprints shone in the snow.

The children knelt, one on each side of Jenny's broken, burnt form. They reached across her until their fingertips touched, and it was like finishing a circuit: the glow of their tattoos hummed and a balloon of golden light grew between them. After a moment, it detached from the twins and gracefully draped itself across Jenny, shielding her, covering her, shaping its magic to her injuries.

Luc kept his eyes fixed on her as the magic did its work – first the bleeding stopped, and a fine, fragile membrane tinged with gold stretched over her bones. Joey thoughtfully removed his robe – his tweed jacket still beneath it – and laid it over Jenny to preserve her dignity as her body knitted itself back together. The robe rose and fell on her chest, and only then did Luc realize his own lungs were aching. He breathed with her. She was alive.

'She won't wake for some time,' Chloe-Lee warned him. 'But she will heal.'

'Thank you,' was all he could think to say.

The little girl's head tilted as she regarded him. 'Thank *you*, Luc Pyro. If you had not used the Light to break the barrier between our spheres—'

'The what?'

'The Light, dear boy,' continued Chloe-Lee. 'It's been aeons since I've seen it, but I'd know that white heat anywhere. Although, I don't think we've ever seen a case of a Fallen Angel's power passing on to their children . . . let alone skipping a generation like this.'

Luc stared at her like she had two heads. Which, knowing the twins, wasn't far from true. His father had said it was Lucifer's Light, but he hadn't believed him, hadn't even really registered it then. Now, though, it landed on him like a brick. He had Lucifer's Light? *That* was his Demonity?

'Speaking of generations,' Joey said, interrupting, 'where's your father? I understand most of this mess is his doing.'

Luc cleared his throat, which was still sore from screaming a literal void into existence, and winced. His eyes swung over to the Lake of Lament.

'He's in there,' he said.

Luc stayed with Jenny until she looked like herself again. She was still unconscious, of course, so as far as Luc was concerned, that meant she still needed him to protect her.

He was dimly aware of the twins, of some sort of negotiation happening at the lake's edge. Of that hand re-emerging, reluctant, and releasing Seth into their custody. He closed his eyes as they marched his father past, manacled in Fenris silver, through the tear between worlds the Light had created. Otherwise, Luc didn't take his eyes off the golden-shrouded girl.

He heard the twins address the remaining demons on the lakeshore, too, until – boat by boat – they sailed back to the far shore and returned to their circles.

The twins came back to him after a while, sitting quietly until he was ready to talk.

When he was, even Luc was surprised by the words that came from him.

'If my Demonity is Lucifer's Light, that means Lucifer could have broken himself out of his chains aeons ago.' It wasn't a question; the 'unbreakable' metal had crumbled in his grasp.

'It certainly looks that way,' Joey agreed. 'Before he went into his enchanted slumber, anyway.'

'Well, why didn't he?'

Chloe-Lee showed him her teeth. 'I wouldn't like to speak for him. I could take a guess, and if I did it would involve regret, and a huge sense of responsibility for the consequences of his actions. But, as I say, I wouldn't like to speak for him. Perhaps you could ask him yourself?'

He felt dizzy.

'What do you mean, I could ask him?'

The twins shared one of their telepathic glances, and Joey shrugged. 'On balance, I'm sure the Council would see the benefit, just this once.'

Chloe-Lee dipped her head, and gestured for Luc to follow her. 'Come on, then,' she said. 'Let's go wake your grandfather.'

36

JENNY

It had been one of those crisp November days with endless blue skies stretching beyond the city's higgledy-piggledy skyline. Now evening had arrived, that same blue sky remained, just leached of its vibrancy, darkening the Heavens with a wash like illustrator's ink.

There were no stars, not yet, and even the moon looked the other way as a black car with heavily tinted windows ferried an unconscious young woman back to her hometown.

Jenny came round when the Ferrier opened the car door and the glow from a nearby streetlight fell on her. They waited for her to unbuckle her seatbelt before holding out one cloaked arm to steady her as she got out.

She looked around at the street they had brought her to and frowned.

‘Why did you bring me here?’

It wasn’t a street she knew very well. It certainly wasn’t anywhere she’d consider ‘home’.

The Ferrier didn’t speak, merely nodded towards a building behind her. A police station.

‘Am I in trouble?’

Again, the Ferrier didn’t speak, but the front passenger door slammed, and Chloe-Lee’s cheerful voice chirped in reply.

‘No,’ the little girl assured her. ‘But your aunt has been very worried. Time moves slowly in All Hell, you know. As far as she is concerned, you’ve been gone for little over a day, but after calling your mother, some old friends, even your father . . . she panicked when she couldn’t find you.’

‘Why would she call my *father*?’ Jenny asked, incredulous.

‘You should let her know you’re safe,’ Joey said, emerging from the same door as his sister. He stood next to Chloe-Lee and they both beamed up at Jenny, teeth glinting in the streetlight.

‘Yeah.’ Jenny acknowledged Joey’s pronouncement. She glanced down at herself, at her borrowed dress and bare feet. ‘But what should I tell her?’

‘Tell her you were at a party,’ Chloe-Lee suggested.

Jenny stared at her in surprise. ‘Are you telling me to lie?’

Joey shrugged. ‘Would the truth help her, do you think?’

No, Jenny thought. *It really wouldn’t*. She was going to have to keep that to herself, secreted away in that still-present gap where her soul was meant to be. *God*. After everything, she was right back where she started, homeless and soulless. *Great*.

As though reading her thoughts, Chloe-Lee stepped forward, batting the Ferrier out of the way, and laid a small hand over Jenny's heart.

'You don't need it, darling.'

'What?'

'That can. What Pyro took from you. You don't need it.'

'I don't understand,' Jenny said. 'How can I not need my soul?'

Chloe-Lee tilted her head, and Joey stepped forward to answer her.

'Sweet girl. Do you really think you only get one chance? Pyro was right, when he said you could become demonic. Where there's a space, something will try to take root, and you were in All Hell for long enough . . .'

'Except,' Chloe-Lee interjected, 'that couldn't happen in your case. Because something else was already germinating.'

She tapped Jenny's sternum twice.

'There.'

'But . . . I thought there was something wrong with me. Something . . . missing.'

Joey shook his head. 'There's nothing wrong with you, Jenny Hall. Not a single thing.'

This was so close to something Luc said to her once, and now – she found herself struggling to breathe.

'I thought I was broken,' she whispered.

The twins shook their heads. 'Never,' Joey said. 'You are

strong, and adaptable, and *growing*. All the time, growing. And that's all you need to do right now. Be yourself, and let yourself grow.'

Chloe-Lee's hand found its way to stroke Jenny's cheek.

'We know what you think of yourself. But walk into that police station and I promise you will discover none of it's true.'

They stepped back, in unison, and Jenny found herself staring at them as though seeing them for the first time.

'What are you?' she heard herself whisper.

Somewhere to her left, the Ferrier snorted. Chloe-Lee shot them a Look, and Joey rolled his eyes.

'Believe me,' the small boy replied, 'I wish there were a simple answer to that question.'

'Figures.' Jenny chewed the inside of her lip, unsure how to properly thank these creatures who saved her life, and the Ferrier for bringing her home. And then there was everyone else who had helped her, like the trees . . .

'Oh,' she remembered. 'Before you go – I made a promise, and I think you might be able to help me keep it.'

'We will do what we can,' Chloe-Lee smiled.

'I should think that's the least we can do, under the circumstances,' Joey agreed.

'I was told that a living human can ask for a file to be reviewed, on behalf of someone condemned to All Hell. Is that true?'

'Yes,' Chloe-Lee said. 'The Celestial Council would have to take on that work.'

'Are you two on the Celestial Council?'

The twins shared another Look.

'Whose file did you have in mind?' Joey asked, instead of answering.

Jenny swallowed, suddenly nervous.

'Everyone's.'

Next to her, the Ferrier made a sound like choking.

'Everyone's?' The twins spoke in unison, disbelief in stereo.

'I . . . well, yeah. Originally, it was the trees. They helped me. Then it was Cleo and Fran, you know, the waitresses at the Hopeless Heart? And then, this Seer, at the bottom of the Narrows, he was kind to me – I thought he was just winding me up at first, but he was *helping*. And . . . now, it's not *just* them. I don't *only* want to help souls who helped me. That wouldn't be fair, would it?'

There was a pause.

'I suppose not.'

'No. And it's also not fair that Hell is for ever, but the crimes – sins – these people were condemned for, they might not be sins any more. But they're still there, being tortured. That doesn't seem right at all.'

'I see.' Joey sighed. 'I can tell you, we are not going to be popular when we bring that request to the Celestial Council. Do you know how many files you're asking to be reviewed?'

Jenny winced.

'I'm sorry,' she said, but she wasn't really.

Chloe-Lee raised an eyebrow at her. 'Don't apologize,

you're doing what you think is right. As it happens, we agree with you. So, we will take this to the Council. We will ensure your request is fulfilled.'

'Really?'

'Truly.'

A lightness filled her. She'd done it! She'd given hope, a *chance* to those condemned souls in Hell.

'If that is all,' Joey said, 'we will take our leave now.'

He made a gesture towards the Ferrier, who dipped their head at Jenny before lumbering back towards the driver's door. Chloe-Lee reached out for the passenger door handle.

'Wait,' Jenny said, suddenly sure she couldn't let them go. Not without telling them—

'Thank you,' she said. 'You know, for saving me.' She looked up, into the Ferrier's hood. 'And for bringing me home.'

'It has been our absolute honour,' Joey told her.

'And mine also,' the Ferrier intoned, their voice gravelly and low. 'I hope you don't mind that I asked to be the one to drive you home; I am very glad you are still alive, Jenny Hall.'

Unable to speak, Jenny nodded, then stepped forward and hugged the Ferrier. They seemed surprised, but after a moment, their arms patted her shoulders. Then she watched the three of them climb back into the black car with the tinted windows. She watched until they turned the corner at the end of the street. Then she walked into the police station.

*

'A party?'

She was in a grey room, sitting on a rigid plastic chair under fluorescent lights that made her white skin look grey as well.

The police officer across the table from her was frowning.

'What kind of party?'

'You know,' she hedged. 'Like . . . a rave. It was in a field.'

Seated next to her, Auntie Vee squeezed her hand and mopped at her eyes with a tissue in her other hand.

'I'm just so relieved she's safe,' she told the police.

'You've worried a lot of people,' the officer said sternly to Jenny. 'A phone call to your auntie here might have been nice, don't you think?'

'I lost my phone,' Jenny mumbled, and this at least was true. It had been in her pocket all the way to the Ninth Circle – albeit smashed to pieces – but when she walked into the Hellfire, her phone had disintegrated along with everything else.

But, even though she'd worried Auntie Vee, she hadn't actually done anything illegal. After making some notes, the police let her go.

Vee drove them carefully, like Jenny was somehow precious, an egg just looking for an opportunity to crack.

'Where are your *shoes*?' Vee squealed. 'And your glasses?'

She had a feeling this was only the start of a series of questions she wouldn't be able to answer, and unconsciously lifted her hand to the conspicuous absence of glasses in front of her eyes. How was she meant to explain she didn't need them any more?

'Where's Charlie's car?' she asked as Vee backed into the drive, as much as a distraction as anything else.

'We, um . . . we broke up,' Vee said. 'Yesterday.'

'Oh.' Jenny arranged her face to hide her real feelings on the matter. She reached across and patted Vee's hand on the steering wheel. 'I'm sorry to hear that.'

'I'm not,' Vee said, holding herself straight in the driver's seat. 'He was a prick.'

Jenny considered this for a moment. 'No one in this car's going to disagree with you there, Auntie Vee. What happened?'

'You know what happened.'

She wasn't sure she did, but before she could ask again, Vee climbed out of the car.

Another surprise waited for her inside.

'Where's my stuff?' she asked, gesturing to the empty spot at the end of the sofa where her bin bag used to live.

'Nip upstairs,' Vee grinned. 'Connor and Tyler can answer that for you.'

So, she headed up the stairs, suspicious as soon as she saw the boys hiding behind Tyler's bedroom door. In the same room? Not fighting? It wasn't *normal.*

'What are you two up to?' she asked, but before she'd even finished the sentence both boys came barrelling out of the room and enveloped her in an awkward, gangly hug.

'I'm glad you're safe, Jenny,' said Tyler.

'S'good to see you,' Connor grunted.

Jenny had to blink back the weird feeling in her eyes. Must be dust kicked up from the carpet by their exuberance.

'Your mum said you know where my stuff is.'

Eagerly, Tyler grabbed her hand and dragged her down to the end of the hallway, to Connor's room. What were they doing with her stuff in there?

Tyler opened the door, and Jenny froze. They'd painted it; gone was Connor's superhero wallpaper, replaced with a sage green colour Jenny distinctly remembered telling Vee she liked one time in Homebase. A matching rug covered the spot on the laminate where Connor had dropped Vimto last year, and when she stepped inside, she had to fight the urge to cry. The bed was covered in brand new bedding and a new wardrobe and dresser sat in place of Connor's Lego table. When she opened one of the doors, her clothes hung neatly inside.

The room still smelt like wet paint, and none of the furniture was pushed right up against the wall.

'What is this?' she asked quietly. Both her cousins were staring at the floor, refusing to meet her eye.

'You needed a bedroom,' Connor said.

'It was going to be for your birthday,' Tyler added. 'Mum already had the paint, but then when you didn't come home, she said . . .'

'She said it was a chance to get it ready. To surprise you.'

'Well, I am surprised!' Jenny blinked rapidly, tried to swallow down the feeling in her throat that made it suddenly difficult to speak. 'But where are you going to sleep?'

'We're sharing now,' Tyler burst out. 'It's OK, though, we got some chalk from school and drew a line on the floor to mark our territory.'

'Oh my God.' Jenny sat down on the bed, that *dust* irritating her eyes again. 'You guys . . . this is . . . this . . .'

'This is your home,' Connor said firmly, and he fixed her with a serious expression. 'So please don't go away again without telling us.'

'I won't,' she promised.

'Also, your mum rang,' Tyler said with a grimace. 'But I hung up on her.'

Jenny laughed, the sound strangled through tears. 'Good lad. Although, I think maybe I should forgive her, one of these days.'

Tyler grunted, clearly unconvinced.

For the rest of the evening before bedtime, Connor and Tyler took it in turns to escort her everywhere she went. Connor went with her when she wanted a glass of squash. Tyler stood guard outside the coat cupboard when she went searching for her school bag.

She drew the line when Tyler tried to follow her upstairs when she went for a wee, though.

It was sweet, but also a little stifling.

'I wasn't even gone that long,' she protested.

'But we missed you!'

When they'd gone to bed, Vee sat down on the sofa next to her and handed her a Sports Direct mug of tea.

'They were worried about you as well,' she said.

'I didn't mean to worry anyone.'

'What have I told you, madam? You just assume we won't be worried. That we don't care. But we *do*, Jenny. Those two think of you more like a big sister than a cousin, you know. And as far as I'm concerned, you've always got a bed here. Always. Please don't ever think otherwise.'

This was about Charlie, Jenny realized. She caught her auntie staring at her school bag and understanding hit her. She'd left it on the sofa when she ran away. Vee must have seen it, realized Jenny heard what Charlie said, put two and two together. *You know what happened.* That's what she meant in the car: she knew Jenny had heard them arguing. That's what prompted their break-up.

She put her mug down on the floor, reached forward, and hugged her auntie. Hard.

This whole thing was a wall of emotions, everything happening all at once, and Jenny was secretly glad when bedtime rolled around so she could close the bedroom door. *Her* bedroom door. She changed into pyjamas and crawled into her new bed. The sheets still had that *new* feeling to them, and she tried to sleep, but it was elusive. After everything she'd just been through, maybe it wasn't surprising.

Was Luc OK? He'd sat with her for *hours* while the twins worked their lifesaving magic. Demon hours, at that. He hadn't left her side, not once.

He'd saved her life, just as much as the twins had. She understood that in the very bones of her. And after he'd done it, he'd protected her, murmured soothing things, promised her she was going to be all right. And now . . . was she ever going to even see him again?

And what was *his* life going to be like, now? He'd basically foiled the best chance the demons might ever have to break out of All Hell. How would the rest of them take that?

And, more importantly, would he . . . miss her?

Tears streaked on to her pillows, and it was a long time until she got any sleep.

After a few days, she was practically drowning in her cousins' love. They meant well, but Jenny was getting claustro, so one night after they'd gone to bed, she slipped out the front door for some fresh air.

She didn't go far, just to the end of the road and round the corner so she could sit with her back against a stranger's wall and breathe. She let out a shaky breath and rested her head against the wall.

'What do I do now?' she asked herself, out loud.

She needed to go back to school, soon. Face the music. She wasn't particularly looking forward to it, except that now she knew Amber was behind the text messages she felt lighter about that whole thing. It was the not knowing that had killed her.

'Anything you like,' a familiar voice said, and Jenny squealed in shock.

Luc dropped down to sit next to her, flashing his trademark sharp-toothed smile in the process.

Jenny stared at him before flinging her arms around him and burying her face in his neck.

'You're OK,' she said into his skin. 'You're OK.'

'So are you.'

'And you're *here*. How?' She let go, but only so she could keep staring at him, scared, somehow, that he might vanish.

'Nice to see you too,' he grinned, his pupils dilating past his irises.

'That's not an answer,' Jenny pointed out, refusing to fall into those tempting black pools.

He stretched. 'Wanted to make sure you were all right.' He chewed the inside of his cheek, as though considering saying something else, but stopped himself.

'I missed you too,' Jenny said, jostling him with her shoulder.

'Figured you might.' Cheeky wink. 'Like, don't tell anyone I said this, but I think I might be your best friend.'

Jenny snorted. 'Best; only – it's all the same really, right?' Then, 'But seriously, *how* are you here?' An awful thought crossed her mind. 'Your dad isn't—'

'Trying again? Nah.' Luc shook his head. 'He'll be chained to that mountain a long time, I reckon.'

Jenny's eyes widened. 'The mountain? With your grandfather?'

'Yep. They're neighbours.'

'Chloe-Lee said you met him. Your grandfather.'

Luc nodded. 'I did. It was . . . weird. He looks *exactly* like me. Like, same age and everything – apparently his long sleep on the mountain is more like suspended animation than an actual sleep.'

She wanted to ask what they'd talked about, but somehow this felt too personal. He could tell her, if he wanted to.

'To answer your question,' Luc smoothly changed the subject, 'I found a loophole in the whole *no demons allowed on Earth* thing.'

'You did?'

Luc's grin widened. 'It seems someone asked the Celestial Council to review everyone's files. And, despite their misgivings, they're doing it. They're even going to let *some* demons decide where they want to settle. Like Earth.'

Jenny's stomach dropped. 'Are you serious? That's so dangerous!'

Luc snorted. 'You asked for this, lady. That's your lookout. Anyway, you know better than anyone, most demons are more like humans than they ever were like angels. They've got hopes, dreams, ambitions . . . they just didn't want to be stuck in the Abyss for ever. Can you blame them? For the most part they just want to settle down with human partners and have a bunch of half-demon babies. And the deal is, I'm here to keep an eye on them.'

'Like a demonic social worker?'

'You could say that.'

'Jesus,' Jenny muttered.

'Yeah, he might help out too if he's not too busy.'

She glared at him, and he laughed.

'I'll tell you who won't be getting a total free pass anytime soon, and that's Zillah.'

Jenny stared at him like he had two heads.

'Zillah?'

Luc touched her shoulder, affectionate. 'She's not dead.'

'What?' Jenny reeled.

'After you left, Lilith and Zillah's sisters swarmed the Ninth Circle, demanding to know where she was; I was trying to calm them down when she just came wandering in, covered in snake bites. She'll be fine. The Succubae are not known for being easy to kill.'

A weight lifted from Jenny that she hadn't even known she was carrying.

'I left her there,' she whispered.

'Don't blame yourself,' Luc insisted. 'Even she said you had no choice.'

'I *always* have a choice, Luc.'

They sat in silence for a while. Then, 'I should get back,' Jenny said. 'Will I hear from you again?'

'Try and stop me,' Luc replied. 'Oh, before you go—'

He clicked his fingers, and something glowed white in his hand. It shuddered, before coalescing into a shape so familiar it made Jenny's heart ache. A can, with a sealed aluminium tab and a sulphur-yellow label.

'Is that . . .?' Jenny reached for it.

'I thought you might want it back. Chloe-Lee said you don't really need it, something about souls growing back if a person's full of good energy? Still. It's yours. Had to make some pretty promises and flutter my eyelashes to get it out of the lake, but . . . well, you're worth it.'

She took it from him with shaking hands. It was warm to the touch, and something inside her pulsed in recognition. She swallowed down the lump in her throat, and then she leant forward and kissed him.

It was nothing like kissing Caspian that night under Scarborough Bridge. That had been unexpected, wet and a bit gross. This? This felt inevitable. Warm. In fact, it felt a lot like coming home.

ACKNOWLEDGEMENTS

Firstly, thank you to the Chicken House team and everyone involved in making this happen. Special thanks to Barry Cunningham, Kesia Lupo, Ruth Hoey, Laura Smythe, Elinor Bagenal and Esther Waller. I am indebted to all the judges on the Times/Chicken House Children's Fiction Competition panel, to Micaela Alcaino for the gorgeous cover art and to my agent Louise Lamont; no one could ask for a better guide through this process.

Thank you, writing coven: Jayne Rice, Julia Boggio, Jo Lyons, Amanda Scotland, Farrah Riaz and Cristal Philips – the best beta readers a girl could ask for, and to Hayley Dunning, for taking me out of my flat and my own head so often; you are excellent at both writing and friending.

I'm a very lucky and grateful girl, so in no particular order I'd also like to thank my parents (for loving me through everything), my aunties Eileen and Lindsey, Naomi Booth and the rest of the York St John Creative Writing teaching team circa 2014, the English and Creative Writing department at Lancaster University, Charlie and Amie from the Urban Writer's Retreat, former colleagues at YSJ, current colleagues at Imperial College and the Debut Authors 2024 Twitter group for the hype and the community.

I started writing this book because I didn't know where I belonged. Three families showed me huge kindness when I needed it most, and without that this book couldn't have happened, so thank you Marie, Julie and Man; Morganne, Helen and Brock; Millie, Alice, Kev and Tracey. There is good in this world, and it's all of you.

Jade. Cal. My Bad Rat. I'd be lost without you. I think this is what people mean when they talk about chosen family, and frankly I couldn't have chosen better. Thank you so, so much for choosing me back (except you, Christina, because we're related so you don't have a choice, but I would choose you a thousand times anyway).

Finally, but totally not least-ly, Steve. Everyone needs at least one person on the planet to believe they're a genius and bring them many, many cups of tea – and you've nailed both of those fronts. Thank you for being my biggest fan; conveniently I'm also yours.

TRY ANOTHER GREAT BOOK FROM CHICKEN HOUSE

ALL THE HIDDEN MONSTERS by AMIE JORDAN

A grisly murder. A detective warlock with a dangerous past. A girl out of her depth. Can they solve the case?

Sage is an ordinary girl and a werewolf, moving between worlds, desperate to make sense of her life. When her supernatural friend, Lucy, is found murdered in the human domain, Sage is determined to be part of the investigation headed up by the attractive but arrogant warlock, Oren Rinallis.

Sage is neither magical nor immortal, but she knows right from wrong – and can scent a killer like no other . . .

This book is the perfect combination of fantasy, true crime and fun-filled chemistry.
ALEXANDRA CHRISTO, author of *To Kill a Kingdom*

Paperback, ISBN 978-1-915026-11-8, £8.99 • ebook, ISBN 978-1-915947-42-0, £8.99